THE NEW GUARD

LITERARY REVIEW

P.O. Box 10612
Portland, ME 04104
www.newguardreview.com

Writers for writers' sake.

FOUNDING EDITOR & PUBLISHER
Shanna McNair

JUDGES
David Plante, Machigonne
Charles Simic, Knightville

EDITORS
Sarah Kowalski, Fiction
Shanna McNair, Poetry, Fiction
& Special Sections
Bill Roorbach, Fiction
Suzanne Strempek Shea, Fiction
Scott Wolven, Fiction
& Special Sections

COPYEDITORS
David Scribner
Sherry Whittemore

TYPESETTING
Melanie Kratovil

COVER, LAYOUT,
WEB & AD DESIGN
Shanna McNair

VIDEOGRAPHY
Patrick Rioux

ANIMATION
Diana Choksey

WEB ART
SergeiChaparin
James Provenzano

For David, Joel and Sean with love

TABLE OF CONTENTS

TABLE OF CONTENTS

WINNER OF THE MACHIGONNE FICTION CONTEST
JUDGE: DAVID PLANTE
Dan Marmor, RECIPES FOR DISASTER

WINNER OF THE KNIGHTVILLE POETRY CONTEST
JUDGE: CHARLES SIMIC
Kathleen Spivack, THE GREAT RAILROAD TRAIN OF ART

MACHIGONNE FINALISTS
Allison Alsup . . . . .A GOOD LIKENESS
Amina Gautier . . . . .MOST HONEST
Caron Levis. . . . . .LATE PASS
Lisa Locascio. . . . . .AMERICAN HOSPITALITY
Greta Schuler. . . . . .WITCHCRAFT
Brent van Staalduinen. . . . . .BUDDY'S MIRROR
Michael Caleb Tasker . . . . .THE VISIT
Kirk Wilson . . . . .THE STORY YOU NEVER HEARD ABOUT LATTORIAL
Sam Wilson. . . . . .MAYBE IN CASPER, WYOMING

MACHIGONNE SEMI-FINALISTS
Jackie Zollo Brooks. . . . . .CHINABERRIES
Soma Mei Sheng Frazier. . . . . . . .SHE MUST REMEMBER
Gwendoline Riley . . . . .A. BORN ETC
Mitchell Stocks. . . . . .WE CHINESE

KNIGHTVILLE FINALISTS
Ioanna Carlsen. . . . . .TWO VARIATIONS ON A BORROWED PHRASE
Kevin Carollo. . . . . .A THEORY
Mary Christine Delea . . . . .MY VILLAIN
Rob Dennis . . . . .WHY I AM NOT A TECH WRITER
Jaydn DeWald . . . . .EPITHALAMIUM (OR, LANDSCAPE WITH SOLDIER)
Nicole DiCello . . . . .THE LONG EMERGENCY
William Doreski . . . . .CONFESS TO ME
Iris Jamahl Dunkle. . . . . .HOW TO COPE IN A NEW LANDSCAPE

Soma Mei Sheng Frazier . . . . THE DEEPEST HOURS
Robin Michel . . . . THE BOY AND THE MOON
Marcia Popp . . . . when she died she took her best stories with her
Melissa Roberts . . . . RESURGAM: PORTLAND, MAINE
Don Schofield . . . . SHEPHERD
Terese Svoboda . . . . CAR PROBLEM
Ken Taylor . . . . foursome
Elaine Zimmerman . . . . THE FLOOR RATTLED WITH US

KNIGHTVILLE SEMI-FINALISTS

Austin Allen . . . . VALENTINE VARIATIONS
Heather Altfeld . . . . ANNALS OF THE ORPHELINES
Luke Bramley . . . . ALL THE PRETTY LIGHTS
Mary Christine Delea . . . . PURR
Lynn Tudor Deming . . . . IN GIPSIE'S CANT
Chad Frisbie . . . . Q
Lyall Harris . . . . ETCHING
Kenya T Jennings . . . . EPIPHANY
Matthew Keuter . . . . VERISIMILITUDE AND OTHER UNTRUTHS
Desmond Kon Zhicheng-Mingde . . . MARLENE DIETRICH MEETS DIETRICH BONHOEFFER
Wulf Losee . . . . THE NAUTILUS MOTEL
Shahé Mankerian . . . . THE MOSAIC OF THE MISSING
Nikolas James Perez . . . . DEDICATION
Jeanie Tomasko . . . . CROSSWORD SONNET: CODES
Julie Marie Wade . . . . GRAMMAR

One recent morning, I got a manila envelope in the mail from John Callahan, the literary executor of the late writer, Ralph Ellison. John and I had agreed that *The New Guard* would feature the never-before-published story, *A Storm of Blizzard Proportions*, and—there it was in my mailbox. To my delight, it was the story as taken from Ellison's original manuscript: a photocopy of a photocopy in Ellison's hard-hitting type. The story is pre-*Invisible Man* (1952) and written nearly a decade before, in 1944. The type—from an Olivetti? Back then, Olivetti made nice portable typewriters, and Ellison was in Wales when he wrote *Storm*. Could he have borrowed a typewriter? A Royal? A Smith-Corona? These happy questions made me feel closer to the man, closer to Ellison's private writer self. I squinted at the manuscript's pencil marks, from "R.E." at some corners to cross-outs, to a long penciled paragraph on the final page.

My partner in crime and fellow *TNG* editor, Scott Wolven, read the story aloud. Here and there, he looked at me with astonishment. Wow, we were raving, this is right from Ralph Ellison's desk—how did we get so lucky? Later, I was to find out that only a handful of people had ever even seen the story. As Scott read, something happened to me. *Storm* has an allegorical tone; the dialogue, the setting—seems otherworldly. Ellison switches from third to first person and back again, creating ever more intimacy between protagonist and reader, as the allegory churns. This is real experiment, with nods to many great writers' styles. The ending is reminiscent of James Joyce's *The Dead*—too, there is the brooding tone of Hemingway. The protagonist is a young man, who's questioning conventions, culture, race; and through the boxer Jack Johnson—the great fight of being alive in his time, or arguably any time. Throughout, Ellison's narrator is aware of a creeping, distant thunder, which suggests the brink of change, a pending shift—a storm, gearing up. War is in that thunder. Life and death. Love. Fear. At only seven pages, this is a story to be studied deeply.

Maybe Ellison does not have a publishing history to equate with artistic proliferation, but he was always writing. He surely knew that the real work of a writer stems from quiet resolve, loneness; and a sort of creative-minded and vigilant attention to the world. Ellison seems a prime example of this writing life, which on its surface is romantic, but at its core is only work. To me it is Ellison's seriousness that is romantic, and his clarity of his purpose.

How did we come to acquire this story? I'd sent John a copy of *The New Guard* to see if he'd be interested in a second interview with Scott (Scott interviewed John for *Columbia: A Journal of Literature and Art*, some years ago). John was more than kind, saying "I believe *TNG* is the sort of enterprise Ralph would have been proud to be associated with…" and that our review's title, *The New Guard*, reminded him of Saul Bellow's magazine, *The Noble Savage*. High praise. I'll take it! Also, I am grateful for the friendship between the two men, who seem to share faith in *TNG*.

Beyond Ellison, who has inspired me beyond telling, we have a tremendous book here. We've instated our themed letters section as an every-issue feature, the theme of which will change each year. We've started up an interview section just for writers who've lived and worked in Maine. In this book, you'll see the old and the new guards—a delineation that is meant to honor and respect all writers in all stages of career.

Judges this year judged on submissions that came in from around the world. Our fiction judge, David Plante, said he was looking for "...a voice that called out with originality, with what I can only think of as resonant with life, with death, with something even more that I risk naming the soul...Though I had to choose one call, it was because that was what was required of me. I would like to have had all the voices calling out, all together in a chorus." While Dan Marmor's short story, *Recipes for Disaster*, "moved" Mr. Plante "deeply," it is in his spirit of a wide-singing chorus that I chose to publish all of our finalists and semi-finalists, in both genres.

Charles Simic, our poetry judge, said his chosen winner, Kathleen Spivack wrote a poem that was "interesting" and "original," certainly the case. One of the things I wanted to do this year was lobby for the long form poem, which is so rarely published, and extend our poetry contest's line limit to 300. I also changed the fiction word count to 7,500 and we now accept flash fiction as part of the fiction contest. Wonderful, various entries came in as a result. Very exciting.

As I write this note, I think of *The Little Man at Chehaw Station: The American Artist and His Audience*, an essay Ellison wrote in 1977. The essay covers a lot of ground in terms of culture, class, race—but what I'm focusing on is the actual little man at Chehaw Station. He is an allegorical, universal figure; an unassuming person, hidden in some way or another, and is ever-present. The little man understands the profundity of form and of discipline and artistic dedication. He sets the highest standard. This seer is the seer in all of us, and he is the conscience of art itself. Ellison had this conscience. John Callahan said Ellison used the term "conscientious consciousness" after Emerson and James. Writing is art and it is craft and vocation, and writing is the eye of the world, a portal to the soul of things. A conscientious consciousness. I am more than proud of this collection of stories, poems and interviews. Enjoy.

Shanna McNair
Knightville, ME 2011

Type Smash!
© dave naybor, 2011

Dear Peter Parker,

Come to me. This is my gentle but unremitting demand. Come here. Now. I am waiting, my heart delicate and shivering as one of your webs. I am here; I know you; I will be true.

But first, to be entirely forthright, I want a particular Peter. I seek no live-action man. Toby McGuire with his oily sheen and earnest gaze won't do. Nor do I desire some hyper-angular, pouting anime edition, a feminized simulacrum. Not an action figure either. Oh! The worst! I couldn't bear it—you, plastic, neutered, mass-produced; meant for the clammy hands of prepubescent boys, you—a thing they'd grab in those last ten minutes, before they start grabbing themselves.

This missive is for a particular you, and if it winds up in the hands of another, if Toby Maguire comes upon it, or if God forbid it gets shuttled down the wrong aisle and winds up among the G.I. Joes—those trash-talking, chin-jutting xenophobes—I ask that this is kindly delivered to its intended recipient. I want Peter Parker, animated, circa 1967, from the Marvel Comics television show.

Are you reading this? You, 1967 Peter Parker, you're who I want. You with the delicate bones, you of an era when cartoon men were allowed to be pretty (but not too pretty). You with the natty suit and Brylcreem hair. You with the guileless Chiclet smile, a pre-Crest White Strips smile, the genuine article. You, a little slow on the uptake. So endearingly slow! You, immune to the charms of 1967 Marvel television Betty Brant, that red-headed, tiny-waisted secretary (wait until you see how she was co-opted by Mad Men). You, before steroids. You, before Twitter. You, before political correctness, before workplace ethics, you, abused by J. Jonah Jameson, that fool who'll never survive the hippies. Compose your letter of resignation, Peter.

Come to me. I'll make you a martini. We can talk about evil; there's plenty here. I'll make a darkroom in my basement. And you won't have to hide from me! Imagine it. I mean you won't have to hide your dual identity. These days, we're allowed dual identities. They're encouraged! Hang your spidey-suit in my closet, among my leopard prints and trousers (your Betty would never wear trousers), among my ethnic prints, my neo-hippie dresses, my ironic suspenders.

Come play house with me, 1967 Marvel television Peter. Escape the cold war. Yes, I understand you may have some concerns, may fear a certain disorientation, but I'll tell you how everything turns out: Vietnam, the Space Race, MLK, Elvis. You won't be missing anything. And the best stuff is still available: Cool Hand Luke is on DVD now. And Bonnie & Clyde. Forget those silly fights with the Vulture and Doctor Octopus and Mysterio. We've got real fish to fry, to use the parlance of your world. We've got the War on Terror and toxic plastic and dirty bombs and anti-immigration legislation in Alabama and Arizona that'll make your sweet radioactive blood run cold, that'll make the dangers of Electro seem quaint. We've got gang warfare, class warfare, drug warfare. We've got melting ice caps. We've got skinny jeans, Citibank, BP, Justin Bieber, the prison industrial complex.

The modern world needs you, Peter. And I need you too. You can fight crime, and then, at the end of the day, come to me. Hang your suit in the closet. I'll be wearing my vintage pink slip. Put your feet on the mid-century coffee table. I'll lean into your body; I'll breathe your Old Spice aftershave, I'll listen, I'll commiserate, I'll serve you the food you love, fondue, pigs in blankets. We'll listen to records.

I will do things to you.

Come here, 1967 Peter Parker. Stay close to me. You're the only future I want.

Yours,
Sarah Braunstein

August 22, 2011
To: Miles Morales, the New Spiderman
From: Carolina De Robertis
Re: ¡Héchale fuerza!

Querido Miles,

You could be my son. I never thought I'd have maternal feelings for Spiderman, but here I am, looking at the pictures of you that burst into the press this summer, and all I can think of is the brighter stronger world you're helping create, not just for me, and not just for the Faceless Others Out There, but for my own son. You'd like my boy; he's two and a half years old; he's an excellent singer of "Twinkle, Twinkle" and other classic jams. He's got a phenomenal sense of humor and, just this week, told me a story in which Ishmael, Queequeg, and Capitán Ahab jumped in a fire truck and rode off in search of Moby-Dick. Like you, he's smart, and an avid reader. Like you, he's Afro-Latino, with one African American parent and one Latina. He has two mommies; there you differ. But still, that's more than enough to see that you are members of the same tribe.

There are those who already hate you. That's old news. When you draw the venom of Lou Dobbs or Glenn Beck, it generally means you've got a leg-up on fighting evil. Don't let them stop you. You matter more than many people realize. Folks of color are constantly discounted in mainstream society; so are fictional characters. They aren't real, commentators say. But what could be more real than fiction, with its narrative explorations of humanity's most unshakable dilemmas and desires? There are few things in the world more vivid than a good read. Because you are fictional, you interact with readers from within their minds, where you hum and pulse with life as they turn pages, transfixed by you, transported. This is an ancient and primal form of power. Look at Capitán Ahab. How many millions of minds has he sailed through, carrying his vaulting passions, speaking volumes about human daring and impossible pursuits?

And so: you matter. And we need you. I say that we are members of the same tribe, but in fact you're of a tribe with all and any readers who connect with you—that, too, is the strange and joyous alchemy of fiction. Along with many others, I am cheering you on, dándote ánimo, from this spot in Oakland that is not only mi casa but also la tuya. If your heroic ventures ever find you swinging through the Bay Area, and your battles leave you wiped out and wanting a taste of home, you know where to find us. There'll be a place for you at our table, a plate of down-home goodness, and, if you're lucky, my son might even treat you to a song.

Un abrazo fuerte,
Carolina

Dear Wonder Twins,

You're born into this world—or, you know, Exxor—and at some point you begin to believe that you'll be allowed to live your own life, that your hopes and dreams and ambitions will be yours alone, that you won't have to answer to anyone else's preconceived notions of who you are, that you'll be able to find yourself. Back in the 1970s, when you two first came to this specific world, the idea of "finding yourself" meant a lot of things—I remember when my mother decided to "find herself" in 1977, the process involved fucking a lot of guys with perms and getting involved in EST, which, as I recall, required her to not urinate for hours on end, to purchase a lot of protein drinks through the mail and force all of us to go on diets consisting primarily of grapefruit—but here we are, decades later, and you two are still trying to make sense of your identities, still taking the form of other things, refusing just to be you, still calling yourself Wonder Twins, as if anyone still believes there is much wondrous about either of you anymore.

That's what this is all about, I suppose. I'm writing to you not because I want you to save me from something terrible, but because I want you to save yourselves. How long can you two live this parasitic life, each of you bound to the other by some pallid sense of duty, some antiquated idea of heroism?

I remember when you joined the Super Friends as impetuous shape-shifting alien teenagers, as if you'd ever fit in. Yes, yes, they called themselves the Super Friends, but these heroes were grown men and women with lives of their own, with anger and sadness and bitterness in their past: Superman with his father issues and the sure knowledge that he wasn't half the journalist Lois Lane was; Aquaman, with his webbed hands a persistent reminder that no woman would ever be able to hold him, his gross deformity no more heroic than a bleeding cyst; Batman and Robin, mere men in capes, nothing special about them at all, except for those nights in the Bat Cave when Alfred would quietly masturbate them both, the millionaire and his boy companion play things for their butler...a man who knew their darkest secrets and preyed on them; and dear, sweet, Wonder Woman, the sadist, with her golden whip and false jingoism, claiming to love America and yet flying an invisible plane. Who was she hiding from? What was her secret?

Oh, Zan and Jayna, how they fooled you into believing you belonged with them! How they pretended to love your space monkey, Gleek! In truth, you were bit players in their drama, veritable chew toys for the big dogs. Didn't you ever wonder, Zan, why Aquaman treated you with such barely-constrained malice when you turned into a bucket of water? Jayna, when you became an eagle, did you not understand that the Hall of Justice had a ceiling...and that ceiling was the height of Superman's facility for mendacity? How they forced you into battle with their arch villains! You came to this planet in peace and what did it get you? A life fighting insurmountable evil.

Your space monkey had a prehensile tail. What grasp did you two have?

So you were heroes for a time.

I can still see you, Zan, taking the form of an ice giant. How good that must have felt to finally stand tall, to not be held in your sister's beak. Did you see the world for what it was that day? I hope you did. I hope you felt like a man for once, and not merely an element.

Jayna, I must admit, I blame you for so many things. It was you who frequently brought your brother into battle when it would have been so easy to simply fly off and let Superman face the music for his petty rivalries and interstellar pissing matches. Instead, you allowed your brother to become an ice unicycle that you rode into the teeth of danger. (That you rode your brother is a Freudian puzzle that I hope poor Zan never pieces together.) Yes, Jayna, it was you who brought a water spout—in the form of your brother—into an android fight.

I hear that Gleek has turned mean with age. I'm not surprised by this. You dressed him in clothes that matched your own, paraded him around your Super Friends like he was nothing more than a mascot...and really, was he more than that? He should have been. You know it. I know it. The world knows it...and yet: he saved you from the circus you two were forced to perform in back on Exxor, but once you brought him to Earth, things changed, didn't they? He did your bidding and provided you with love, but to what end? To suffer at the whims of Wonder Woman's perversion? To be mocked and teased by Apache Chief? Gleek traveled across the universe, through light years, to be with you...but there was never room for him in your personal lives, not once you became heroes, was there? Is it true he lives in a cage in Florida now, after he ripped Black Vulcan's fingers off in 1996? Why don't you form a flood, Zan, and drown your old friend Gleek, put him out of his caged misery? Don't let him go mad, like poor Hong Kong Phooey did: blind and deaf, showing up in other people's filing cabinets, covered in blood and feces.

It pains me that for all the times both of you took the form of other things, you never managed to be something larger than yourself. Zan, Africa is filled with people dying from lack of water, and yet you never once landed in Ethiopia and brought forth a blizzard, never bothered to drop even a bucket of water to a traveler lost in the Serengeti. Jayna, for all the time you have flown above the land, have you ever once plucked a child from the hands of their kidnappers? And maybe it's the question no one wants to ask you, but I fear I'm the only one with the guts anymore: where were you on 9/11?

The wonder of your lives is this: you wasted so much potential, content to serve first and foremost each other. Hundreds of researchers have asked you to sit down with them, to finally understand the secret of your twindom, to see if there exists in you a genetic abnormality that might help the people of your adopted planet...but no, no, you refuse. Those simple words you utter—"Wonder Twin powers, activate!"—may well hold the medical secrets to finally curing Parkinson's, cancer, AIDS, Alzheimer's, or something as seemingly negligible as eczema, but we'll never know.

Tonight, I stood outside and watched the moon rise. It was cool out, summer having finally left us, and the stars glittered like shards of broken glass. I'm told one of those stars is Exxor, though I'm not sure if I believe that anymore. Your mythology, I've come to conclude, might be a lie. Perhaps you are from someplace like San Jose or Reno or Portland. Perhaps you grew up downwind from a nuclear plant—my extended family, who grew up in Walla Walla, Washington, claim that most of their problems, be they medical or financial or mental, stem from having lived downwind from the plant in Hanford—and your powers are the result of shitty parents who weren't smart enough to move you away from the gamma rays. I suppose it doesn't matter. We live under the same sky, in the same world, and we all have regrets. I guess what I'm trying to say, Zan & Jayna, is that there's still time for you. There's still an opportunity for you to become singular, to see what life might be like if you couldn't activate any powers and were forced to simply be. Who might you be if you could only be you?

I, for one, would like to know.

My very best wishes,
Tod Goldberg

An Open Letter to Wonder Woman:

Twirl, twirl, twirl.

When I was in elementary school, I used to come home from school, eat a snack, and then run out to the backyard. Then, after making sure no one was looking, I began to twirl in a circle, as fast and as hard as I could.(I thought I was unique in this, but years later, I found out that in backyards, parks, and living rooms all across America, gay boys like me were twirling their hearts out.)

Here's what I hoped would happen. My mane of long, smooth black hair would loosen itself from its ponytail. The white orchid tucked behind my ear, the nurse's cap perched on my head, or the oversized glasses hiding the beauty of my peach-colored cheeks would fall to the ground. There'd be a bolt of lightning and a burst of pink light. I'd hear the triumphant blare of trumpets, a rumble of bass guitar, and the thump of a disco beat. And then my elegant brown pantsuit with cream-colored rayon blouse, or fluttering dusty pink sundress, or stiff maid's uniform would transform itself into a red, white, and blue bathing suit with gold accents outlining the bustier. A gold belt would appear around my waist, while a magic lasso of truth would dangle against my hip. I'd fluff out my hair, put my hands on my hips, scan the horizon for trouble, and then leap into action. Just like Lynda Carter did when she played you on TV.

Twirl, twirl, twirl.

Here's what actually happened. I'd get painfully dizzy, run out of breath, and tumble to the ground, while the sky above my head continued to spin until I closed my eyes to make it stop. The smell of grass, which had been cut by a crew of rough, muscular, non-Jewish men from some other Detroit suburb whose name I'd only heard of on the news, filled my flaring nostrils. The swing set shrieks of the neighbors' kids (whom I'd never met and wasn't likely to befriend) filled my ears.

When I opened my eyes again, I was still who I'd always been: a pale, awkward boy with short, shaggy brown hair who hid behind books, terrified of meeting new people and only happy when I could retreat into the secret world of my imagination.

Frustrated by the failure of my desired transformation, I twirled harder, faster. I worked hard to focus my thoughts like your younger sister Wonder Girl did when her first few attempts at twirling failed. Debra Winger did such a good job being Wonder Girl, why couldn't I? Hurry up and change, I told myself. Become a beautiful superhero who performs graceful gymnastic leaps and fights evil without committing acts of violence or mussing her hairdo. Because at any time or in any place—an alley, a forest, even while tied to a chair or locked in a wooden box or rolling down a hill—Diana Prince could become a superhero.

As long as she was alone and unobserved.

Twirl, twirl, twirl.

Still nothing.

Actually, I'd have settled for turning into your alter ego Diana Prince, whose clear, straight-laced beauty I preferred to your bounty of black hair bouncing above a golden tiara. Diana always dressed at the height of 70s fashion, and she spent a good deal of her time in close quarters with her boss Steve Trevor, played by Lyle Waggoner, Playgirl's first centerfold model.

Besides being handsome, Steve Trevor was smart, kind, brave, and not too macho to accept the aid of a glamorous female superhero. I imagined he gave warm hugs. In my family, at my Jewish Day School, at camp and after-school programs at the Jewish Community Center, or at synagogue, I had never met anyone with a name like "Steve Trevor," nor was I likely to.

Maybe that was why I had such trouble making friends. All the good-looking boys I knew, with names like Jason Levy, Dave Cohen, and Jonathan Schwarz, were crass, inconsiderate jocks who sneered at sensitive nerds like me. They picked me last when divvying up teams in gym class, laughed in my face if I raised my voice, pinned notes to my back, tripped and shoved me or knocked my books out of my hands as I walked down the school hallways. Each day, I prayed I might pass through life unnoticed, just like Diana Prince was able to hide her special, secret identity.

But somewhere else, in a city with no middle class Jewish children, perhaps I could make friends with a Scott or Chris or Justin with soft blond hair and brilliant blue eyes, a handsome boy in need of saving, like Steve Trevor. Maybe I could find my own Paradise Island, if only I could spin fast enough.

And so I kept on twirling.

Sincerely,
Aaron Hamburger

Dear "Superman"—

The only thing I'm angry about are the shoes. I'm not angry about the Waterford crystal—we have extras. Actually I wouldn't mind getting rid of the whole set. They take up room and we only use the champagne flutes once a year. And I'm not mad about the curtains either. They're not nice curtains, they came with the house. Believe me, I'm not a materialistic person. People matter more to me than things.

I'm just wondering why you can't act more like a full grown adult when you're around people whose feelings and opinions I care about deeply. And a child's birthday party! Thank God Karen was in the other room. You can't just get drunk like that and expect others not to notice or care. And these were people who were actually looking forward to meeting you. What am I supposed to say to Rick Fraser on Monday? Did you know he lost his wife in a drunk-driving accident last February? How do you think it made him feel to see you bobbing and weaving and spilling your amaretto on the kitchen floor? I'm so annoyed with you right now, I could just—.

You need to realize you're not like everyone else. People expect a certain standard of behavior, children especially. The comment to Mary Orenstein was inappropriate. You shouldn't even be going into people's cabinets if the liquor bottles aren't set out. One beer or one glass of wine should've been plenty for a party that began at four in the afternoon and was over by six. And where did you go after that? I called your cell three times before Lois was nice enough to tell me you got home okay.

Look, I understand you're upset about the whole "Axis of Evil" thing, and Christa and I have tried to cut you some slack. But I have problems of my own. I just had surgery three weeks ago, I've been sick for the past two years and I've got no teaching lined up for the fall, and you don't see me making morbid comments to strangers and getting belligerently drunk in public. If you're really that depressed, do the world a favor and just stay home.

By the way, those shoes meant a lot to me. They might not be worth a lot of money, but Christa bought them for me in Santa Fe and I'd been hoping to wear them to my cousin's wedding in New Jersey next month. Thanks a lot.

MH

Dear Mr. Radd,

I hope you'll understand if I do not call you the Silver Surfer. I don't believe in space surfing, but I do believe in you, Mr. Radd. I encountered you at a time when you affirmed everything I had come to believe.

I was seventeen, a college freshman away from home for the first time. In just two months I had lost my belief in everything I had been taught about right and wrong, about God and religion, about America and war and morality, justice, sexuality, drugs, even about reality and the nature of existence. And Superman.

Amidst a teenage reality cobbled together by assassinations, family upheaval, musical obsession, psychedelic drugs, and naïve teenaged ravings about revolution. . .at least I was sincere. I was deeply committed to a personal philosophy, an astounding paradox born of a psilocybin trip, that the only certainty in life was uncertainty, and in that broad light, I made myself a moral code with one commandment: Don't stand on others to elevate yourself. And I stopped eating meat.

"You what?" My mother's voice, fifteen hundred miles away. "Did you say, 'Superman's a pig?'"

I was young and smart and energetic and defiant—a completely disinterested student. I was playing music every day and night and feeding my head whatever I could get, and hanging out with the most fascinating people I'd ever known. It was Adventureland, Funtown; we were shocking the straights, breaking laws and conspiring to break more. Yet in the quiet of my bed, I passed many nights feeling lost and lonesome—I mean, way, way out to sea.

Then one day I happened to pick up a new comic book: The Origin of the Silver Surfer.

I read about how you saved your home planet by challenging the cosmos-roaming, world-eating colossus Galactus, how you stood up to him and told him that what he was doing—devouring whole planets—was wrong. His reply was as simple as it was profound. "If your life required you to step on an ant hill, would you hesitate?"

In a comic book! The whole right-wrong relativity thing. And I watched you stand there slack-jawed. We were treading the same wide waters, Mr. Radd, you and me, so out of our depths. Can't depend on anything anymore.

You made Galactus an offer: "What if I could find planets to sustain you without your having to kill living things?"

Zap. He accepted your offer, gave you powers over time and space (and a surfboard, which even then was pretty much bullshit, right?), and made you his herald so you could search for planets he could eat without killing living beings. With that act, sacrificing your happiness to save your home planet, you gained his respect. And everything was okay for a while, not great—I mean, you're roaming the cosmos all alone—but things were bearable at least. Then you happened upon Earth.

It's been a long time, Mr. Radd, so I don't remember the details, but I do remember that you were fascinated by us Earthlings—and confused. In fact, I think you may have fallen in love with a woman here. The point is, Galactus started getting hungry, and you had become mired in another conundrum. You told your master something like this: "Look at these people. They've been given a paradise! Yet, everywhere I go they are destroying more and more of their planet and killing one another. What kind of madness is this?"

You told Galactus that you couldn't leave—not yet. He told you that you could not stay. He took away your keys and stranded you on Earth with the rest of us. For the last time, you stood up to him. You refused to go. So he marooned you on Earth with the rest of us. As I recall, you ended that episode sitting alone in some isolated spot, probably the Arctic, brooding. A brooding superhero. I bet I slept with that comic book. Eventually, I loaned it to an English professor, who never gave it back.

Years later, I came to realize that you were suffering from depression. At the time, I felt like I'd found a brother. I subscribed and read all about you for, I don't know, years. Eventually, Marvel pulled the plug on you, ennui not being a big seller in the Home of the Brave. But you were there when I needed you. Thank you for that.

Kindest wishes,
Mike Kimball

Dear Moses Herzog:

Ah, you are long dead I know, but that never stopped you, did it? I don't think you ever did write a letter to anyone who wasn't real, who was more or less totally imaginary. Anyway, it doesn't matter to me if you are alive or dead, real or imaginary, part Saul Bellow or simply your own good self. We are all alive more or less in the warehouse of dreams, down on the docks at the edge of that grand old Republic of Letters, and you are as real to me as you ever have been. And that, my friend, is very real, very present. So much so that I can't believe this is the first time I have written you.

The odd prompting of this is from an editor who asked various writers to compose a letter to a "super-hero or super-villain." I don't know what got into me to make me say yes, but I said it, and for about a month now I have earnestly tried to play it straight. First I wrote a snarky little note and quoted a Stafford poem, saying it is "time for all the heroes to go home, / if they have one." I said the whole business of comic book heroes and villains, despite the way they embody our anxieties and yearnings, is just too juvenile to worry about. The whole business of our popular culture in 21st century America bothers the child's imagination with too much of too little. Let the kid go to sleep, I wrote, and let the dreams find their own weird, idiosyncratic villains and heroes.

But then the editor, blessed with an infinite patience and optimism, said she'd be happy to publish my note, but that she was hoping for something a little more substantive, a genuine reflection on heroes and villains in our time. Ach, I instantly recalled all the times I myself have given students assignments on heroes and anti-heroes, and how I most often commented that I had hoped for something, well, a little more substantive.

Worse, she was right at the core of things. There is significant inner work to be done in this post-industrial and post-everything-else imaginative landscape we uneasily inhabit. Perhaps now more than ever we need to renew and refresh and restore our imaginative grasp of the concept of hero and villain. The impulse to commodify is the impulse to simplify, to make palatable and tolerable some part of our ongoing collective dream of saviors and monsters. The comic book world of super-heroes and super-villains provides the data of decadence peculiar to our time. For those who take upon themselves some little shred of the unacknowledged legislator's mantle is to put some weight back into the airy nothings generated by the popular culture. Mr. Moses Herzog—professor of nothing useful, nebbish and schlemiel—this is where you come in, you most unlikely of super-anything. Mr. Moses Herzog—fictional and literary hero of mine—I am conferring on you the honorary degree of "super," at least for now. You will be puzzled and embarrassed, and will say you are, at best, a poor schlub.

Heroism is not—despite all the press releases and opening night galas—a matter of identity, not even the hidden identities of so many Batmen,

Supermen, Ironmen, and Hulks. Whatever heroism really is, it is inevitably a flickering, ephemeral moment. What that moment does is provide us with evidence that upon occasion we might as individuals be more than, as Yeats said, "the bundle of accident and incoherence that sits down to breakfast." And truly, even in the sociological realm, does not the story of a hero always try to outline a new or extended horizon of human possibility? And does not that image sift down in our consciousness, floating just a few feet above one of the vents of the unconscious before it settles in almost forever?

As I said, this is where you come in. One moment, one action that has been with me for all my adult life. I am in your novel now. It is toward the end. You are broken-hearted, cuckolded, and falling apart. Your wife is now living with your ex-best-friend. You have gotten that Russian pistol from your grandfather's desk. You are going to go kill the adulterer Valentine Gersbach. For all the pain this man has caused you; for destroying your life and marriage and career. You climb the back stairs of your old apartment. It is Chicago, Hyde Park, and the alley is quiet and empty, secluded. You look through the back window and see into the bathroom. Your little girl Junie is standing in the tub, and there in the white light, is Gersbach bathing your daughter. Sexual weirdness hovers at the edge of what you are seeing.

You ready to shoot the sonofabitch, but you notice that he is actually bathing her, scrubbing her, even her private parts, with brusque paternal care and efficiency. You could, if you were in your right mind, even call what he is doing decent, loving. You put the pistol back in your pocket, and you go back into the night to face as best you can all the remnants of your life, including all those letters to important thinkers that you have been writing, letters that will, as this one, never be answered.

You were very much alive in American literary culture when I first met you. I was on Okinawa, and it was 1969. I was a lieutenant in the USMC, and had a kind of adolescent desire to go to combat in Vietnam, perhaps in order to write about it. But for a few months I was "stuck" on Okinawa. In my free time, I picked up the book named after you. My girlfriend then had mysteriously stopped writing to me, and so I identified with you in your romantic dilemma, and well, Saul's sinuous sentences just carried me along until that scene. Honestly, I had—as a child of *Gunsmoke, Have Gun Will Travel, Battle Cry*—and of course all the superheroes of the day—never quite registered a moment when someone decided not to shoot, not to pull the trigger.

A few months later, I want to tell you now, that moment became part of the narrative of my own life. In late 1969 the My Lai massacre stories and photos made their way into the greater American consciousness, including the United States military. I saw the photo of the dead Vietnamese women and children on the path, and I looked up at the ceiling and declared myself "not a Nazi," and this was not what I had joined for. Six months later I applied for conscientious objector status.

I did not feel heroic, just as I am sure you did not either. But in a strange way your no prompted my no. This was the chain of imaginative connection between us, and with Bellow. Saul and I never shared the same politics, nor would I think you a pacifist in any way, but when you decided not to shoot, you enacted a way of being that heretofore had not been present, or present enough, in my imagination. You and Saul have both probably read Simone Weil's *The Iliad, or the Poem of Force*, the essay she wrote in 1939 shortly after the Nazis invaded Poland. In her reading of the epic, Weil says that those in love with combat never pause, or are never forced to pause, and thus never experience that "interval of hesitation wherein lies all our consideration for our brothers in humanity."

A pause on that order was what happened on the back steps of your Chicago apartment as you looked in on Valentine and Junie. When you hesitated and decided not to shoot, my guess is you were shedding false images of manhood, and how a man, especially a deeply aggrieved one, should behave. I actually wrote to Saul once about you, and he said that when he thought of you, he thought that he had at least shown you shedding the more obvious falsehoods of your life. That too was how I understood your story, and how I understood specifically that moment. It also turned out to be a prescient moment in regard to my own life. I had it in mind, for instance, as I began the long process of obtaining Conscientious Objector status and a discharge from the Marine Corps. You were in my mind as what I wrote was in effect a long letter to the Commandant explaining why I could no longer participate in this unjust war, or in any war thereafter. It was a memo, I admit, but in the Defense Department's world, it was a Herzog letter, for sure.

And it worked. In the fall of 1970, I became the one of the first—if not the first— Marine officers to be honorably discharged during the Vietnam War. And so this, my letter-writing role-model, this is my letter to you, so long overdue, and brimming with my most sincere thanks.

Fred Marchant

Registered Letter from Maria Astrid Schumann-Spiderman
June 18th, 1968

Dear Italian Spiderman, I'd like
To say I've left your things in the garage:
Your green Ducati (half of it), your chains,
Your socks, your guide to Indian massage,

Your chicken (known for laying packs of smokes),
Your girdle and the large electric wheel
You use for moustache sharpening. Your gloves—
I know about your extra loves, you eel.

All I ever wanted was the truth.
My therapist had warned me that a guy
With psychic links to penguins and a paunch
Was nothing but a rich, exotic lie.

Damn you and your beer, your sick guitar
For serenading babes (imagine how!)
I know what kind of untermensch you are;
And yes, you blob, I'm using German now.

My lawyers will provide you with the key.
The asteroid is sitting in the bank.
If Goblin calls, please tell him I'm in Paris.
I find it is my duty to be frank:

You cannot love with just a poison bite.
You'll need to get yourself a new ragazza.
Romanza: gone. Velocita: I'm off.
Terrore: you were loved, but I was pazza.

Ahoy Green Lantern!

Loved the movie—seriously. Loved that you played yourself, authentic: I mean the part where you're chosen for the lantern, chosen to have the power to conjure any kinda whatever—with a thought, on a whim! Whoa! And your shock at the sudden red carpet of possibilities sprawled before you, the mix of panic and thrill as the good news ripened. That's the moment. Like a first wet dream, when life became different than it was the day before (though one is still human after such a dream) but you, my man, were hardly still human, given such abracadabra to run with. And you played it small. You could've told Captain America to kiss your green ass, and he would've too—sat on his mighty shield and puckered the fuck up.

That's the thing I couldn't resist if I were you: cruising around all swollen with such stupendous potency and begging some once-thought-to-be-tough-guy to start some shit, just so I could go green, summon up some kinda savage weed-eater for him—I mean I'd get straight-up green eggs and ham on a Snidely Whiplash ass! That's the thing. Seriously, though, I wouldn't really spend too much time on the daily thugs. They look in the mirror and their hearts go flat. They wish they were someone else.

I'd spend most 'a my time prowling the halls of Congress, and hanging out in the White House foyer waiting for some pointless war to be declared or some prune-hearted legislation to pass. And if I witnessed anything adding measurable hurt to the globe, after one of those all-in-favor/all opposed aye and nay, I'd kick down the doors with emerald boots the size of Honda Civics, tie up every business be-suited dickhead, gag 'em and start strolling the aisles eye-pokin' and water-boardin'. What could anybody do? Call the Fantastic Four? They're not Real! But I'd be real, and by the time I was through—oh, we'd have world peace, no poverty, and a three-day work week, believe me. See that's why the powers fall into the soft hands of guys like you: cuz ya never really do nuthin' big enough to do nuthin'!

Sincerely,
Michael Moore

To Namor

Atlantis will rise again. —Charles Olson

In the morning we find a speedboat

smashed on the rocks of Lost Boy Bay
after heavy storm clear the sand

ruined ships sometimes emerge
near where the old remember
mackerel-sharp this our true fleet

I have seen those touched the evidence

migration and capital leave behind
boats of small archaeologies

some weekend aluminum toy
may the dispatcher understand me

I pause between each number each letter
phone in the registration

Listen through that aquarium window before I knock

Atlantis down again
wait for the play to finish

old domestic animal on the couch
blue plates diffused to the wall commemorating
(surely something) starboard

a few blocks from the condo where the body

not until after the holiday was discovered
when I come back to this level of attention
sky means ground sun means shore

what I recognize as human what I recognize as
stop light in rain

below the flying design of kingfisher no swan

it's true I own a lamp
lamp's on the table

I'm excited the table also holds
two coasters a magic book a remote
the remote does not point at the tv

the table is a kind of monster island

were the items monsters
the only monstrous presence

an absence monster

two dogs sleep on the couch
they are remotes

the remote monster
towers over us
saturates the atmosphere

this time of year I receive catalogues

few letters the cards are tinged
I listen to a playlist of songs titled "can't "

I say can too
someday I will take that cookbook
back to the kitchen

it's true that I own

nine hundred dollars
the exploitation I do

is done far from me
my bumper sticker says that

green light fathers snow on your waves

or rain soaked streets in a desert town
a winsome lintel a little bushel a gigantic bustle

listmaking animals live in rage
counteragency and nimble bird sidereal comedy
play out under the crèche

we pretended not to be ourselves

as we walk out of the ocean
certain tangoings may be permitted

either my head is just what I look out of

like the spires of your lost cities at low tide

or because I put water in one opening
it is a watering can
concatenating in barber mirrors

like fossil section

the scientist who is about to be turned into a hero
attends to with white smock fine brush green potion

your painters are cleaning yellow pigment

from one another's hands
at the center of a plum

while thieves fill pillows
willows hum love song to the carpenter
out in the tallgrass between red thunder

truck tire rolls in surf

beyond the housemartin savagery
twice I've hid a tutelary noun feathery

in an albeit Wednesday beside a statue
a noun good enough to fix my hometown
a breadcrumb romance amid mustard

street stretched out to disobey

and so might we reach an alliance
did not tell us where

the path beneath the sphere
would lead him just roaming there
until his figure became unclear

every gem came tumbling from her hand

into the prepercieved

color tensed inside her fist
like green panthers

Dear Red Mist:

I'm concerned about your character and some of the issues surrounding it. Or saturating it, maybe, is better, as saturation is more in line with dissolution and diminishment, whereas surrounding seems to ensure that there is some steady quantity of something that is there to be surrounded.

Your character begins with a mixture of both qualities: as the evil and vicious billionaire drug lord's pampered son, you are excluded by your father from his business (diminished), and at the same time surrounded (protected, ensured) by his bodyguards. The boy heroes who attend your high school cannot approach, nor do you endeavor to allow them to. To them you are nothing and everything. The hypothetical person. They try to approach, and they are thwarted. You move not toward them but toward your father's numb gory work.

At first this intrigued me. It resisted the expectable, at least, insofar as your pampered life did not turn you into a romantic. But what did it turn you into? That is really the question. What did your pampered life make you? Your father scoffs at the idea of your inclusion in his brutal business—his identity. He flicks you away so casually and so profoundly. And yet, you do not subsequently move further away from him of your own accord—you do not have any interest in the heroes. They are so nice, so kind toward you.

And then, your father is suddenly faced with someone who is able to go on killing his men routinely. Then—and only then—is it possible for your father to include you in his business. You see the opportunity and you take it. Okay, the *prove myself to my father idea*—a reasonable premise, the arc of which still allows for proper revelation of your real identity. So off we go. You will pose as a hero and befriend the heroes who need to be killed. You will deliver the good for execution. An act of supreme evil. Here, you are being set up to fail, to turn toward the heroes when you see their basic decency.

This seems to be what might happen, when you're out cruising and smoking weed together. Listening to music—great times, those. When you pull up to the kill-site, it's already in flames, and all your father's men are dead. Coupled with getting high together, this turn of events accentuates your vulnerability, which seems like it should make you paranoid about your whole effort to join with evil—to actually kill someone good. There you are: the pampered kid, suddenly faced with dangers unlike any he has seen before. And you go on posing as a hero.

There may be something to be said for your effort to rescue your father's men, but it pales in comparison to your failure to form a bond with the person you are actually with—the person you are deceiving and would have seen killed. Why has no bond formed? You simply take what you have learned back to your father. You went out from your father as no one, in your fancy car, and now you have come back to him as no one, author of a failed plan. Identity still pending. And then what? How can we heap more shame upon you?

Let's have you sit beside your father to watch the heroes be tortured to death live on the internet. You voice your displeasure about killing the hero who "isn't really" a hero, but you lack the conviction to act on this displeasure, to make a response out of it. You sit there with your make-up halfway removed and you are not on the side of the hero or on the side of the villain, your father. No, you just sit there beside him, vaguely aghast. You certainly aren't enjoying it like your father is enjoying it.

And then of course when all is lost—when your father is blown to bits between skyscrapers—you are the only survivor on the side of evil. There you stand in your lair, suddenly thrust into the bad guy mastermind cliché. The same old vengeance over a murdered father. This cliché follows the other cliché, the *prove myself to my father* cliché.

But they don't really work together. How does the unexpected death of your father complete the effort to prove yourself to your father? Or fail to complete it? And what does it mean that you are the supreme villain now? If we are able to keep ourselves from seeing it as merely the slapstick level confession to an intended sequel, what can we say about you? How can you, "Red Mist," be the face of profound evil?

Your fateless drift—your sudden and meaningless movement from one cliché to the next—your having lost nothing and your having suffered nothing—is this what we are to think of as evil? Is your lack of believable conviction a symbol for evil? *The* symbol? This is as far as I've thought this through. I hope you can help me, and help yourself, too. Maybe it is that evil is being caricatured, as with Dr. Evil and so many cartoon evil geniuses nowadays. A loveable evil. A bumbling evil. But then why aren't the heroes' intentions caricatured in the same way?

The question of risking your own well-being in order to help someone who badly needs help…this is a difficult question to make fun of. Beckett has come closest, I think, in Endgame, in the story Hamm tells about the father who comes begging bread for his son. You make no such effort to scoff at the heroic father, and in your world the heroes don't come off as pathetic.

We have seen no evidence at all that you are even capable of such scoffing. If you were capable, you could then begin the arduous task of motivating yourself to make an attempt at it. This task is rarely completed by those who are capable of it, and like I said, we have no evidence that you are capable of it. So I am unsatisfied with the comedic reading of you.

Sometimes I think I have no reading of you at all. Like you remain—no matter what—some irreducibly vague presence on the fringe of the narrative, vulnerable at every step to whatever cliché response is called for to advance the plot. If this is what you are, I expect that perhaps you can't know it.

But maybe I am wrong? Maybe it is possible for you to smoke some weed with someone and just let all the good and evil shit go? I mean, maybe take on some more realistic desires?

Sincerely,
Joe Wenderoth

Schumaker P. Fitts
Vice President, City Council
Gotham City, NX 10101
fitts@council.gotham.gov

July 30, 2011

Bruce Wayne
Wayne Manor
Gotham Heights, NX 10104

Dear Mr. Wayne:

It has come to my attention, as Vice President of the City Council of Gotham City, and as representative of the district of which you are a constituent, that there have been numerous complaints in recent months regarding activities in the vicinity of your personal residence, Wayne Manor. These complaints center on the presence and behavior of an individual who calls himself Bat Man. Allegedly, he resides in the basement of said property.

First of all, as you may be aware, zoning in Gotham Heights does not permit subdividing a residence for the purposes of creating a second living space or apartment. Unless Mr. Man is a blood relative, it is not permissible under zoning code GC-6442R for him to reside in your basement on a permanent basis.

Second, Mr. Man has been observed leaving your premises on several occasions in a black vehicle which violates Gotham City's emission and noise abatement standards code GC-4241N. Third, he has been clocked by police radar traveling at over 120 MPH in a 35 MPH zone, endangering the lives of the women, children, and beloved pets residing in our great metropolis. In fact, it has even been reported, although without corroboration, that this vehicle has been driven so fast as to rise into the air.

Fourth, there have been frequent sightings in the night sky of a beacon emanating from an unknown source, which seems to inspire Mr. Man to appear on Gotham's streets in his black vehicle. This violates code GC-1034L, which regulates the use or promulgation of beams of light which may interfere with air traffic control over Gotham City's Archie Goodwin International Airport. In addition, the design of the beam of light has come to the attention of several multinational corporations, including, among others, Bacardi Rum and Motorola, which claim that it infringes on their trademarks and branding, leading them to threaten Gotham City itself with legal action.

Finally, Mr. Man has appeared dressed in a costume which has been experienced as unsettling and even threatening by the good people of our fair city.

Schumaker P. Fitts
Vice President, City Council
Gotham City, NX 10101
fitts@council.gotham.gov

This is in violation of local ordinance GC-1313C, which addresses the daily comfort and well-being of our citizenry.

On a more personal note, Mr. Wayne, as you know, the metropolis of Gotham City holds you in very high esteem, and greatly values your contributions to the wealth and welfare of the city and its people. I myself am more than grateful for your many years of support of civic and economic development, which have made Gotham the crown jewel of our great and free nation. That is why I am writing to you personally, to ask you to convince Mr. Man to cease and desist in his unruly behavior. It is my fervent hope that this will quell the groundswell of opposition to his presence at Wayne Manor, and will preclude the need for intervention on the part of the Police Department of Gotham City. In this regard, I am quite convinced that Police Commissioner Gordon would not want to find himself in the position of being required by law to pursue such a course of action.

As you know, you and I have discussed this matter off the record several times. Regrettably, I am compelled at this time, given that there has been no apparent change in Mr. Man's actions, to address you more formally. Further, I'm sure you understand that there are political forces at work that are less supportive of your ideas for the economic development of certain tracts of land in Gotham City than I am, and my influence would be diminished if the "Bat Man" issue is not resolved in the near future. I trust that you understand my position, particularly in an election year such as this, and are not offended by the official nature of this letter.

I am hopeful that, when this matter is resolved, you will drop by the club for a drink or two. I trust that this letter finds you in good health, and please give my regards to Alfred.

Sincerely yours,

Schumaker P. "Shoe" Fitts
Vice President, City Council
Gotham City

Dan Marmor

RECIPES FOR DISASTER

PART 1. APPETIZERS

Cocktail March 24th, 2012

Jim Jones' Kool-Aid

1 tall glass

1 half-empty bottle of sleeping pills

4 shots of the Jameson

1 bud light

2 cubes of ice.

Drink ½ the beer. Take 2 shots. Mix the rest of the ingredients in tall glass with ice. Stir. Sit back.
Take a deep breath. Drink, and wait.

Hors d'oeuvre March 23rd, 1988—March 26th, 2012

The Phil Martin Monroe Platter

1 part sperm

1 part egg

4 parts Daddy issues to make the concoction more wayward and frightened of the future

A dash of pessimism

1 overprotective but alcoholic mother with a short temper

1 older brother with a superiority complex

1 girlfriend you met in college

A healthy dose of that feeling that everything is against you

2 parts apathy

1 broken cross for mixing

1 house in Queens that needs repairs

A splash of self-consciousness after a fourth grade teacher called you worthless

Crushed dreams when after realizing you'll never become an astronaut

1 combination of sparse facial hair, a horrible fashion sense, passivity, a feeling of victimization, a round face, and a very wide smile

1 slice of pineapple for the rim

Combine sperm with egg in the restroom of *Pio Pio*, a Peruvian restaurant near the city, or in the taxicab after dinner on the way home. Pop out of your mother nine months later covered in placenta and blood. Sneeze. Your dad will say, "Your kid's gonna be a stubborn son of a bitch." Your mom will get offended but she'll be too tired to say anything. When you arrive at your new home in Queens, don't forget to make a bad impression on your older brother, Edward. He will say about you, "He's so boring. He doesn't do anything. When can we return him?"

Attend Daly Elementary School. Play I'll Show You Mine If You Show Me Yours with Samantha during naptime. Make sure to be best friends with Robby, but be just acquaintances with him after that year. In second grade, jump out of a first story window to escape math class. Break your leg from the fall. Miss a week of school.

Attend Marie Curie Middle School. Fall in love with Lindsay. Give her a necklace you found on the ground with a mood ring that you bought from the stationary store down the block from school. When she leaves you for another kid after three months, pretend you don't care. Care. Secretly, start a journal of awful poetry about how sad you are. Think about running away for the first time. Don't. Your dad will.

When your dad has a midlife crisis, he will buy himself a ticket to Israel "to find his God," as your mother will put it later. He won't say goodbye. He'll just pack up and leave. Your mom will be sad. Try to console her. Your brother will turn sour and avoid contact with both you and your mom. She will be upset with him, and she'll tell you all about it. She will drink Bourbon Old Fashioned with a slice of pineapple on the rim during breakfast to make it look healthy so you'll drink your orange juice. Get horrible acne.

Attend PS 156. Hate it. Have very few friends. Study to get by. Pass all your classes. When your dad returns, be outwardly angry with him. Obviously, love him though, and hope for a better relationship. Start to do better in classes even though your parents constantly argue. Return home one day to find your father hanging by the neck from a pipe in the basement. Attend the funeral with an air of disbelief. Stop accompanying your mom to church. Start experimenting with drugs.

Go away to California for college. Meet the girl of your dreams, Sarah. Ask her out. After dating for a month, have sex for the first time. Tell her you love her after two months. Major in Psychology. Get decent grades. Work a part-time job at Jamba Juice. Sarah will talk to you about the future. Genuinely smile for the first time in years. Take a German cooking class in your senior year. As the Great Recession hits, graduate with no honors or awards.

Move back to the house your mother has abandoned for an apartment in Florida and your father has left for a grave in Jackson Heights. Edward will join you. He will be worried about you, but he will pretend not to care.

Try and cook for yourself more than you eat out, but spend the majority of the money you've saved on booze and Sarah. Although still sad, feel a bit of hope for your future. Think, Life isn't all that rotten. Believe it. This optimism will change very quickly.

Unemployment may not have been a problem before, but allow your anxiety to slowly creep up on you. Call yourself a pathetic loser in the bathroom mirror almost every morning. Doubt yourself. Blame society for the mess you're in. Write essays about the need for governmental reform. Talk about this with Edward and Sarah constantly. They both will roll their eyes in response.

Listen to all of your old music, any angsty punk band to indulge your anger. Read novels by misanthropic authors. Watch a lot of television. Drink a lot in your spare time. Eat unhealthy food all the time. Try not to notice that the lawn is covered with tall grass, weeds and garbage. Notice, but don't do anything about it. Always forget to take out the trash. Disregard the flies and ants that accumulate in your kitchen.

One day in late January, decide that your life would be so much better if you made Sarah your wife. Edward should be in Boston for the month visiting his girlfriend. Go out and buy roses, champagne, whipped cream, condoms, and strawberries. Turn the heat way up in your house. Invite Sarah over. Make every inch of your house scream love, condoms on the table, candles lit, light music playing from another room. Wear your tightest underwear. Comb your hair.

Decide that you will present her a ring inside of a cake. Preheat oven to 350. Spread butter on 9 x 11 baking pan. In separate bowl, combine cake mix, eggs, milk, and vanilla extract. Beat until batter has no hard lumps left. A few lumps are okay. Pour into baking pan. Place baking pan in oven for 35 minutes. Watch TV. Take cake out of oven. Spread frosting and sprinkles on top. With squeezable frosting tube, write Marry Me, Sarah. Below the last word, place the engagement ring.

Wait anxiously for half an hour.

When she arrives, give her a long hug. She will push you off and say, "Why's it so hot in here?" Apologize, and turn down the heat. Pour two tall glasses of champagne. She will turn on the TV. Watch it until you can't take anymore. She will be entranced by a show about two rich women who moved to New York and can't help but whine about it.

Sneak into the kitchen, and prepare the cake. Enter the room with gusto, with passion, with love. Get down on one knee. Hold the cake out to her. Say, "Sarah, will you marry me?" She'll look at you in shock. She'll begin to cry. Ask, "What's wrong, baby?" She'll look at you through her tears and say, "Phil, I've met somebody else." Look shocked. She'll say, "It's over." Don't say a thing. When she walks out of the door covering her eyes, lose your last ounce of dignity and weep. Drop the cake and the ring into the garbage.

Very important: stew for five minutes. With relish, contemplate suicide.

Now, incorporate Jim Jones' Kool-Aid as shown on page 1. Go out to your backyard. Things should go black as you pass out on your back patio. Go into a coma and think over your entire life in the sequence as written.

Unbeknownst to you, the real world will continue on. One of your neighbors will see you and try to say something to you. She will check on you, tell her husband that she thinks you're dead. They will carry you back to a guest room in their house. The woman is a nurse. She, her daughter, and her husband will take good care of you until you recover after two days of unconsciousness.

PART 2. ENTREES

Breakfast March 27th, 2012

Recovery Fondue

1 curious Catholic angel

1 drip bag saline solution

1 dimly lit room

Open your eyes for the first time after a long sleep. Don't really know how you got wherever you are. It is important that you be too exhausted to fully open your eyes or move at all, too beat to really understand the situation. In what you think might be a dream, see an angelic figure at the side of your bed praying. See the lamplight from behind her head as a halo.

Hear whispered words, "Dear God. Please guide this young man to safety. Guide him to a meaningful life under your watch, a life dedicated to you... Please make him better. Please, God, make him better." Watch as the beautiful girl kneeling beside your bed crosses herself and continues mouthing religious blessings.

Breathe slowly as you watch her hands fall from the prayer position onto the sheet-covering the flank of your leg. Admire her cheekbones, and curled hair, and slender fingers as she slides her hands under the sheet. Feel the coolness of her palms as they slide up your thigh.

Shut your eyes tightly. She should be looking at your face now, hoping not to wake you as she moves the sheet back from your body to expose your naked flesh. Feel ashamed, but stay still… As she starts touching you, examining you, try to stay as still as you can. Meanwhile, feel an erection starting.

Peek at this girl's face as she holds your cock in her hands, rolling it, stroking it, enjoying it. Stifle the groan you feel erupting from your throat as she teases you more. She will look pleased. Hope for more. But, she'll just touch you for a little while longer. Then, she'll turn off the lamp and leave.

Feel your heart pounding, more in your crotch than in your chest. Feel yourself slowly fade back to sleep. Look around the room, but feel heavy in the darkness, and feel lonely. Contemplate the afterlife just before you fall asleep. Debate whether celestial nymphs would service you constantly in heaven or whether you simply wouldn't need sex at all. Decide you're in a hell where beautiful women leave you with a constant state of blue balls. Go back to sleep.

Dinner March 28th, 2012

Cougar Stew

1 glass of water

1 TV playing static

Weakness

1 hot MILF

A carpet from the 70's

Revelation—You are alive!

Your sleep will be disrupted by a shocking light, a persistent white noise, a brilliant crackle, and a throbbing headache. Lift your head to see that the television across the room is playing static that reminds you of a torturous snowfall. Attempt to kick your legs off the side of the bed. You will be tucked in tight though, and it won't be easy.

Try again. On your third try, however, you should finally free yourself.

As you attempt to stand, brace yourself. Your legs are weak and will crumble beneath you. Hold onto the bed frame to regain composure. Make your way towards the TV. Stumble. Knock a vase to the floor, shattering glass and spilling water all over the place.

Continue your mission towards the television. Your headache will worsen when you realize that you're wearing a hospital gown. A light will turn on in the hallway outside, but you will only be able to see the light from under the closed door. A sickness will creep up on you with the realization that you are, in fact, alive.

The door will open. A beautiful, older woman will enter. As you crane your neck to see if it's the angel from your dream, feel your knees give out. Fall face first onto an orange and red shag carpet. The static of the television will be the only noise you can hear.

The woman will delicately pick you up by the armpits. She is skilled with her hands, but they are thinner than those you remember from your dreams. She is real. She'll put your arm around her shoulder. Each strand of her hair is thin, and it will feel like satin against your face. Your hand will fall onto her breast. Feel your fingertips again as they touch her shirt.

Try to look at her face as she walks you back to bed. Admire her angular cheekbones and large lips. She will smell like maple syrup and flowers. She will place you back into bed. Your limbs will become limp.

This woman will look into your face with compassionate eyes and a concerned brow. Enjoy the moment as you fall in love with her. Enjoy her hair falling just above your face, and almost smile when she tucks the stray hairs behind her ear. She will have freckles and sensitive eyes. She will be beautiful. "Go to sleep," she'll say to you as you try to whisper something to her. Try to ask her to confirm that you're still alive. Try to ask her how it could be possible. Try to ask her why. Don't. Not because you don't want to but because you can't. You will be too weak.

As she strokes your head, feel your eyelids get heavy again. Think that this could, after all, be heaven. But, for some reason, it will feel real. Know it is real. Know this woman is your savior. Know that you are alive. Sleep will return even before she turns off the TV.

Pre-Breakfast March 30th, 2012

Coffee, and A Hard Morning's Work

1 hefty father figure

1 thermos of coffee, black

1 headache, stronger than said coffee

A begrudging smile

A hazy morning drive

The sun, not even close to rising yet

A fish market that seems more like an Asian bazaar

A heavy bag of fresh halibut

An empty kitchen, spotless and silver

Two Tylenol

Abrasive cursing

An apron, an oak chair, a white tablecloth, and an inappropriate nap

Wake up to an obese man with a white goatee and a nice smile punching you in the arm and handing you a thermos filled with hot black coffee. "Wakey wakey, son!" he will shout in an unusually low baritone, "time for work." He will have laid out fresh clothes for you on a chair, clothes from when he was younger, clothes from what he calls the clothes museum. Groggy, let your eyes adjust to the brightness of the artificial light. "If you don't get up soon," he'll continue as your headache gradually returns, "you're going to make us both late." He will walk to the door. "You've got five, kiddo," he'll say. Have a bit of trouble understanding what in the world he's talking about. It shouldn't really make sense.

Think semi-logically, late for what? Where am I? Who is this fat man? Let your legs swing over the edge of your bed, and get up. Wobble for a second, but be surprisingly okay with fighting gravity. Take off your medical apron, and throw on your clothes. You should remember how to do this. You've been doing it for 23 years now.

But, for some reason, it will feel odd, foreign, like you haven't dressed yourself since you were a child. Once the final touch of the shoe-tie is complete, the fat man will reenter with a broad smile and rosy cheeks.

His hair should be sparse and short, but if it's longer, don't worry. Everybody's life turns out a bit differently. He should have that hair halo, with a bright baldness at the crown. He should be supportive, holding onto your arm as he guides you to his Escalade, helping you up onto the riding boards and into the passenger seat. It will be dark out. Don't look at the clock, but deduce that it's fucking early.

"I'm gonna straighten you out, boy, give you something to do," the fat man will say. "The name's Ken," Ken, the fat man, will say. He will look you in the eyes while driving. He will ignore the road. Don't feel any ounce of fear. Trust him completely.

Slouch in your chair, and watch the passing signs, buildings and bits of worn rubber from busted tires on the side of the road through uneasy eyes and a pounding headache. Feel the buzz of the city as cars start to fill the road. The sun will begin to peak over the horizon, but not enough yet to be seen over the skyscrapers.

When he stops, be surprised. Think where are we? Why did I get in this car? Are the people outside even speaking English? The answers to these questions are: At a Chinese fish market; Because you don't have the mental capacity to think for yourself just yet; and No, respectively.

As you get out of the car, see hundreds of Asian men running to and from a tiny rectangular room, screaming in a language you will think is from Star Trek. Ken will usher you into the madness. The odd men in strange aprons will be throwing fish back and forth, wrapping them in wax paper, shouting at each other, and pouring buckets of ice into larger buckets of ice. Ken will nod his head at a few of these scurrying men with bad teeth and bad eyes.

He will stop at one section that is the loudest of all, where the buzz of the crowd is startling. He'll throw a few little men out of the way with his burly arms, pulling you along with him. Don't apologize. Don't even realize that this is improper etiquette at one of these gatherings. Ken will shake the hand of the man behind the counter, introduce you to him, and get a huge bag of halibut, or some kind of fish that you imagine halibut should look like. Ken will put the bag in your arms and usher you back through the chaos to the large car. Inside the car, feel safe. Inside the car, it will seem like the city is whispering.

The car will reek like fish within a minute, and your headache will come on stronger than ever. Your eyes will struggle to stay open, but make sure to keep them open. Keep them open so Ken won't worry that you're dead if he looks at you. Drink your coffee.

"We're almost there," Ken will say with a smile. Nod and smile back. As the car shimmies down some city streets, forget its real life, and feel like you're in a video game, like the buildings have turned into bad graphics of buildings, and the cars have turned into pixilated images of cars. Feel like you don't belong. Recognize, though, that you are driving down city streets that seem too crowded. The streets will get somewhat less crowded as you drive down a row of shorter buildings separated by small alleyways.

When Ken puts the car in park, get out with him. Hold the bag of halibut over your right shoulder. Ken will guide you down a back alley into a side door of a brick building. It's a grimy door that will have graffiti on it. "Fuck you," it will read.

Follow Ken through a small corridor with a bathroom on the right and a light switch on the left. He'll throw the switch and the darkness will suddenly turn to a blinding brightness. The room will look fairly similar no matter how you get to this point. Bright silver sinks and rows of silver surfaces, a bright silver double oven and three grills with matching pots and bronze spoons, spatulas, and whisks. Pots will be hanging from the ceiling from every reachable spot. It won't make sense yet, but when Ken throws on his white apron, dirtied with years of grease and oil, realize Ken is a chef, and that you have become a part of his crew. You will become a chef's assistant.

"Grab an apron," Ken will say as he takes the halibut from your back and brings it into a spotless silver door that releases a vapor of sorts. Think, walk-in fridge. You will have regained some reasoning skills over the last couple hours. Grab an apron as you hear Ken cursing crudely on the other side of a steel door.

When Ken reappears, he'll be carrying two gigantic burlap sacks. "These fuckers!" he'll say with a smile, "never fucking prep. Can't trust a goddamn Indian." As he plops the bags down onto the floor, he'll walk to the grill. "I'm kidding of course, kind of."

"You want some eggs?" he'll say nicely, softly. Say, "Yes and some Tylenol if you have it." Your voice will sound weak, but don't be scared. It's the first time you've spoken in a long, long time. Your voice will sound scratchy like when you're recovering from a cold. Ken will smile, turn on the grill, and walk into his office in the back.

Suddenly, feel like you're about to collapse, but brace yourself on the steel workstation marked #3. Ken will give you a glass of water and two Tylenol. Drink the water first. Throw the Tylenol into your mouth one at a time, and swallow regularly. The pills will remind you of your last moments of depression, of desperation. Gulp down the rest of the water, and shake your head so the pain will make you forget.

"Over-easy and some toast sound good?" Ken will ask. Nod. "Go sit out front. I'll bring it to you," Ken will say. Think about that for a second, what does he mean by out front?

Walk through a swinging door that's marked OUT, and sit down at a large round table, white cloth draped over and about eight chairs surrounding it. Look around.

The place is beautiful, oak chairs, large windows, small, steel chandeliers. It's a little, fancy dining room. It's chic, with avant-garde art placed almost haphazardly on the walls. Feel like you don't belong here either. Put your head on your arms as the place starts to spin, as your headache hits you hard. Close your eyes for a second, and, in a moment, fall asleep.

Breakfast March 30th, 2012

The Staff Meeting

A staff meeting over breakfast, which will be eggs over easy, toast and butter/jam for you but leftovers for everybody else

1 large redhead male with rosy cheeks, gelled hair, an anchor tattooed on his forearm, and bright blue eyes, called Steven Swagger

1 Hispanic dude, short black hair, black eyes, olive skin, no accent, named Andres Cegura

1 cute black-haired girl, looks kind of like Jennifer Lopez but a more nasal voice with

a large smile, named Maria

2 little Mexican fellows, Juan y Carlos

1 elderly Indian guy, heavy bags under his eyes, and eyebrows that loom over the table, oddly named Philip, too.

Ken at the front of the table with a frown

Dim lights overhead

Open curtains allowing the rising sun to pour in through the windows

Wake up. Again, wake up! The sudden roar of conversation around the large table should be enough to get your eyes open. Your eggs should be right in front of you, and the smell should ease you back into reality. Everybody at the table will be having a great time. Everybody will be talking and laughing, recounting anecdotes from their weekends as you lift your head.

The commotion will cease. They will see that you are alive. Everyone at the table will clap for you as you engage with consciousness. A puddle of drool will be hanging from your lip and trailing onto your shirtsleeve. Everybody will laugh. Smile with them. When Ken says, "Eat up," and then goes through introductions, try to follow him. Yet, the whole time, be more worried about whether or not you have drool on you anywhere rather than trying to remember their names.

Nod your head at each of the members of the table. You'll soon see firsthand what each man and woman's role is in the kitchen.

Ken will then introduce you possessively. "This, everybody, is my boy, Phil."

Everybody will say, "Hi, Phil." Wave. "He will be taking over for Rob. He's a good friend of mine so, everybody, take good care of him. He doesn't know much about the industry. Help him out if he needs it. We need an extra set of hands tonight, so treat him like one of our own. Welcome, Phil!" Ken will start clapping, and everybody will join him with wide smiles. Feel like you belong. Feel good that you belong. It's a new start for you. Smile! Smile widely! Smile genuinely! Ken will say, "Now to business..."

Ken will then shout at Philip for not prepping his station, shouting about how he has two bags of onions still not prepped. Phil will say that it should have been Rob's duty. Ken will say, "Rob is fucking gone! He's in jail. Get over it." With Ken standing, there should be only one chair empty. And, when they all start cursing about Rob being absent, realize that you must be in his old chair. Feel an eerie sense of shame, which will soon pass.

"Today, we're not going to have another shit show. Are we, boys and girls? We've got Phil to impress," Ken will say pointing at you.

Eat your breakfast. It's going to be a long day. Trust me.

Pre-Lunch March 30th, 2012

Working Snack

1 disgruntled employee

2 gigantic bags of onions

1 huge butcher knife

1 white bucket

A whole bunch of time

The day will have started, and you should feel like a mouse in a maze or more just like a scared kid in a strange kitchen with strange people running around that have objectives you can't seem to fathom. This will remind you of high school. You were always lost, while everybody else seemed so aware of themselves, like they knew exactly where they needed to be and what their futures held.

"Go help the Indian guy, Phil," Ken will say to you in a rushed but considerate tone. He doesn't remember what it's like to be new to a kitchen. All he sees are the patrons and the completed dishes and the money at the end of the day. It is, after all, his kitchen, his staff, his place. He flashes you a smile, and you appreciate the kindness.

Approach Philip with an air of caution. He should be staring at the two burlap sacks on the floor. He'll look at you confused. "At your service," say, your voice suddenly working again. Try to be humorous despite the timidity and fear this Indian man inspires within you. His brow will lower with concern, an air of suspicion as he leans toward you, knife in hand.

"Cut these then," he'll say handing the knife to you, not pointing at anything in particular but somehow implying the bags at your feet, the same bags Ken brought out from the fridge earlier. Nod, and take the knife from him.

Untie the string from one of the bags. See what must be a hundred or more large white onions. You know a little bit about cooking, but you don't know how you're going to dice so many onions. It will seem like an endless task.

Ask, "What do you want me to do with these?" "Cut them," Philip will say. Ask, "How?" Philip will sigh at this awful question. "I'm not here to baby-sit," he'll shout to Ken, dropping the hardboiled egg he's started shelling into the sink. "Help the kid out," Ken will shout without taking his eyes from the fish he's filleting.

Philip will roll his eyes. He will think you're an imbecile, but he won't know that you'll be wondering what an old Indian man is doing working as a prep guy in a kitchen. Philip will show you how to prepare onions. He will peel an onion and cut it all at once, chopping off the head and base, and then slicing it in half. He'll toss the waste into the garbage, and he'll drop the two halves into a large white bucket standing between you and him. He'll hand you the knife, blade first. "Got it?" he'll say. You'll want to say yessir, like you've been brought up to do by your mother, but don't say anything. Be too frightened to say anything.

Just mimic exactly what he did, slowly. Peel the onion, tossing the yellow film into the garbage bin. Chop off the head of the onion, slide that piece with the back of the knife into the garbage, chop of the base and slide that into the garbage. Slice the onion in half, and put the good part into the large white bin.

Do this cycle on repeat for what feels like seventeen days. Lose yourself while cutting onions. Forget who you are and where you are. Forget about the strange dreams and the nights of fear and depression. Forget the anxiety that's been building up inside you throughout the day. Forget that you actually care about what's happened to your dad. Forget that your brother must be home by now. Forget that your mom will never know any of what has happened to you because she's always with her new boyfriend somewhere in Miami and you don't really talk to her anymore. Forget about your ex-girlfriend and all the rejection. Forget about what you've done. Forget the world. Forget everything.

You could be cutting onions for days or minutes. You wouldn't care. People fade into the background, and you don't even notice when Juan has turned on the Mexican radio station. Don't realize that Ken has filleted all of his fish and has moved onto other things. Don't even think about what anybody else is doing, the mess that's being created all around you, because all that matters is that you cut two huge bags of huge white onions. You've never cut so many onions in your life, but you've never felt so weightless and timeless either.

All you can see are onions, tears building up in your eyes, tears that never would have despite all of your personal tragedies. Enjoy the tears as you slice each onion in half. Each cut will feel like a fresh start. Slice your finger once. Suck on it as the pain brings you back to the kitchen. Philip will be laughing at you. Don't say anything. Nobody cares about your pain. Wrap your finger up in a paper towel that you grab from behind a sink.

Finish cutting. Your eyes will be red and dripping with tears. You will hardly be able to see. Snap back into reality. In the instant, remember where you are, who you are, that you tried to kill yourself. Picture your father's lifeless face, veins almost protruding from his bloodshot eyes. Philip will begin taunting you as others look on, "Try and be a little more careful next time." He's still working on his eggs. Grind your teeth, and look at the huge basket of onion waste to your left and onion fruit to your right. Feel a sense of accomplishment.

Ken will say, "Good work, Phil." With a hint of spite, move on to help Philip shell the rest of his hardboiled eggs. He will not be happy about it, but realize why he's on the lower end of the totem pole. He's slow. Out of spite, join him in his duty of shelling hard-boiled eggs.

Shell the eggs like it's your business. Lose yourself in it. There are just so many eggs. This time, there's no onion juice to make you cry and no knife to make you bleed. Philip will be looking at you with anger and disbelief. Think, Why are you making an enemy so quickly? Why, Phil? Only later, with a knife to your throat, will you realize that this probably wasn't the best idea…

Dinner March 30th, 2012

Rush Hour

Missed lunch

A few bites of random vegetables that you sneak

8 people working hard to prepare for a large function

1 big helping of surprise when you are asked to join the line

Surf and turf

Although you didn't know what to expect, you absolutely will not have expected that there would be a charity-sponsored dinner at the restaurant that night. Having eaten nothing all day, sneak enough of the vegetables you've been chopping and dicing to hold you over. Your knife skills will improve by the second. Even Philip has stopped scowling at you, not because you're good, but because he will be busy.

You've joined the whirlwind. You've become an element of the chaos. Try to keep your area clean, but the black rubber mats under your feet will become coated and sticky. Juan and Carlos will also try to keep the mess at bay, but even their efforts will be thwarted by the amount of pans and dishes Chef Ken and Chef Swagger run through.

Ken will be working hard. Take a second to admire his skilled hands. Maria, the pastry chef, will be doing the same. She will be admiring him, too. She will brush by you, while you're not so hard at work over some carrots. She will make her way to the far end of the kitchen where Ken is stewing something, preparing something into something else. Whatever he's doing, you know he's doing it right.

Maria will turn the corner, and squeeze in front of Ken and his workstation. He will stop working as he sees her approach. She will push her ass into his crotch as you look on. He'll put his arms around her, blocking her exit. She'll blush and giggle coyly, "I just needed a spatula." "Yeah, I believe that shit," Ken will say as he brushes his lips against her neck, breathing into her ear. She will turn to him with visible chills down her spine. Be intrigued. Be turned on! It's hot in the kitchen. She will move on, and Ken will look at you almost frightened by your voyeurism. He will go back to work, and you should follow suit.

"Alright fuckers," Ken will shout. "Man your stations." Ken will then point at you, "Phil, you're on the line now. Take this. You're on the string beans." Ken will hand you a pair of tongs and stand you behind the green beans. Feel a sense of pride as you stand there over the garlic-sautéed greens. Look around the kitchen. Chef Swagger will be dishing up the steak. He will look tough almost grimacing as he reaches for the first plate. Ken will be dishing up the fish. He will have a serene smile on his face, calmly placing the halibut on his plates. Philip will be slopping the mashed potatoes onto every dish like he could care less. Andres will be dishing up the side salads. His fingers will work quickly to make each one look exactly the same. It will finally be your turn to place the green beans onto the plate. Using the tongs, place an assortment of string beans onto your first plate. Feel insecure about it, and decide you will put less on the next one. Do it again, and feel better about it. Do it again, and try to make them all parallel. After your duty is fulfilled, pass the plate down the line. Juan and Carlos will be waiting, working hard to clean the sides of each dish to make them look pretty. The waitresses, whom you will soon meet, come in and pile four plates onto their trays. The three women look gorgeous, but do not be distracted. Do not look away from the plates. Work diligently so you do not fall behind.

Without even noticing it, allow a smile to creep onto your face. While your arms swing in rhythm, in concert with the line, feel comfort. Feel fresh. Feel born again. Think to yourself, This is your new beginning. This is what you were meant for. This is exactly where you are meant to be.

Mary Christine Delea

PURR

1.) I am sorry about the broken glass. I was interested in examining Shin Yoon Bok's painting, *The Pleasure Boat*, and I accidentally knocked over the vase, causing it to fall and shatter. I am guilty. I feel guilt.

2.) The artist Shin Yoon Bok was born in 1726 in Korea. No one knows when he died. His birth year is always followed by a dash and a question mark, as if we should all question whether he is dead. An ingenious use for punctuation, causing us to reconsider the finality of our own demise. And death is, after all, our greatest fear.

3.) *The Blob* introduced Steve McQueen to the world. The movie's final shot: **The End?** jolted me to question my safety in my living room on Long Island, watching alone on the black and white TV. That giant ball of solidifying blood could easily get in through the baseboard heating. My fondness for horror movies as a child kept me from sleeping soundly for years.

4.) On the plane, a dull man sitting next to me bores me with his obsessive talk of a complex indie film I have never heard of. I yawn. I will never know if his intense love of this movie is warranted, as he has taken away any desire to ever see it. Without his noticing, I turn up the volume on my headset and focus on the music the airline has supplied.

5.) The musicians in *The Pleasure Boat* are already playing as the passengers board. Three couples. My knowledge of 18th century Korean art being what it is, I do not know if the women are wives or prostitutes. Does "pleasure" in the painting's title mean relaxation or sex? Will the boat drift along as three musicians serenade three couples who will whisper sweet nothings? Or will they play "Afternoon Delight" because when that boat's a'rocking, you shouldn't come a'knocking?

6.) It is a rock 'n' roll, easy listening, reggae, country, jazz, blues, standards, hip-hop, operatic, classical world. One culture's guilt is another's shame. The unknowing of death. The childhood fears that stay with us. How a yawn is contagious. The desire to understand what we see overpowered only by the need to feel so safe, so content, that we actually purr.

Mary Christine Delea

My Villain

I cannot deny you are lovely: your face is balanced
in the style our society elevates and likes to photograph.[i]
Your beauty is matched by your practiced charm,
the ability to flatter crowds and squeeze on the guilt
napping in their hearts.[ii] You smile from the podium
and are forgiven your lazy knowledge of history[iii] and gender.[iv]
I stand at the back of the room, forced to attend you
for tenure, for goodwill, for all the reasons junior faculty
must show up at events[v] from which they will take only
so much stress a mouth guard is necessary for sleep so as
not to grind their own teeth into graveyard dust.[vi]
I lean on the exit door as if to keep the truth
from sneaking in. I want you to read the part
where the master rapes[vii] the slave, an act you refer to
as "love." But you skip that, and I later learn you no longer
read it, ever,[viii] you stick to the men saving the world.
Or at least this hemisphere. You smile with your last words
and the audience almost swoons. You thank us
for our attention and our love of words. But I know
what that thanks is really for: you want us to love you,
you want to master us, your words raping us again and again
until, in your fantasy, we will throw roses instead of rocks.[ix]

---

[i] What a strange illusion it is to suppose that beauty is goodness.—Leo Tolstoy
[ii] Liberals feel unworthy of their possessions. Conservatives feel they deserve everything they stole.—Mort Sahl

[iii] Africa only matters as the creator of African-Americans—Mr. ___, classroom lecture
[iv] Women's brains are smaller than men's brains; women are vindictive and cannot be trusted; white women in particular are selfish and conniving—Mr. ___, paraphrased from department meetings, reading receptions, and actions
[v] See "Handbook for New Faculty Members," page 82
[vi] "graveyard dust" is a term made up by the author for poetic drama
[vii] The master subjected her to the most elemental form of terrorism distinctly suited to the female: rape.—Angela Davis
[viii] AP: Police were called to a disturbance in the Rivendale Community College parking lot after a woman, angered by an earlier poetry reading, threw a rock through the window of a car rented by that night's visiting speaker, Mr. ___
[ix] It's possible to love a human being if you don't know them too well.—Charles Bukowski

48

Kevin Carollo

A THEORY

After you die, you will meet God,
but God may not recognize you.

Forgetting who you are might
be written into the very fabric of

Intelligent Design. He—or she—
might say gender in heaven has

never been necessary either and
it is possible that you won't know

how to feel about this. You might
think to yourself that you cannot

remember a time when you did
not have one. You might even

say something to someone like
"Gee, I've always been all boy,"

or "Weird, I've always been all
girl," and then you might have

to move on because there is a
line. Or you might have to wait

because even heaven uses a kind
of elegant protocol which requires

you to be alone for a time. Then
again, you might consider the

possibility of not being able to
think to yourself in heaven, of

having no free time or too much,
or the option of calling out to

someone in your situation. Another
possibility to consider about you

and God once you get inside:
the complete and utter absence

of any separation whatsoever
between the essence of things,

a lack of definition so shocking
and terrible that you might not

realize at first that you are saved.
You might expect God to finally

make things explicit. And God
might, in turn, say, "Here, we're

not that into names." And that
could be the least worst thing

about getting acclimated to
forever. If you're lucky, then

there could be angels who
say "your Grandma Nancy is

a saint" and then disappear so
you can hang out with your

Grandma Nancy. Some monk
or priest might intone "everyone

can wear a hat, but not well."
One option could be to count

and love everything equally:
the osprey and its prey, macro

and micro, groundhog and
narwhal alike. Even the humble

chipmunk might decide for once
to say, "Fuck it, I'm not moving."

Maybe you will wait an eternity
in an etherworld of morphine

before God comes to you and
says that you are loved and

that is forever. Perhaps God
appears to you as a tiny clay

figurine on a long wooden
mantelpiece. Perhaps God lives

in the plaster dolphin over
the TV who will never reach

water. Maybe God has decided
to keep you in your original

packaging, or maybe God will
put you in charge of pushing

the reset button. Let us say
that Our Father is an ordered

hoarder committed to working
harder, and you are one of God's

better sorters. Perhaps there is
no paper in heaven, and therefore

no ledgers. Maybe "ledger" only
refers to those angels who spend

forever jumping and jumping
off the celestial windowsill.

But only those "ledgers" would
know whether there are windows

in heaven or no. Maybe you will
meet God and make her a window.

Amina Gautier

MOST HONEST

MY WIFE'S VOICE COMES ACROSS THE
receiver, plaintive and unforgettable. "I need a favor. Can you
take Marissa tonight?"

"Good morning," I say. Divorce or not, I am still
worth the common courtesy of a greeting.

"Sorry," she says. "So…can you? I'd really appreciate
it."

We are no longer married, and that is why we talk like
this. My wife does not indulge in idle chatter. When she calls,
there is always a reason, always an explanation. Me, I never
have to explain. I never call.

She says, "I know it's not the weekend, but I
wouldn't ask if it weren't important."

"Who's the lucky guy?"

"I don't think you should ask that sort of thing."

"Should I pick her up from school?"

"If you get her around six, it's fine."

"Must be a dinner date," I say. One annoyed breath later she hangs up.

Conversations with my wife are among the things that I don't miss. Had she not called, I'd still be asleep. That's another thing I don't miss. Waking up early because she has to get up at five and have lights and music in the morning.

Every morning now, I wake up reminded that I am newly single and that it is a good thing. I always wake up on the side of the bed farthest from the door, the side that used to be hers. Having to sleep on the lumpy side is another thing I do not miss.

I start each day enjoying my new small freedoms. I keep a list of them on the refrigerator where I can be sure to see it each morning as I take out the milk for my cereal for the breakfast I eat in a kitchen free of the clutter of useless appliances for extravagant dishes that no one but an accredited chef actually knows how to make. (I do not miss the garlic press).

It seems like I should have a say in this, like she should need my permission to go on this date.

Once a week, I add a new freedom to my list, but today I can't think of anything to add because I am looking at the list and thinking of this date and pouring milk over my cereal and missing my wife and now the bowl is filled with milk and my cereal floats in the milk and milk is now spilling over the bowl and down onto my bare feet and I'm still looking at the list and missing her hard, so hard.

Now I have to knock on my own front door. No use trying my old key. My daughter comes out bundled, dragging a bag seemingly meant for an extended stay. Marissa watches me uncertainly, then drops her bag and runs to me.

"Hi, Pumpkin," I say, all of my life in the words.

I've never picked her up from home before. My wife always drops her off at an innocuous location, like McDonald's. That way, I have no excuse to drop by my house which is no longer where I live. That she is allowing me to pick Marissa up here means something. Maybe the guy is such a loser she doesn't want Marissa to meet him. Or maybe she's so eager to get to him she doesn't want to waste time with a drop-off.

Marissa pulls off her hat and asks, "Daddy, do you like it?"

My daughter's hair lies smooth against her scalp. Parted down the middle, her hair is gathered at either side of her head and pulled up high and then braided, secured at the tops by brightly colored bobbles resembling gumballs and at the bottoms by plastic barrettes in the shape of butterflies. Always before—when we lived as a family—my wife had braided Marissa's hair into elaborate and pain-staking patterns which her hair would hold for weeks at a time until the braids grew too fuzzy to ignore and had to be redone. I'd watch the two of them seated in the living room, my wife on the sofa and Marissa on the floor between my wife's knees, her head leaning back as her mother fashioned her a surprise hairstyle. Now my wife takes Marissa to the salon and has them put a relaxer in her hair. This is to make things more manageable, to free my wife up from one more task now that she is a busy single mother with much too much to do.

"I like it." I smooth down Marissa's already smooth hair and hug her to me.

I need these minutes with my daughter, hugging her, to brace myself. When I finally look at my wife, her appearance comes as a surprise. She'd stopped wearing makeup because I'd once complained about all the smudges left on my clothing and the expense of the dry cleaning bills. Now, here she is, lipsticked and powdered, her brows tamed into thin, arched lines. She's poised and grim, as if meeting me at our house is a battle she's had to train for.

"You look nice," I say, unable to help it. Too late do I recall her disdain of the mediocre compliment. "If 'nice' is the best you can do when I'm all dressed up, I'd rather you just didn't say anything," she'd once told me, pointing out that I gave her the same compliment when she was dressed in jeans or sweats.

"Thanks," my wife says, making a moue of displeasure. Apparently, she remembers that talk, too.

Marissa says, "Oh Daddy, I forgot Munchkin." Dropping my hand, she runs back into the house for the stuffed elf I'd won for her at an amusement park when she was three. Holding Marissa's bag, my wife guards the door, blocking it. According to my wife, Marissa began sleeping with this elf again soon after The Divorce. (Divorce is my wife's word. I prefer dissolution. It makes our marriage sound like a crystalline substance, glittery yet hard, succumbing to forces greater than itself.) Now she refuses to sleep without it. According to my wife, Marissa clings to the thing all night, holding tightly, needing it.

Marissa gets into my car and pulls on her seatbelt. "Daddy, can I get a milkshake instead of a soda with my Happy Meal this time?" she asks. "I want strawberry, okay?"

"Pumpkin, we're not going to McDonald's tonight. We're going home." She climbs up onto her knees to look out the passenger's window at the house, then turns back to me and says, "But we are."

The outing with my daughter, if it can be called such, doesn't go well. I usually have grand plans, but today was a surprise and I'm strapped for cash. I've never brought her back to my apartment until now. The disappointment starts before Marissa even sees the place, once I tell her that her bedroom and the living room are one and the same. When we go inside, she takes one look at the apartment's ransacked appearance, at my socks curled in a hallway corner with my underwear and soiled tee shirts, at the puddle of milk pooled in front of the refrigerator and says, "I want to go home. Now."

Back at our house there is only one light on in the living room; its dim yellow haze shows through where the blinds stop short. I know the lamp, an ugly little thing my wife inherited from her college roommate. My wife and her date are probably seated next to each other on the couch near the ugly little lamp with the stereo behind them tuned to something mellow and commercial free. They have likely come to the part of the evening where people say the clever yet noncommittal things that increase the likelihood of sex.

I ring the bell.

I didn't mean to come here. After two hours of the cartoon channel, I gave Marissa a bath and put her to bed. Now here I am. I didn't mean to leave my daughter alone and asleep back in my apartment. I only meant to shower after dinner and settle in for the night, but when I stepped out of the shower, I'd felt the way I had when we were dating in college and my only thoughts were of seeing her. I didn't mean to come here. I am no longer in college on my way to pick up my girl. And she is no longer my girl. We share only the merging of our genetic makeup and even then we merely take turns.

My wife opens the door. "What are you doing here?"

"Can I come in?" I step into my old house. There is no one else in the living room with my wife. Her shoes curl on their sides beneath the coffee table and a nearly empty glass of water sits beside a hard-backed book above the table. The stereo is off, its face silent and gleaming.

"Where's Marissa? Is everything okay?"

"She's fine," I say, taking a seat. "I put her to bed for the night. I just needed to drive around for a while."

"So you came here?"

"I didn't mean to." It is a strange feeling, sitting on my own couch in my own house with my own wife when neither one belongs to me. Her glass of water rests atop a hand carved coaster that resembles kitchen countertops. I lift the glass and hold the slippery, disc-like thing. "Is this new?"

"This isn't funny."

"So where's your date?"

"Is that why you're here? You came to meet—"

"—That's not why," I say.

"Well?"

"Sit down." I pull her down beside me.

"Okay, I'm sitting." She looks at me in a way she hasn't in a long time, like she's really listening, like she really wants to hear what I have to say. She has eased her shoulders back against the couch and her hands rest softly against her thighs. For the first time I can remember, I have her full attention. This is the closest we have been to each other in far too long. Two people on a couch, inches apart, not separated by the steel and metal of the car doors we use as barriers. I am taking a picture of her as she is in this moment. I snap the shot in my mind where I hold all of my pictures of her, since my wife kept the albums, and I lodge it in a far corner where I know it can't run amok and crush me like only a fresh memory of her can.

"The night I moved out, I got drunk," I tell her.

"You don't drink," she says.

I'd never been one for drinking, but before I'd even bought cookware or groceries for my new apartment, I'd bought alcohol—rum, vodka, whiskey and scotch (I have no preference, no signature drink. Drunk is drunk is drunk to me). My wife would never let us keep alcohol in the house, not even safely stashed away, for fear that Marissa would get into it and become a closet alcoholic. Moving into a one-bedroom apartment that day, I'd finally realized that my wife would never be my wife again and I drank myself into a stupor. My inebriation made me fearless enough to call her. I called her over and over again until she eventually stopped answering the phone. Then I just lay on the couch, calling her name until I passed out. I awakened alone the following day feeling sore and smelling sour, with an imprint of the couch's cushion on my forehead.

"Is that what this about? You want a drink?" she asks, as if I am a stranger and she a hostess gracious enough to oblige.

"No, that's not it. I—"

"You're in a very strange mood."

What I want to say to her is, I want you. I want my old life. I want what we had even though you think it was terrible.

I reach for her hand. "You look beautiful. Really beautiful. Your date—"

"There wasn't any date," she says. "I just wanted some time alone."

"You could have told me. I would have still taken her."

She leaned down and slipped her shoes back on. "Talking to you isn't so easy."

I should have known better. Random and impetuous dating was not her thing. It had taken me three months of trying to get her to agree to go out with me. She'd wanted more from her life than to end up as her mother. Instead she'd gotten me.

"You can talk to me now," I say. "I'm listening. You can say whatever you like. Whatever you need."

"You don't mean that."

"Honest," I say. "You can talk to me." But I am looking at her and seeing the picture of her in my mind and realizing that I am inches away from my own wife in my own house and we are not mad at each other, not hating—not loving either— but not hating. We are not cutting each other's words off, not slamming doors, not walking away. We are not keeping our distance. We are here. We are home.

I kiss her.

My wife's lips know the man I am and the man that I could be if she didn't push push push. Now I am pushing, pushing through all of our layers of accusation and guilt and blame, pushing through layers of clothing to find my wife, to join her until we are no longer separated.

"I still love you," I say.

She pulls out of my arms. "Don't say that. Please…just don't, okay?"

"What's wrong now?" I brush a few strands of hair off her face. "We just made love."

"We had sex. We did not make love." My wife reaches for her clothing. She struggles into her top and smoothes down her skirt "We're divorced. I don't love you anymore."

To her, it is that simple. You divorce someone, sign the paperwork that severs what God has joined, divide your assets and possessions less than equally and that is that. Affection, emotion, memories, all the byproducts of love become null and void. We are divorced, dissolved; therefore we no longer love. Yet I still do.

"It's not that easy," I say.

"Sometimes it is," she says.

"Even now, you could be pregnant," I say, although it is a dumb thing to say and I took Sex Ed like everyone else.

"No, I can't," she says.

"You're right. It's too soon to know."

"No, you don't understand," she says. "I can't."

Leaning up on her elbows, she tells me she aborted a child of ours two years ago (I hadn't even known we were pregnant) and shortly afterwards had her tubes tied. She didn't want me to father any more of her children. I don't believe her until she reminds me of a particularly rough patch, weeks of arguing to no end.

She says, "That's when I just knew I couldn't do it. Not with you and the way we were. You wouldn't talk to me. I kept trying to talk to you. I kept trying to talk. Remember when I told you I needed to talk to you and said that it was important?"

"I think so," I say, hedging. There had been many times she'd said something of the sort to me. She'd been unhappy before she left me. That much I remember. She'd wanted to talk and I'd evaded, believing as I always did that problems would blow over or take care of themselves.

"You promised we would talk. You promised."

I am willing to believe some, but not all of it is my own fault. I know she's made sacrifices for me, though I've never asked her to. Before she asked for the divorce, she'd trotted out a string of my infractions. Things I couldn't even remember saying or doing. Things that sounded like something I'd said but not meant. Events, fights, and conversations that had long slipped from my memory. Promises and guarantees and assurances unkept. Admittedly, I could have been a better husband, but I was not all bad. I did not deserve this.

"Why tell me now?"

"It just seemed the most honest thing to do," she says, so calm.

I reach for my clothing. This is not real, I think. My daughter is sleeping alone in my apartment and I am here and this is not real. My wife is calm so calm I want to kill her. Her naked back bespeaks vulnerability as I search for a soft spot between her shoulder blades, a pressure point at the base of her neck. All the parts of her body that I used to trace and kiss now suggest possible ways of extinction. I can squeeze. I can kill. I touch her shoulder blade with my fingertips, brush the ends of her hair, curl my fingers around her soft pliable neck. She looks at my hand, not bothering to remove it. Speaking over cool bare shoulders, she says only "You won't."

I slam my fist into the stereo to feel something other than this, and my fourth and fifth knuckles explode with pain against the sturdy metal of the display panel. My wife crawls to the stereo and runs her hands over its face, gingerly testing the stop, play, forward and rewind buttons, smoothing the stereo's face lovingly like a child's.

I head home, trying not to think of the last hour. Instead I think of Marissa and how terrible it was to leave her, feeling it deep in my stomach. As I drive, I keep my foot on the gas and imagine all sorts of atrocities that end up with my daughter dead or assaulted. My building has a security system and an intercom, yet I imagine pedophiles scaling the walls and climbing in through windows to get to my unprotected daughter.

Maybe she's had a bad dream. Maybe she is sitting in front of the window crying silently, trying to be brave. Maybe she needs me. Maybe there is something I can do.

Marissa is sound asleep, her face turned to the window, her hair mussed, her cheek pressed against Munchkin's. I sit on the edge of the pull-out couch and watch my daughter sleep, scared to lose her, too. I am scared that there will be other prices to pay for my negligence, only I just won't be able to see them, just as I couldn't have seen that I'd have to mean the things I'd said long ago on nights I couldn't remember just as I couldn't have seen the things I couldn't see until it was too late.

I lie down by my daughter's blanketed feet and fight to stay awake. From this moment on, I will be vigilant. I will keep watch over all that I can ever have.

Rob Dennis

WHY I AM NOT A TECH WRITER

—after O'Hara

I am not a tech writer, I am poet. Why? I think I would rather
be a tech writer, but I am not. Well, for instance, your ex-boyfriend,
the tech writer, he's working on a study of green. When you decide
to reanimate that relationship, I drop by his web site. I sip my drink.
"You've got GREEN all over it," I say, sipping my drink. "I guess
you needed something there." Days go by, and I drop by the site.
Cyanobacterial biofuels, geothermal desalination, and the promise
of synthetic photosynthetic systems. I navigate away, and days go by.
He blogs, he tumbles, he tweets. I drop by. Hydroelectric envirotech,
hybrid batteries that power cars, and dreams, and the renewable miracle
of the composting toilet. Days go by like this. He rides his bike to work,
I bet, towing the toilet. When next I drop by the site, his study's finished.
He's making a book out of it, printing it on biodegradable post-consumer
eco-friendly compostable magical tissue paper. It's got GREEN everywhere.

And really, it's too much. And you – you he doesn't mention even once.
But me? One day I'm thinking of that color, and I start up a poem.
I write a line about the unrenewable miracle of your greenhouse eyes.
Pretty soon it's a whole page of words, not just lines. Then another page.
Thunder snow and corroding copper and the atmospheric magnetism
of being in room with you. How nothing like the sun, your aurorean flairs
still warm me so globally. The days go by. Days like this. And in my brain
all that's unreclaimed stays unreclaimed, for a thing observed risks being

changed by observation: the uncertainty of searching for something that was
or wasn't. Our quantum entanglement. So instead of picking up the phone
I practice action from a distance: write pages. Green sweater, jeans just tight
enough, and how I made you scream. I am a real poet. I place the nothing
between us into a sealed box where in other -verses it's either something
or no thing at all. Paradoxing probabilities. And there should be so much more.
Not of green, of words, of worlds, of how terrible green is, and life: the space
you cut, the shapes you left in time, and that zombie love you've settled for
in this lonely version of our universe, why you won't let what's undead die.

Days go by, and my poem is almost finished. I haven't mentioned green yet.
It's seventeen poems, and I think I'll call it GREEN. I keep writing. The days
go by: with me getting out of bed and drinking too much coffee and smoking
too many cigarettes and thinking probably too much of you. The days go by,
and yes, I put all my cans and bottles and crappy drafts in the proper receptacles.
All that can be trashed, I trash. As for love, I want one that hasn't been salvaged
or recycled, one that doesn't run on rechargeable batteries. No, give me a love
nuclear and environmentally unfriendly, one to stamp a giant carbon footprint
on my heart, to ruin me with its ozone-ablating rays; a love like a mad landmine;
a love that quakes and razes with waves that drown and decimate and yet dazzles
with its life-giving vulgarity; a love that's an outrage, an affront; a covetous love
to deracinate all other loves, matchless in the way it lays waste and wreaks havoc,
levels without pity, gluttonous even in ash and rubble; a terrifying and filthy love
to blow me back to a darker age, to wipe me out; a love that will never be a rescue
but a devastation so excessive it will create a space for us that's uncluttered finally;
a juggernaut love; a love that is a world wonder, rising not from all the old pacts
but from their wreckage, full of every great green feeling. Unjust, unsustainable:
a love that can't exist but somehow does. A singularity: unstable, unfabled, new.

Nikolas James Perez

DEDICATION

To Rob—not you. I understand we made a deal four years ago, but things have changed. My alcoholism has become much more manageable and I don't just go around promising book dedications for pitchers of beer like I used to; though, to be fair, you're the only one I did this with. And yes, I know you lent me $300 at the time, too, which actually seems like a reasonable amount to be paid for a dedication, but if we both stop to think about it, what would the proposed allegiance even mean? While I still have only the fondest memories of you, it's been over a year and half since we've seen each other, and I don't know about you, but my person has significantly changed since our drunken promises to one another. I now make much more sensible drunken promises. Let me say this, however: you are a kind soul, who witnessed me at the height of my indignities, and still did not judge. Please don't think I don't realize this. But Rob, you're not getting a goddamn book dedication.

To Mom—this one's gonna be tough. The fact is, you're probably all over this thing, in ways only Freud and Jung could begin to understand. You've done more than right by me; the life, the shelter, the love, however unaware it sits between us. I am always grateful, my debts unmanageable. Of course this is a testament to you, but not a dedication. Poets tend to bestow their inspiration upon the Sun, but what of the shadows it creates, and the refuge they may offer? Therein, we lie.

To Dad—let's not pretend.

To Artists Before and After—You swirl in me kaleidoscopic. You have granted me access to caverns within myself I never would have known without you. You have complicated me and set me free. You are my Chateau D'If. That being said, I'm not talking to you, Dumas.

To My Friends, Innumerable—I know you don't need it. I've never truly believed in science, as it's as constantly changing as any rhetoric, and I don't need a type of blood to tell me who my family is. It is you. It is those of you who have gleamed the very pits of me—the addictions, the absence of worth, the infuriating destruction—and remained. No dedication is enough, and no work of mine is untouched by your collective graces. You've raised me, and every day I work to elevate you all in return. Also, you've all smoked me up countless times. Praise be.

To Evan—I stole this idea from you. Ethically speaking, the dedication should be yours. It's not.

To God—I fully believe you're worth the dedication, but I'm holding out until we get to know each other better.

To Myself—well, that's complicated. For the first time in my life, I can say you are deserving. You are a slow creature. You lose yourself too often, though more and more, your disappearances march towards something still unnamable, something, maybe, transcendent. But you have not come far enough—perhaps you never will. Be patient. I will be, too.

And so, I dedicate this:

To No One—I couldn't have done it without you.

Chad Frisbie

Q

As a president, he doesn't do a damn thing like you're supposed to. He doesn't wage war. He doesn't sing the national anthem. He doesn't even believe in God. Instead, he forms long, slow opinions of babies and clouds.

As a president, you're supposed to form long, slow opinions of citizens expressing emotions. But President Q can't help it. He loves babies. He goes absolutely crazy about the clouds.

The weird part is, he only likes babies doing the most normal things imaginable. A baby giggling at clouds is a major political event.

Is this a crisis? President Q opens a speech then gets sidetracked by a roving cloud. Stick your head in that cloud and you'll hear babytalk leaking through a very long wire that really isn't a wire at all but a kind of atmosphere of clouds.

Decisions, decisions. When choosing between plan A and plan B, he snorts a few babies then watches the clouds parade out his nostrils. When choosing between plan Y and plan Z, he inhales a giant fluffy cloud and exhales a giant fluffy baby. It's like technology, which is awesome!

Suddenly it dawns on President Q that he can't make decisions of the logical kind. Perhaps because his cabinet is filled with babies, we can only experience the President's choices as rapid sensory flux, like clouds coming and going so fast you can't see them. We have no say in the proceedings. We shut up.

Since enduring so many babies and so many clouds, people learn to call his policy experimental. That's how they make sense of his behavior. But he isn't experimental in the least.

He knows exactly what he's doing.

Caron Levis

LATE PASS

DO I WANNA PASS?

Don't even bother to turn my head, cause Ms. Anders like one a those automated announcements in the subways nobody listen to less you a tourist or lost. And you know I no tourist to lateness in these halls. And I not lost. My direction been mapped out for me in permanent ink. Today's the day and none of her little late, bathroom, or hallway passes gonna do nothin for me.

She not pausin anyway. Her heels just keep on clickin. Been weeks since anybody bugged on me bout anything in this school. Nothin like a shot up dead brother to keep teachers off your back, right Ms. A?

Click, click.

Yeah, thas what I thought.

Head on into the stairwell and pull the c-bun outta my pocket. Same 99 cent shit I always do, but today this frosting lookin like pus, for real. Rip the plastic, and chomp this sweaty cinnamon anyhow. Just gonna haveta deal with the fact that when you don't catch enough sleep your hunger hides on you and you start hearin the ghosts of bells hangin round.

Do I wanna pass. Please. Head up the down case two steps at a time.

I mean to go inta class but somehow I'm pausin at the door, lookin through the glass at how the colors on the girls sweaters is so bright today. Everything so bright today. Even dull-boy Angelo at the sharpener. And those shavings falling in slow-mo. Everything's slow-mo. Ms. Diamond scratchin on the board, Cherish pourin her gossip inta Monique's ear, Hector slappin Dwight on the head every time he turn around, Raz goin to town tagging up his desk, Shawanna, Daiquan, and Kendell sittin real serious as usual, and my girl Kiarra readin away and sucking on one a her cherry suckers with that cute, I-Concentrating, look. Everything same as same as.

Cept nothing same as.

Used to be we in the same video game but now it's like I'm watchin a movie from the very last seat. Outside the theater, even.

Kiarra look up and mouths me a mornin, baby, then she go back to reading. But knowin that I watchin now, she sucking on that cherry sucker real sexy. Sliding it cross her lips. Wrapping her tongue round it all slow. Wouldn't mind getting sucked like that till I disappeared. Course, if I was a sucker I'd wanna be grape.

Tower was always sayin grape the best flava. Tellin me how ladies in Italy stomp on grapes under they feet to make wine. Said he learned that from some TV show and when he had the dough, he was goin straight to Italy where you pound the food all day while the ladies with the big tits pour the wine and you drink and get mad drunk and just look at the stupid vines growin up to the sun. And then you play on the PlayStation when all that gets old.

Maybe he with the grape ladies right now.

Ma likes to talk bout heaven. But you believe in heaven, you gotta believe in the other and I don't know how Ma fools that it's upward T going. But maybe Italy. Maybe he get that chlorophyll in him and turn into something like a vine that don't gotta do nothing but grow up to the sun. Maybe Mr. Fadden know somethin bout that. I'll ask him bout it in science. That's the only class worth comin in for. Even when nothing's making sense, things be making sense in science.

An science be soon I guess, cause everybody's jumpin, packin up they ELA shit now and headin out. Even in slow mo this day's moving fast. Bells. Guess I'm saved by them again.

Don't remember much about the funeral cept those bells. And lottsa black clothes. Ma yellin in the morning tryin to get my feet in some shinies not gettin that these the last sneaks on his feet and I'm gonna wear em till they fall off, a'ight? Then some words fallin out the preacher's mouth and some lady sayin that you can never read enough Bible. Horns on the highway, one freak bird somewhere squawkin, and the noise coming outta my Ma—

Damn. That sound scrape out your insides. Pull the pulp outta you like you nothin but a pumpkin on Halloween. And ears don't got no off buttons so when they start chiming those bells I busy myself with findin the place where the sound ends and the silence begin. I'm not hearin ma's pain or nothing else that's goin down on the ground. Jus seein. How it's time now to go. Walk away. Leave my brother here by himself. His boys, my boys, all walkin in they big glasses and big jackets, shakin heads, lookin at me like yeah, you know. And me knowin. What all I gotta do now. Dust for dust. Eye to eye. Ye now I walk.

The old ladies they say God have a plan.

Mr. Fadden say every action got a reaction.

The boys just come tap me on the shoulder and say—

"Let's go, baby."

Hands so tight around my neck almost lose my air. Kiarra pulling me outta my mind, quick kissing my face, tellin me, come on—then remembering how shit, she got to give something to somebody so, shoot, nevermind, she'll see me in science. Gives me sticky cherry lips but before I can get my tongue in there she gone.

Everybody scurrying round the halls to get to class or somewhere good to cut. I just walk mad slow through all of it cause none of it matter. Kids given me a wave or just gettin out of my way, depending. Thing is I only seein them below the neck. Looking for that place where the heart's sposed to be. Under those tight t-shirts with the bra's edging through, under the hoodies, and the jackets. Got to be able to take aim no matter what's on the outside. Lift my arm at this green parka covered spot to practice. Line it up right. Close my hand around this trigger made a air, give it a pull, and the invisible bullet it goes racing right through the hallway; past girls laughin and tuggin they braids, past punks rappin, home work swappin, but nobody even twinge. Which is crazy. Cause you ever heard a gunshot up close?

Make all your cellular activity stop.

Open the door to science and see straightaway that Fadden not here. Some scrubstitute all up in my face asking me bout what's my name and where's my late pass and talking bout how even though she just fillin in there no reason not to be answerin her and the way she tryin to look me in the eyes, I see she don't know. She don't know. Everybody in the school know, but she new, so she don't know.

Kiarra up and pulls on her, whisperin some stuff in her ear and the way scrubstitute back off quick and let all the air outta her body, you can tell that she know now. And she will be leavin me be like the rest of the teachers been leavin me be. If Mr. Fadden was here like he sposed to be, he'd be leavin me be too, but he leave me be like I'm a man who need space, not like the rest of em leavin me be like I'm a bomb. I walk on to the back.

Fadden the only one still on me to graduate. Get to high school. But he's absent so guess we not coming up with that topic for my exit-project today. Not coming up with—

What the fuck all these tissues doin on my desk?

Raz. He over there sittin by the door crackin up his shit and slappin Hector some palm. Cuppin his hands and yellin to me like I mad far away or deaf or somethin.

"Thas so you can wipe it off, son."

He did not just say that shit. Damn. Chicken-legged little sucker gettin too bold. Now I'm gonna have to do somethin bout it, cause thas what you do in this life. I straighten up justa remind him of my height. Raz, barely makin five feet himself.

"Shut the fuck up." I tell him.

"Whatchyu gonna do?" He push his chin up at me. "You gonna jump me or you gonna sit your ass thinkin on it for your lifetime?" He grinnin big now. A buncha Awww *shiiiiitttttttsssss* risin up from the room. No he didn't.

I toss the desk over and bam—tissues fly all up in the air. Everybody look up like damn. I lookin right at Raz, but out the corners I see Kiarra lookin worried at me and scrubstitute froze like a popsicle. Tissues the only things in motion, comin down like giant snowflakes. Thas the power. When you can freeze time and people's breath you know you got it. For this second it's all mine. Not that I asked for it.

I just look Raz up and down. And watch the way he is scared. Maybe nobody else see it, but today my eyes like a close-up camera, and I can see how his breath is makin that cross on his shirt go up and down like it's trying to pop on up to heaven in a hurry. It's funny how we all dependin on something so invisible. Only time you notice breathin is when it—

Damn—Raz askin me whatchyu gonna do. Why don't he just quit it? Why can't nobody ever just quit it?

I kick the desk at him. Hard. Tell him he better get that fuckin smile off his face or I'm gonna have to smack it off. Let some words fly about him watchin himself and needin those hankies for his own ass and to quit playin me.

Fuck Raz. If he'd been born my way stead that Dominican cocoa-powder, we might be runnin crews for the same gang like back when we was playin on that basketball team together. But, you know. Things the way they is, he on the other side a my fist, deservin the beating he bout to get, cause fuck him talkin like I'm not gonna do what I gotta do, fuck that. You know I'm not about to let this shit go down without the proper protocol. Please. He was my brother. I'm gonna do him my respect. Just been takin my time, thas all. Cause it's got to be done right. Want my brothers killer sweatin himself near to dehydration fore I come to put him out of his miserability. I do it when I'm good and ready.

Which I guess I am since, yesterday, Skillz, he call up sayin that today the day. Been long enough he said. This shit need be wrapped up. People startin to doubt. Gonna pick you up for the drive, he said. After dismissal, he told me, you be first one out that door. You. Be. There. And I said, yeah, fine by me. Cause I am good and—Raz don't know nothin bout nothin. He just got a big mouth and it's right here, in my sites, wide open for me to slam closed. I grab his collar. He put up his hands and I stomp on his foot. His face twist all up—so baby face, it's like we still on the playground with him cryin bout big kids stealin his hoodie—this hoodie thas slippin outta my hand, why's it slippin and and why my steppin back, and why my lettin him go? I'm the big kid, lettin him go. Cause though I smash Raz's face a buncha times before this day, I'm tired, mad tired and I just don't wanna.

Hope to hell I didn't say that out loud.

Everybody in freezeframe—for a second—then Raz duck away, Shawanna giggle, somebody walk out the door, and it's over. Kiarra trying to get my attention, but I just sit back down in my chair wonderin what the fuck is wrong with me that I can't do the most regular things you supposed to do in a day like eat my breakfast and crush Raz's face.

Scrubstitute tryin to get back control. Leaning down to pick the tissues up offa the floor. When she come up she lookin at me and I see that curious kinda look on her face. Noticing the ink under my eye. The outline of my tear. Yeah, I could tell her, it's real. It's permanent. But she don't ask. She the skinny, blouse tucked in but always droppin pens type. Kind that just asking to get mowed. She not gonna do nothin. Nobody gonna do nothin. Fadden absent and he the only one and fuck Fadden. Fuck Fadden. He don't get it. This like ancient, old time shit now. Gang rules like the last remnants of the gallant ages. Somebody disrespect your family, the damsels, the treasure, then the knights step up. You step up. You do what you gotta. You can't just be absent. Fadden say it himself. Objects in motion stayin in motion.

"Would you hold up?"

Turn around and see the door shuttin right on scrubstitutes frownin face. Kiarra comin after me.

Let her grab my hand and slow me down.

"Where you going?" she wanna know.

Let her run her arms round my waist and up and down my back one time before I shrug her off and put my hands safe in my pockets. Her softness too contagious to take part in today.

"You a'right?" she asks.

You know how if you stare at somebody's eyes close enough you can see them seein you? I am lookin at the me in her eyes and he is so small, and far away, and lost lookin that if I didn't know who she was staring at I wouldn't know it was me. Couldn't pick myself outta a line up today.

"Tired," I say like it's the usual. Can't tell her. Not spose to tell nobody. Wonder what would happen if I didn't tell her at all and tomorrow I just come to school and she jump and hug me same way she doin today. Wonder if she could tell the difference. If touching me will feel different tomorrow. Maybe my hand'll be rougher to hold.

I take my hand out my pocket but it's kinda shakin so I put it back. Look up to her to see if I can tell her somethin without telling her.

"What is it 'Lique?"

She grab my arm and it's too much. My knees almost bring me down to the floor.

"Nothin," I say. Shouldn't tell her cause she might not let me go through with it. She might try to stop me somehow.

"What is it, 'Lique? For real? I do something?"

"No. Nah. Jus I can't do nothing after school today with you, thas it."

She smile and laugh a little. "That's it? I got practice anyways, so I not gonna cry for your absence, no need to worry. I'll be okay."

I nod. She not hearin me.

"Won't be able to answer the phone, either. Ima be on business."

"Well okay, fine. I'll be too busy to call you anyway." She tryin to be all sass. She don't like it when people say how she overboard for me.

"Might not be able to call for a while. Dependin…."

"We better get back in—"

"Damn girl, I'm tryin to say..."

"So, what are you tryin to say?" She roll her eyes at me.

"That I got somethin to do today."

She frown at me. Startin to get it.

I wait for her eyes to fill with those tears and start beggin me not to like she did when she first heard what I was meant to do. Maybe if she shed enough of em she could convince me. But all she do is take in one slow breath through that pretty nose of hers and say,

"Well, I'll leave my phone on loud. You do what you gotta do, and call me when you can."

Then she let go of my arm.

"I better get back to class, you coming?"

Shake my head.

She stick her finger in my face.

"You be careful. Hear? And then you call me." She drop her finger on my chest. "Real, careful." Then she turn and go.

Damn. Look at her handling it professional, just like I told her to. Told her I wouldn't stand for no drama. Never thought she'd actually listen to me, though. Thought she'd keep cryin and beggin me not to do it. But there she goes. I watch her back-pockets weaving down the hall till they disappear, thinkin about how we never even did it yet. She keep sayin we will but always she got some excuse about why not. She a good girl. Studies. Got all these future dreams about shit. Maybe I'll go off to jail and never do it with this girl. Damn. My stomach droppin like an elevator cut loose. Jet myself around the corner into the bathroom and make it to a stall to toss my breakfast.

Teacher bathroom may look cleaner than ours but it still smells like shit under all that rotten lemon ammonia crap. Rinse out my mouth and check out the mirror. First time I took off the gauze, and saw this drop inked under my eye, it was like seeing some birthmark I never knew I had. But still, I always gotta double glance like how you do when you forget you got a new haircut and you not yet knowin yourself. I look good in my brothers hoodie even if I don't fill it in the shoulders like he did. Don't know what's wrong with me, gettin all sick like this. Cheap-ass bodega bun probably expired. Settle myself on the radiator by the window to chill for a sec. Last time I puked was that night after I got inked.

The boys'd been fillin me up with hard stuff taste like fire since we got outta my house away from the napkins, and the food, and the damn shames. Passed me the blunt saying I won't feel a thing. Won't feel a thing and laying me down on the table on that paper that crinkles like in a doctor's. Photos on the walls of people showin off they fresh tats. Some of them real nasty. And it's too late when I remember the reason I don't smoke much is cause it do the exact opposite of what they saying. Make me feel everything more. Feel my own liquids sloshing, my skin sweating, hair growing, I swear. So when that needle come down, my skin it scorches and that pain under my eye not dulled by nothing. Feel like lasers be slicing permanent holes for my everything to leak out of. And I am wishing that all my years be leaking out, bringin me back to before when I knew nothin bout how much this world isn't and how much I want and how much I won't.

"Keep your eyes closed, kid," they sayin. "Les a spark jump in."

So I do. And this tear's being etched into my face forever. For always. For Tower.

"Just the outline for now," they reminding the man giving me the pain, "He be comin back for fillin it in."

Fillin it in.

After I even things up for T, I come back and ink man be fillin it in.

Remember beach one time and Tower diggin the hole, to the Chinese, he say,

"All the way," he's grinnin and telling me, "look down in there and you can see it."

"See what?" I ask him.

"The other side," he says.

So I look down and it's cool on my face and then he shoving me in, crackin up, and pouring the sand in on top. And I am yelling I HATE YOU I HATE YOU.

And the louder I get the more he know I'm loving it. T never push me into a hole he couldn't lift me out of and his arms they are skinny but they are strong as I want my arms to be some day. So I start laughin and with two hands, he's tossin piles of sand and keeps fillin it in, fillin it in till feels like a hug to tell the truth—and I hope that's what it feels like for Tower now he's down there in that ground. It'd be okay then. All those dirt clumps. Like a hug.

Who the hell's touchin me?

Open my eyes and some Mr. Idunno, shakin me and telling me this for faculty only. Nasty taste in my mouth. Itchy hot.

Get to class, teacher's sayin, you know what period it is?

Damn ringin in my ear, always got to be ringin. I shake this motherfucker off and tell him to fuck himself. Yeah, I know what time it is. I know.

But now I'm wonderin if it got to the end of the day already somehow, cause not even one ass is sitting in the hallway cuttin. Then I see it's cause security up here for a stroll and I flip quick to walk away, but hey, what I got to be worried bout security for?

"You got a pass?"

It's the dumpy one with the braids who don't even try to pretend he like us and who always eating some sandwich dripping with eggs.

"What for?"

"Get to class."

He eyeballin me toe to head. Cause he know me too. He know it all. Just nothin he can do bout it. I hear them sayin it. How even though they know shit's bound to go down, all they allowed to do is wait for it to happen.

"You kill somebody ever?" I ask just to mess with him. And cause I'd like to know.

He don't answer, just look me up and down, deciding how he want to take this shit today.

"Get to class," he says.

"I got to go to the nurse," I tell him.

He just grunt and let me go.

Even if he guessed what day today was he'd still have to let me go.

Might as well go to the nurse for real cause in fact my stomach still illin.

Watch my feet goin down, down, down the stairs in T's shoes. Try breathing through my mouth cause smells in here like kids who don't shower. Everything metal and dirty. Skillz joke that jail just like school cept you don't got to worry bout what to wear. Come out on the bottom floor and go over to the nurse. Line for a mile. Mostly fakers, probably, tryin to get outta a test or homework or somethin.

I'm just gonna get me an ice-pack to steady this hand and cool my head a bit.

See some sixth-grader baby up on the wall holding his knee. Got blood seepin through his jeans. Looks scared. Looks familiar maybe. Rest the kids mouthin bout who beatin who in what game, and that girl said you not gonna believe what she said, and how wack ELA is, and I am seeing all these words they saying, like you see breaths in winter. What they talking bout sounding like fairytales. We might be in the same building but I in a whole other place.

This baby be tearing over his trickle of blood. Kid shoulda seen what come outta my brother's head. It didn't come out all pretty like in the movies neither. It thump out with this weird beat, like a cripple walking down the block makin progress one clumsy spurt at a time. Wonder if NME's gonna bleed the same way. He best bleed the same way.

Malcolm. Somebody told me that. Skillz told me to forget it. He NME and thas that. He don't need no other name. He just a blurry motherfucker in my mind, but somebody told me it's Malcolm. Wonder where Malcolm spending his day. Last day. He don't know it. But he spending it. Hope he not wasting it in some nurse's line.

"Are you kidding?"

Nurse rollin her eyes at some kid telling him there's nothing wrong with him, but damn, you know there's something's wrong with me. Thinking like this. You got to keep your mind narrowed on NME just like your weapon, Skillz says, and don't let nothin distract. It ain't no thing. He says first time you fire that piece in your hand you feel a crown come down on your head like you King of the whole damn planet.

T told me about everything else—weed, sex, stealin, everything, but when he did his first blast and I asked what's it like? He just act like he didn't hear me.

Which is kinda fucked up, since—damn. Nevermind. May he rest in peace, I love him my brother I do.

"You do not get a nurse's pass for a papercut." Nurse's lookin mad tight.

"Okay, people, we're almost at the end of the day and I am out of ice-packs. So, unless you require actual, honest to goodness care—unless you are bleeding, or burning up, do yourself a favor and get back to class or I will write you up like you have never been written up before. I am tired of making excuses for you all. You are not excused."

She sits back down. That kid hobblin to the front of the line, trying to show his knee. She glare at him and suck her teeth. "This is not what I was set on this earth for. Don't know what it is, but lord knows it can't be this."

Can't be this.

Look at the clock and wonder if it's right. Cause if it's right, then it's 17 minutes till the end of the day. How'd that happen? 17 minutes. In 17 minutes you not allowed to be in the building less you got detention or on a team or something. I'm not bleeding and I don't got a fever. Guess I don't require honest to goodness care. Guess I don't got no excuse.

Walk the hall, bang, bang, bang, my knuckles on every locker. Pass by the dean's door and door's closed. Must be he got Other Matters. Thas how he put it when the teachers complaining about him doing nothin. I give a good slam on his door. See if his Other Matters get shaken up. Nothing. Slam one more time. What I'm here for.

Door jerks open, Dean Lowell bout to shout at whoever—till he see whoever is me. He pucker his face instead and glaze over his eyes.

"Malique, why aren't you in class?"

I tell him I don't know what class I got.

He don't say nothing.

Tell him I don't know where I'm sposed to be. Tell him maybe I not even here, maybe I'm absent.

"Fine," he says, "I don't have time for this. Bell rings in a few minutes. Just quit the banging till then, and you're free to go do whatever you want."

Whatever I want.

He start to shut the door, I stick in my foot.

"Don't start," he says.

"I not starting nothing," I remind him.

He pausing now. Deciding if he gonna fess up to knowing what I'm talking bout. Cause he knows it. But then he'd have to let me in that office and all those Other Matters of his would be piling up to the sky and his day never be over.

"Just get back to class, Malique, and finish the day, okay?"

Finish the day.

"If I don't, you gonna give me detention or something?"

"Detention's filled to the brim. Six-oh-four decided to have a brawl." He rubbing his hand over his face. "I can't ask any more teachers to stay today."

How the hell you sposed to get to the top of his pile a Matters?

"Cause you know I already throw a desk at Raz's face. Maybe I go back and finish that. Should I do that?"

He just sigh. "You want me to put in a call to your mother?"

My mother.

Everybody always like to talk about my mother like she the answer to the problem of me. Please. They been trying to get her to come to the phone for years. That counselor tried to be all sneaky by sending that slip she wanted signed inside a pretty condolence card with blue glitter flowers. My ma even looked kinda pleased about that card till she saw the slip the counselor wanted her to sign so I could go to see her steada class sometimes. Ma cracked up then. "Counselor?" she says, "what the hell you need a counselor for?"

My mother.

That night they got me inked, by the time they drop me off I mad drunk and can't believe we in the same day we started in. Don't know how I made it up the stairs. Walk in and there platters and napkins all over, but only a few women left, cleaning. And Ma. Ma over on the couch alone. And sorrow not a bird, like T once fuckin wrote up on a test. That's a sparrow. Sorrow somethin else and ma don't got no wings. I am illin big time now. All that booze crashing round my insides. This burning skin under my eye, and everything spinning but there's my ma and I am thinking maybe she can make the spinning stop. Like when she used to stop the fever by pressing that damp rag on the sides of my head and saying, ah baby, baby, baby, ah baby.

Fall over the carpet on my way over there and end up on the floor with her looking into my face and I am waiting for her to fill my hole up with sand but she just takes in the mess under my eye which of course she know what it means. After all she been in this thing longer than me or T. She nods. And she go away. Come back with that damp rag in her hand that's going to wipe the fever tears away, make all the spinning stop.

"Keep it clean, son." She reach out like she gonna start dabbin, but she stop. She don't touch nothing on my face. She just toss me the cloth and sigh.

"Maybe it gonna hurt less when you fill it in."

I throw up all over the pillow and the spinning never did stop.

"Call your mother, you fucker." I tell Lowell and walk away. Hear him sigh and close his door. Go back to his Other Matters. School day almost done.

11 minutes. Skillz probly waiting outside. I walk on down the hall toward the front doors. First floor security getting ready to let everybody out so they can go home. End of the day. Less the bells just don't go off and we stuck here like in some kinda frozen state like what Fadden say happened in the Ice Age.

Who in charge of the bell anyway? I poke my head in the front office.

She don't even see me comin in. Busy scribblin at some papers. All alone at her desk there, doin whatever it is she do that I don't know what it is other than sign the late passes, mark people absent, give em a tissue for their gum when she catch them smackin it. Confiscate stuff. I don't really know. Maybe there's something else to it. I just don't know.

So, I close the door and walk myself over, even though students not sposed to go behind the main desk, cause I got this question. And she look up ask me what can she do for me?

But I know you don't mean it, Ms. Anders, I know what you meaning is step back and get lost. So maybe you shoulda said that. Cause look what happens when you don't say what you mean and somebody takes you serious and tries to give you an answer for real.

I wanna pass.

Don't say what, you heard me.

You telling me it's too late in the day for passes. You say the dismissal bell's going to ring any second. Well, what if it don't?

That comes outta my mouth meaner than I mean it to and now I see how you registerin who I am. Gettin scared. You a teacher and I'm a kid and here you are scared a me. But I'm just tryin to tell you. What you can do for me.

Let's make an experiment.

No, don't ask me what class am I supposed to be in. Let's see what happens if it don't go off, like a test. You not sure what I askin, but aren't you in charga the bell? I just wanna see what happen if we stop it. Cause I don't know what I'm set for and I just need a little more time to figure it out on this earth and would you quit mumbling and makin me haveta come all close up just to hear what you saying.

Whatchyu mean it's on automatic? On a program. Unstoppable.

Now you lookin at the door, and how I closed it, and being more scared, but I'm tellin you not to be scared, don't be scared, nothing to be scared about, cause see I'm not tryin to scare you. It's for my Exit project. Newton's laws, you know. Objects in motion, right? They stay in motion....less something gets in the way, see? So, like this parta the day—the school part—it's in motion right now. Till the bell rings. So if the bell don't ring, then maybe it just keeps goin. Maybe we stretch out time.

Yeah. That makes some sense to me. Think I just found a project Fadden might like for real. So, you and me, we gonna stop the bell. Freeze time. Ice age this place.

No, don't stand up, don't tell me I need to get back to class, no, you don't get it, we got to fix this bell. Quit shakin your head. You not cooperating. Don't you want me to do an exit project? Don't you wanna see me go graduate? If Fadden was here maybe he'd get you to understand this important. This about science. And even though maybe I'm not makin any sense right now, science make sense, and I was gettin good at science, so maybe I'm set for that. But Fadden not here and you tryin to come around from behind your desk like you wanna leave so I have to put you back in the chair. And all these papers fly up and you gaspin. Tryin to get up. I hold you down and now I got my hands clamped on your mouth to keep it shut, cause what you gonna do, scream?

If I take my hands off, is that what you gonna do? Cause this not what I come in here for, you know that right? Not to get your red lipshit all on my hands, Ms. Anders. You feel me? Don't move. I just came in here for, I don't know what I came in here for, I came in here for, damn, quit it, just let me figure this out, a'ight? Cause we got 4 minutes—damn, now 3 minutes—to figure this shit out. Quit screamin. I feel you tryin, but nobody hearin you and you spittin all over my palm. Feels like I'm drowning.

Which is funny cause when I was a kid I used to think about the Olympics. Yeah. Don't know why. Wanted to be a swimmer. But you haveta know how to swim for that and I never learned and anyway that was a long time ago but sometimes, lately, I have these dreams about it. My arms pumping through water and bringing me to the edge and Tower there with a silver medal for me. Mine always silver in the dream cause his is gold for sure. He's my older brother. Everything happens to him first. T only let me join up once I tested the life out. Said, so long as we stuck together, it'd be a'right. We'd make some bills to do life how we want. I never make it to the end of that dream. Somethin always—

DAMN—

What the fuck you biting—let go, LET GO—DAMN—

Fine, go, GO. I let go, see. Go. Go scream your head off. Out the door. Fuck it. Forget it. Forget you. You go on. You go.

You keep resting in your peace.

I'll be here.

Waitin for security—or Skillz, whoever comes first cause anyway it's too late for the experiment, right? You hear that, right?

I do.

I'm listening. I'm listening real close cause maybe, if I listen closer than anybody ever listened to nothing before, I'll find that place where the loudness stop and the quiet begin and meet you there in that spot where sound goes when it's gone, cause you hear that?

That's the bell.

Jeanie Tomasko

CROSSWORD SONNET: CODES

1 Across: Knot in the middle of the spine. 2 Down: The
spine of the matter. 3. Matter at the corner of the eye.
4. I, you, word for us. 5. Word for tonight. 6. I can't
_____ anyone. 7 Down: The Truth. 8 Down: Word
for wild joy—(see 9 Across.) 9. Across from me at your
shiny steel counter, you, taking orders for fries, burgers;
on our breaks they won't let us talk so we write notes
to each other (10) across: fast food order forms. 11. Words
for can't wait. 12 Across: to meet you later. 13. Under:
the second bridge. 14. Run: Your hand up the middle
of my sternum; turn the key behind the heart.

Nicole DiCello

THE LONG EMERGENCY

My seven year old self
lying in the front yard, back
damp with dew

gazing at the unfurling

clouds, each one driving the other
as an engine, as a human invention—war
for instance—and even then I wondered

if that vapor was in combat
or courting

and I told myself—*remember.*

In this way
I am consolable.

Lyall Harris

ETCHING

A comb and The Lord's Prayer shake loose from the visor.
The trapped miner with a wristwatch was the only one who died.
The Dow is up due to exchanges and cancellations.
Night tide buries phosphorescent sand.

The trapped miner with a wristwatch was the only one who died.
A mushroom-shaped growth at his collarbone.
Night tide buries phosphorescent sand.
A knob, the driveway. The reel of his suicide: an etching.

A mushroom-shaped growth at his collarbone.
Tufts of grass spray, momentarily weightless.
A knob, the driveway. The reel of his suicide: an etching.
Cells multiply from the biopsy site.

Tufts of grass spray, momentarily weightless.
Mower in the back rattling traces of cut hillside and gasoline.
Cells multiply from the biopsy site.
Scratch then flake of paint, metallic shower, mapped glass.

Mower in the back rattling traces of cut hillside and gasoline.
Bark splits and peels, lodges in the gap between doors.
Scratch then flake of paint, metallic shower, mapped glass.
The impact might not kill him.

Bark splits and peels, lodges in the gap between doors.

The Dow is up due to exchanges and cancellations.

The impact might not kill him.

A comb and The Lord's Prayer shake loose from the visor.

Ioanna Carlsen

Two Variations On A Borrowed Phrase

I

How Neatly silence Describes the Thing*

Home

Knowing the place so well it's always a surprise,

returning,

to notice something you had not remembered,

how much work you must have done on the garden,

or something you had forgotten,

a painting someone did when they were ten,

and that old emptiness in the hallway

amid the familiar, the known, the lived-with,

the frequently handled—and

the sooner or later to be permanently left,

the-not-to-be-returned-to.

The dog sniffs something new,

perhaps the strange scent of the sea on you,

and as you unload your luggage,

a tunneling of pain reminds you

how long you have been roaming the earth,

mostly in these rooms,

and this manifests

as a slight apprehension when taking messages

off the machine:

returning to the ordinary, it seems fraught with danger,

extra-ordinary, or more beautiful than you had thought,

and you more lucky to be here,

because instead of living it

you *know* you're living it:

the glinting, wordy, bobbing lake of the day,

the lap of night.

And how does the returned-to receive you?

Like a dog who cannot be told when,

(Wednesday, June 28th, means nothing to a dog)

if ever, you are coming back—

absence just happens to a dog,

and the house and all its objects, the fireplace,

your favorite chair, the green vase on the sill,

the clock,

did not even know you were gone,

how neatly silence describes the thing,

your return.

II
How Neatly silence Describes the Thing

Pleasure

I'm curious about pleasure,

is it a sensation or an emotion

and what is the difference, I mean

what is a feeling, how do you touch it,

how are you touched by one, I'm curious

about how your emotions fit you like what you wear,

sadness a glove you can remove by drinking or shopping,

depression, a dress too tight to get off,

the blouse of laughter—

and where do they all go,

the pleasure you took,

the sadness you felt,

where do they go when they go?

I hope the diver who eventually dredges this corner of the bay

brings up trunks full of doubloons, and the letters

of rapscallions,

and things

of things, artifacts belonging to the dead,

and I hope that ship is sunk deep in the water as a fish,

and that the diver as he retrieves

the belongings of breathers dressed in silence

thinks of pleasure down there in the deeps,

how when sensation sleeps, the world turns into a dot

from which you can see forever,

how you fall asleep saying nothing

and wake to a big dream.

The phrase is Jorie Graham's.

Soma Mei Sheng Frazier

SHE MUST REMEMBER

SHE MUST REMEMBER NOT TO MENTION HER WAKE-and-bake-weed-smoking, jobless Carolina redneck dyke ex-lover's name. She must remember not to draw attention to the heart-shaped marinara smear on her left breast, or to her breasts at all, as the upstanding Dean of Student Affairs has already given her sheer white blouse and slightly visible black bra the stink eye once today, guessing accurately that she dresses this way to gain an advantage over the fearless high school boys in her sophomore English class. She must remember not to show emotion, or lower her eyes, as she threads through packed hallways: shouting kids, scent of sweat, shiny narrow lockers. She must remember not to cuss like a gambler with Tourette's, staring at a 7-2 off-suit hand.

The classroom is yellow with sunlight. This is not a typical secondary school; rather, an elite private institution in a renovated 1920's art deco hotel, all high ceilings and marble bathrooms and dark wood doors.

She must remember that the quiet one is Juliette—for the quiet ones become allies quickly, before the louder ones realize that they love her too; that she is their favorite teacher because she lets them talk. She must remember to let them talk: not while completing assignments, but in the brief moments after the bell rings, when the French financier's daughter catches her by the sleeve, *Ms. Katz*, to tell her how that late-night party, where she ended up the last girl drinking vodka with boys she had thought were her friends, went wrong; or in the early morning, before class, when the football Center who threatened to toss the algebra tutor out the third-floor window is waiting for her with a loaf of banana bread he's baked himself. *Thank you for explaining comma splices without getting mad. You never talk to me like I'm dumb.* She must remember, too, that the charismatic mother of the sociopathic Louisiana implant exploited a tragedy—got her son into the school by claiming he'd been a straight-A student at a school whose records were wiped out in the hurricane, though it was perfectly clear he'd never cracked a book in his life.

The faculty lounge is intimate and warm, connected to an oak paneled reading room and a miniature library. In the library, a classic rolling ladder allows her to reach the topmost shelves, and motes of dust float incessantly, year 'round, on some soft current that circulates from nowhere.

She must remember not to mention her wake-and-bake-weed-smoking, jobless Carolina redneck dyke ex-lover's name. She must remember to label her Cokes, or lose them to the Dean of Discipline. She must remember not to grin as she watches the Coke thief rummage through the faculty fridge, and imagines the contents of his desk drawers: riding crop, paddle, ball gag, nipple clamps, leather gimp suit, hose? She must remember that the Assistant Headmaster is a widow who insists on *Mrs.*, although, if the gossip here is to be trusted, she hated her husband, may he rest in peace, and slept around.

The Rockefeller Room: long conference table, hidden modern lighting, and subtle ivory walls hung with stiff portraits of past headmasters. She likes to sneak in there and stare blankly out the window overlooking the quad, when it's not booked for board meetings (uppity powwows at which manicured suits grip and grin and say things like *I don't want to ant-fuck about formatting* and *tell that idiot bean-counter to get me the goddamn budget* to prove they're still men, or can play ball with the men).

She must remember not to mention her wake-and-bake-weed-smoking, jobless Carolina redneck dyke ex-lover's name. She must remember that it is an honor, and not a fucking pain in the ass time-suck, that keeps her at work late the first Monday of every month, to sit as the sole faculty member on the Fundraising Committee and strategize about how to help a bunch of rich assholes get more money out of their rich asshole friends and contacts. She must remember that she was hired—and for more than even the most seasoned teachers are generally paid—as much for her West Coast connections to wealthy potential donors as for her impressive curriculum vita. She must remember not to push too hard on behalf of the scholarship students: *We really need to provide a study-abroad experience for Amara, because all of the other kids' parents have access to such resources, and...* She must remember to wear the sheer white blouse and slightly visible black bra on the first Monday of next month—that is, if she can get the marinara out.

The detention hall is actually just the well-appointed dining hall, transformed by the magic of the last bell. The solid, dark wood table at which she sits with the sociopathic Louisiana implant is engraved with furtive carvings: *Maya LOVES Adam* and *Fucking Dean Dickwad can lick my scrot'*. (She is impressed by the apostrophe.)

She must remember not to mention her wake-and-bake-weed-smoking, jobless Carolina redneck dyke ex-lover's name. She must remember to convey the egregiousness and foolishness of stealing another student's ideas, and presenting them in a portfolio that was to have been shared with the class, while avoiding ambiguous or incendiary language that this kid's charismatic mom can use to get her fired before the rest of the faculty discerns that he's a sociopath—they've been had by a teenage con and his well-heeled con mom—and he quietly transfers to another school. She must remember the name of the rapidly promoted black New York Times journalist who was fired for plagiarism, in one blow decimating his own career and discrediting affirmative action, at least in the eyes of the reactionary right. She must remember to clarify that there is also a reactionary left, leaving her personal politics obscure. She must remember why she broke up with her wake-and-bake-weed-smoking, jobless Carolina redneck dyke ex-lover.

The parking lot is nearly empty under a vast cobalt sky. It was for her own safety and prosperity, right—not just a thankless future at a snooty school where payday rolled around and most of the faculty lined up to have shit tossed at them?

She must remember not to mention her wake-and-bake-weed-smoking, jobless Carolina redneck dyke ex-lover's name. She must remember that the Director of Institutional Advancement position will open up next week as the current, incompetent director is fully phased out. She must remember not to interrupt *Mrs.* Assistant Headmaster's diatribe about having to stay late to reprimand a scholarship student's single mom for the misplaced values that led her to refuse to miss work at a *gas station* to attend vital PTA meetings with the other, *quality* mothers who *care* about their children's *wellbeing* for goodness sake. She must remember that nobody here could possibly guess how her own mother had raised her on bodega soda pop and boxed spaghetti, the two of them hustling to pay the rent on a South Bronx efficiency apartment; that her wealthy West Coast connections are comprised of strangers she researched online; that her curriculum vitae is a lie and she can always spot the cheaters because she's just like them: doesn't give a damn about the rules that invisible people with power drafted; just wants these assholes to pay her an increasingly ridiculous guilt fee to pay attention to their kids; can't believe a father could avoid raising his daughter to the extent that she thought a home office packed with plastered, entitled, savage teenage boys constituted a fun, safe evening among friends.

The Englander—a stereotype of a pub where the school's administrators get sotted and dish goss about the faculty while the faculty, in an adjacent room, get arseholed and gab about the administrators—is too warm. An apply scent hangs in the cloying air, reminding her of her diabetic amputee uncle Garth, buried in Saint Raymond Cemetery.

She must remember not to mention her wake-and-bake-weed-smoking, jobless Carolina redneck dyke ex-lover's name. She must remember to stick with ale and forego the hard stuff till she's alone, at home, in her black bra and pajama pants. She must remember to be acerbically witty; and to balance that with empathic nodding when her sloshed coworkers start shit-talking the young people they've opted to teach. She must remember to hit the loo and soap the heart-shaped stain out of her blouse, before it sets in. She must remember to prolong eye contact with the Headmaster's Assistant, Ringo, who actually does look like a British pop star and drinks with the faculty despite having the ear of the icy, erudite board member heading up the Hiring Committee. She must remember to hit the hard stuff and soap out the memory of her wake-and-bake-weed-smoking, jobless Carolina redneck dyke ex-lover's name, before it sets in—

The kitchen is her favorite room; possibly her favorite place in the entire world. Its peeling walls still hold the soft scent of her ex-lover's fried hush puppies, and there's vodka nestled in the freezer between frozen peas and more vodka.

She must remember me. She must remember something of the way I gently held her face, like a good mother does her baby's, and kissed her tears away.

The bathroom is too bright. She leans close to the mirror and suddenly realizes she is beautiful, as she does every time she drinks slightly too much ale at the Englander.

She must remember that I need this role, this deception, to ascend socially whereas she, much stronger, is free from the urge to climb.

The bed is soft. Welcoming.

She must remember how hard we fought, and that fights among equals can never be won.

The light is off; the room airy and dark.

She must remember that—though the world is full of trap-doors and idiots will hear her accent and smell the weed that helps her eat despite the chemo and mistake *her* for the idiot and gorgeous teenage girls are brutally gang-raped at late-night parties on the leather couches of their financier fathers' home offices and good mothers are compared unfavorably with bad ones, and people leave one another, even when they love them, maybe especially when they love them—somebody saw her once, eye to eye, and found her lovely.

Austin Allen

VALENTINE VARIATIONS

I

Roses are red,
Violets are blue.
Spring has decided
To try someone new.

II

Violence is red,
Neurosis is blue.
The blood of my heart
Wears a purplish hue.

Frozen with dread,
Spineless straight through,
I drain seven glasses,
Contriving my coup.

Moses's Red
Dividing in two:
The crowd drains around her,
I stride up on cue.

Poses are shed,
Guises torn through.
Lubricant yields
To a warm social glue.

Cozy in bed,
Skylit dark blue...
Sunrise. Her blinds
Bleed a faint purple view.

III
Rosé with bread.
Violins coo.
Candlelight melts
To a pool of white dew.

Goes to my head.
Wine hits me too.
Her eyes are diamonds,
My insides are goo.

Roses are red.
While this is true,
A man's got to do
What a man's got to do.

IV
"Oh yes," she says—
Violates taboo—
Lets me (although
We're allowed now, it's true).

V
Grossness is said,
Vileness spewed.
The door of the room
Of the night of the feud

Closes. A lead
Silence ensues.
A court case blows open.
We're both going to lose.

Noses are red,
Eyelids are too.
The case is straightforward.
My tie is askew.

VI
Roses are blue,
Violets are red.
Meanings are constructs.
The poem is dead.

Prose is unread,
Stylists are through.
Composers are next,
Says the Paris Review.

No, I misread—
Music went first.
I stare at my desk
And prepare for the worst.

Orchids are green!
Daisies are pink!
This wine's so delicious
I can't even think.

Cirrhosis ahead:
Bile will spew.
Saved it for decades now.
Long overdue.

Roses are rose,
Violets are violet.
Love is clear prose,
Even dying won't style it.

Houses in rows—
Twilit, outspread.
The verdict is autumn.
I'm going to bed.

VII
Spring is in session,
The docket is full,
The heifer with bailiff eyes
Summons the bull,

Gold fuchsia indigo
Ochre vermilion
Are phlox poppies hyacinths
Mums by the billion,

Senses are evidence,
X equals Y,
And a couple in Paris
Decides with a sigh

That is subject to further
Judicial review
That roses are red
And that violets are blue.

Luke Bramley

ALL THE PRETTY LIGHTS

From darkened hills where worms glow green

And throb beneath the gloaming trees

I see a stretch of blackened grass

Run down into a grey morass

Beyond which flame the city lights,

An archer's thousand burning flights

And all across from here to there

A boiling darkness, blazing air

The curving sea, a dwindling trail

Of floating quartz and gleaming shale.

But mid this wondrous, glowing place

I sit, a single, muted space,

A charcoal smudge, a grimy root,

A dead thing dressed in nature's suit

And feeling all this nothingness,

This fractious hole inside my chest,

I rise up and I walk upon

Each glowing part, until anon

The hills are dark, the city gone

And all the sea is dredged of stone

And all the sky is blown of stars.

Yet in this hot and ticking gloom,

This man-made night, this dying womb,

In one small hole, life still exists

Where eyes are caught in callous fists

And peeled by cooks and fried in vats

And round these pots, those blind are sat

Who speak of love with great remorse

While nibbling on the second course

Until each spits his tongue and cries:

The truths lie here but there truth lies!

You stop me then, hand on my chest

And feel my heart beat through my breast

And make me hear your eloquence

That for a moment makes some sense.

But, no, you're young and burn with rights

And trust in lies like at first sight,

And I, by God, am past my prime

And cannot stand this pantomime:

The lights! The lights! Such pretty lights!

Just let me see them one last time

Before I must put out mine eyes.

Ken Taylor

foursome

(with a line from Olson by way of Creeley)

retreat to a place out of season.

hint of venom in the nicknames

now. measure of how much whip

still left in the stick. warm up our

hinges for rough dutch art. more

than stance, grip & alignment going

under bucket hats. more than clubbing

up. more than the bet, automatic

press two down, junk, greens in

regulation, number of putts, narrowing

execution. bigger knowing doesn't help

meniscus, rotator cuff, rolled ankle,

tennis elbow. fail points & betrayal of

body is what we know. we transport

better medicine: vicodin, voltaren,

skelaxin. put on c-pap, float cortisone

in blood. our shadows don't resemble
folk of earlier gatherings as if digitally

diminished or engineered away. we are
apposite to light right after sunset: hocus,

locus, polis, pole dance, trance after
the rock, after steak, after whiskey.

gloaming, gloom & self-loathing.
thinking of the times a folded dollar

bill picked front teeth. wish of what's
before to sit on our native DNA & bring

longevity, bitter fruit, bittersweet sweat,
night thrash of the lost days, tossed

with momentum towards what? *we are
as we find out we are*...wake to old

stomping grounds, land of peggy lee &
sinatra & great tequila. gay mecca, über

hip reminding we are invisible to those
we would pursue. we ape elder whining

of the wine pour, crash into our fool

echoes. we work to avoid the middle

of the horseshoe. over tip the cart girl.

replace our divots. play by the rules.

Wulf Losee

THE NAUTILUS MOTEL

I am driving across a bridge of high steel
over a bay where the playful goldsmiths of light
display their wares on the rippled blue;
where stanchion shadows strobe by; car tires moan;
concrete hums; past the fast frames of sky (where
Chagall's cockerels mimic pink-bellied clouds).

The dance steps of my memory move to no clock.
My journey's meditation skips back decades, as I steal
into that first room of our hearts (and become a voyeur)
replaying the time when the smile of lithe Aphrodite
smirked on our couplings as she twisted the motes
of morning dust into her swirls and foam-blooms.

Waking from this recollection is like a flowering bruise
(a welt on my spirit's skin).Bandaged in Time's cloth,
the sting of regret will pass in an infinite moment.
I offer you a million dandelion mandalas instead.
Their parachute caps dry and unfold in the sunlight
freeing our desires to whirl aloft on the air.

God's windy fingers (double-helix cyclones) tear

and batter us with the storm-birds of debris, blown

from the realm where the Archetypes prowl by half-light.

Vicious as any big cat (and as playful as ocelots),

they are thin-lipped chameleons, who seem asleep,

until we are wrapped in their quick and sticky tongues.

I descend the bridge-ramp into night's yawning mouth;

thoughts fly across the six directions of awareness,

the magic net of senses flails on winds of feeling;

but I am the spider trickster skittering on its billows;

my driftnet web snares the flutter-wings of gold.

(and the fly converses with the smiling skull of life.)

I will occupy a room in the Nautilus Motel tonight,

and in my chamber I'll recite the sestinas of insomnia;

I'll chase my thoughts (down tight spirals), and, cloaked

in naked wakefulness, I'll unfocus the gaze of my stare.

The walls of my room will dissolve into night's blueness.

As the moon sinks westward, I will swim with it in the sea.

(Tomorrow) I'll wash dream-dust from eyes with clouds of light;

somewhere within me, though, a steel bridge will moan;

You will swim out to me again where the sea-foam blooms.

Lisa Locascio

I MET HER IN BERLIN IN A BAR CALLED American Hospitality. She was sitting alone on a gray velvet settee with long vertical tears that exposed the stuffing. She was tall and ample in the way a man can be ample: a little stomach, thick legs. Her light brown hair was pulled back into a low ponytail that draped both sides of her face as she leaned over her right leg. From across the room it looked like she might be crying.

When I came closer I saw she was braiding a long cord from several strands of bright thread safety-pinned to her jeans. I stood close to her, exhaling, and waited for her to react, but she did not. "What are you doing?" I asked.

She answered without looking up, in a sharp American accent. "Making a bracelet."

"Who is it for?" I asked. My wineglass felt suddenly heavy in my hand.

"My friend Katie," she said. "Why?"

"I saw you from across the room and I thought you were weeping, with your head down like that." I had meant for this to sound light, with a little rough laugh, but it came out hushed and fearful.

"I'm not." She looked up, hair falling away from her face. She had a long nose, gray eyes, the remnants of a tan on her temples and cheeks. Her lips were chapped and thinner in the middle than at the edges, as if she had chewed them into a different shape. The skin beneath her nose was smooth and still. Her eyes were clear and bright. She was telling the truth.

We considered each other for a minute before she went back to her work on her leg. I stood next to her, trying to see her fingers. "Do you need more wine?" I asked.

Her curtain of hair muffled her voice. "Sure." She held out her glass in one hand. I took it, letting my thumb linger on the pad of her index finger before I went to the bar.

Whether it was the wine or the fact that I fetched it for her, she decided to speak to me for the next hour. I sat beside her on the settee. She stayed hunched over her project, occasionally rearing her head back to sip from her glass or ask me to repeat something. She spoke both English and German with equal unease, sometimes slipping into the former when she couldn't locate a preferred word in the latter. She had gone to boarding school in the north of the country and was now at university for economics, but she seemed bored by her studies. I sucked on my bottom lip as she told me of her minute and peculiar extracurricular pursuits.

With a razor blade, she cut empty laundry detergent containers from trash bins into feathers and kept them, like business cards, in a wallet made of duct tape. As she told me this, she produced one and laid it between us on the settee. It was an exquisite glinting thing. The duct tape wallet was juvenile, unbelievable, but it could not shake my weird attraction to her. I lifted my eyes from the feather and watched her face in the top of my vision. She squinted, then closed her eyes and relaxed her face, as if in deep thought, as she rattled off the rest of her hobbies.

She collected tea cups, rescued chickens from butchers, made daisy chains from waste paper, never flushed urine, read arcane agricultural chemistry ("Black-eyed peas are rich in nitrates and often planted by farmers to enrich the soil"), remembered all of her dreams, and played a lute inherited from her grandmother. Her name was Juliet, and she walked in a shambling gait, with the slightest intimation of a limp. Her father was American, from a faraway California town called San Pedro, about which Juliet dutifully reported her father's joke: "The main exports are fruits and nuts."

We drank a lot of wine, becoming sleepy and argumentative, somnolently turning the names of films over and over in our mouths. When the bar announced last call, I assumed she would take me home. "We are closing. We are closing," the bartender called, and I bounced back and forth on my feet to show that I was friendly, that this would be fun. Juliet hauled herself up from the settee. The roll of stomach that had been settled on her lap for the past hour flattened impressively. Her weight seemed to redistribute as she stood, and I felt embarrassed that I had judged her to be heavy. Her hair fell back, derelict from hanging in her face all night, but she made no effort to rearrange it. Maybe that was what I liked, that lack of self-awareness. This was the moment in the evening when most girls became jumpy, jokey or morbid. But Juliet just ambled agreeably along, smiling at the floor. As we passed through the door I saw the old painted sign hung just above the threshold, the words bright red against the washed-out pale wood:

AMERICAN HOSPITALITY SUITES:
YOUR HOME AWAY FROM HOME

Outside, the summer wind had turned cold. Dust rushed at my face. "So," I said, searching her gaze. She turned to me, smiling, and excitement bubbled up in my stomach. I began to speak again, and then I realized Juliet's smile was for someone behind me. A tall blond man swooped in and took her close to his chest, whispering endearments. When their embrace ended, Juliet smirked at me. "This is my boyfriend, Fabian," she said.

"Hello, it is wonderful to meet you," Fabian said in English. He mistook me for an American. We spoke vaguely about the evening for a few minutes, and then the two of them receded into the night, arms around each other's waists. Juliet turned her head and mouthed "Goodbye." Or at least it looked like it, in the low light.

I walked home. I thought that was it, just another way of getting through an evening. I was not even particularly bothered that I hadn't slept with her. But then, of course, I began to run into Juliet and Fabian everywhere.

When I lived in Berlin, my days began with the fevered clanging of my discount alarm clock. It was made from cheap metal—tin? aluminum? I wasn't sure—that dented whenever it fell to the floor, and it fell often, because my natural response to its racket was to sweep it from my bedside table with my left arm. The wrist of that arm always hurt in the morning. I became aware of the pain again each time I knocked the clock off the table, and then I woke entirely, cradling my left wrist in my right hand and wondering again what I had done in my sleep to cause the ache. In this way, the alarm clock only triggered the actual alarm—the wrist pain—that roused me from my rest and started my journey through the day.

I rented a room in a massive apartment that I shared with three room-mates: a Spaniard, a Greek, and a Canadian, a man and two women. Our foursome produced no social intrigue or late night rendezvous. Every room in the apartment was too big for us to fill. The inroads we made in the project of making the place welcoming—the bathroom plant we hoped would benefit from shower steam, the vaguely Eastern cloth thrown over the divan from the street—always fell short, were awkward or tiny in the room. Like the city itself, the apartment refused to be made ours. Perhaps for this reason, no intimacy developed between my roommates and me, not even friendship, only politeness, gentle nods on the way to and from the bathroom, limp jokes about our nationalities that petered out before the punchline. Mainly we encountered each other in the strangely proportioned kitchen and complained about the lack of hot water, the broken washing machine.

Before I met Juliet and Fabian, I rose each morning without expectation of company. I had no friends. I walked to the shower, I walked out of the shower. I had left most of my clothes and possessions in my old city. On my first day in Berlin, during the same shopping trip that had produced my alarm clock, I had purchased three pairs of dark straight pants and six button-up shirts in shades of gray and brown: a new Berlin uniform, utilitarian and quiet, padded out only with thin white undershirts and the tweed greatcoat I had brought with me. I had my hair cut short and learned to polish my shoes. If asked, I would have denied it, but of course I was trying to remake myself, to be someone different.

When I was dressed I went to the kitchen, nodded glumly at my roommates, if they were present, and ate a breakfast of yogurt and honey. I wasn't particularly fond of yogurt and honey, but they were always in the refrigerator, and after I ate someone else's yogurt and honey during my first week, I was obliged to replace it, a transaction that had grown into a perpetual motion machine. I listened to the radio as I ate. The news was not good.

The economy, in Germany and elsewhere, was not good. Our chances of continuing the lives our parents had led and we had been taught to expect were not good. Things were not good in the wars the United States had begun, and things were not good in the wars the United States might soon begin. In a village some-where, water made an entire school ill. Climate change destroyed the Russian crop and changed wind patterns over a Chinese desert, but people still didn't believe that climate change existed. There might not be enough money for healthcare, for school, for surviving climate change. There might not be enough money, or there might be too much meaningless money. We might all wake from our long dream and not know that we had woken.

I listened to the news on the radio because I did not want to read the newspaper and I refused to watch television. It was a part of my day, like taking vitamins—although I did not take vitamins—that seemed necessary penance for my ability to lead the unfettered life of a young man in Berlin. The news on the radio did not tell me about my day. I was never hungry, and if I was sick I could go to a doctor and be treated. I tried not to let the water run unnecessarily, but it took long minutes for it to heat up in the shower, and I couldn't make myself get in cold water on the mornings that were already so cold and so bright. I tried never to waste food. I told myself that I didn't have a car, that I took the U-Bahn everywhere and ate leftovers and appreciated the silver-blue dome of sky above me. That should count for something. That was almost like doing something.

My new neighborhood was an old area, west of the city center, that self-proclaimed artists had recently begun to resettle after many years of urban decay. The streets were impossibly wide, bearing traffic, families, food vendors, the U-Bahn tracks and their metal supports, and inescapable distracted young people wandering the city. The tall brick buildings were dark walls on both sides of the street, shielding us from the wider world, giving us a smaller world. Some of the streets were paved with cobblestones, and some of the apartment buildings had little gabled garrets at the top, with pyramid windows reaching into the sky. I had hoped to live in one of these garrets, but they were out of my price range; my apartment was on the second floor.

I performed various rites every day to shake the feeling of impermanence. I went grocery shopping at the Turkish store the locals frequented, which had bad lighting and bruised fruit, instead of the new Kaiser's Tengelmann just a few blocks farther away. I took long walks and looked out the windows of coffeehouses. I made sandwiches and ate them leaning on my balcony in the cold morning air. I created reasons to be out and about, errands to the post office and the stationer's that had to be run on a weekly basis. But I couldn't shake the tourist twinge, that combination of embarrassment and longing.

I was in the throes of this emotion the first time I saw Juliet and Fabian again. I had stopped on the sidewalk in front of a travel agency, transfixed by the image in its window: a tall poster advertising a weekend trip to my home city with a photograph of its opera house, a spaceship of modern design promising cool art from across the water. I hadn't missed home before, and I didn't now, I told myself as I looked at the poster. Close up, the edges of the image were clearly pixilated; it was a blow-up of a digital photograph. The opera house had been photographed in the spring, when the color of the water lightened slightly and the harbor filled with visitors. But when I turned away from the travel agency, I realized that I understood nothing in Berlin as well as I did the manufactured image of the opera house. I felt simultaneously distant and near, as if I had a barely-controlled power to manipulate time. I looked at Berlin, eyes hungry for something to recognize, and then they rounded the corner: Juliet and Fabian.

She wore a long green scarf that seemed to be in tatters, a black jacket over a purple shirt, ragged jeans. The bottom hem of the shirt snuck up over her lower stomach as she walked, revealing a tube of skin pinched up by the jeans and whipped pink by the wind. Beside her, Fabian was elegant in a long gray coat and brown boots. His hair seemed fuller than it had been the night we met. I felt self-conscious of my plain clothes, my short haircut. His handsomeness set off Juliet's awkwardness. As it had the night we met, her hair looked as though it had seen neither comb nor soap in several days.

Juliet noticed me first. I watched her eyes stop on me. She looked neither surprised nor interested, just unfazed, content to walk past. I doubt she would have said anything if Fabian had not recognized me when they were just a few steps from where I stood, still frozen in front of the travel agency.

He raised his arm in happy greeting. "Hello! What are you doing here?"

"I work at the university," I said, astonished.

"We are going to lunch!" Fabian said, as if this was an unusual event. "Please come." Juliet looked at me from the side of her eyes: interested, maybe.

I sat across from them and listened as Fabian held forth on his areas of expertise—he was an apprentice industrial real estate broker, a job title he loved to speak, giving me the five words in clipped, smiling English. It was his job to take foreign businessmen to abandoned warehouses and convince them, in one of his many languages, that Berlin was the future of world commerce. While he spoke of his exploits, Juliet kept her eyes coolly on me, as if deciding.

She's not particularly attractive, I kept repeating in my mind like a protective prayer. I was powerless against Juliet's wrists and neck, the exposed roll of abdomen I knew waited under the table. When the waitress came I glanced at the menu and ordered the cheapest thing. Fabian and Juliet didn't even look at the list. Fabian said to the waitress like something out of an old American movie: "We'll have the regular."

I had a strange salad of canned corn and pineapple topped with a thick white sausage while they chewed beautiful pressed sandwiches with creamy green interiors. Over the next month, I would come to view the details of that lunch as prescient, directly determinative of what came after, Juliet and Fabian lost in their lovely food as I knife-hustled yellow nuggets onto my fork, hoping they would balance until they reached my mouth.

We parted, making no plans to meet again, which relieved me. But I kept running into them there in the streets around the university, at least once a week. I briefly entertained the idea that they might be stalking me, but I had to discard this notion for lack of evidence. Fabian always insisted that we have coffee or a brief meal, over which he would hold forth about the developments in his life and career as Juliet glanced at me over the rim of her glass. Both of them had been raised on American military bases; Fabian's parents seemed to have been some sort of cleaners in the compound where Juliet lived, a detail that made his dull ambition understandable. Juliet told long stories about how studying the industrialization of England in gymnasium had inspired her to pursue economics. She wanted to become an accountant and help uneducated people manage their money. They were equally charmed by their boring goals. Fabian automatically tied Juliet's scarf around her neck when it was time to go back out into the cold. It seemed they had been together forever.

I was exhausted after I saw them. I finished my work at the university as quickly as possible, went home, and got directly into bed. As the autumn progressed, the sun began to go down earlier and earlier, and it was often dusk by three in the afternoon, when I left work. It felt right to get into bed when it was dark outside, to turn off the lights, not exactly to sleep, but to think. First I thought about my family, about my mother in America and my father in my grandparents' old house in the mountains. They divorced when I was nineteen, informing me of their decision in a letter written on hotel stationery. My mother had sent me odd gifts since moving to America: glasses, silverware, a crystal vase, the kinds she had sent brides in my childhood. Lying in the dark in my huge bedroom, I reviewed each of these presents, all of which I had pawned immediately. She never included a note. Only the shipping manifest told me where the items had come from. My father sometimes sent cards. Neither seemed to think anything was strange about their complete retraction from my life, and when I thought about it in the dark, I supposed I felt the same way.

I thought about my mother's gifts and my father's cards, and then my mind drifted to women, to the women I had slept with. I could remember only one thing about each of them, a problem that reminded me of the serial killers on television who kept mementoes from their victims, a ring, a stick of gum, a sock. But it wasn't the women's possessions I remembered but their bodies: a pair of thick ankles, a long swan neck, the undersized thumbs I noticed only when a stranger shook my hand goodbye. Then, lonely for a person's entire presence, my thoughts turned to Juliet, the woman whose complete body I could remember. I saw over and over her elegant hands, her gray eyes, her belly. I imagined holding her in my arms, but the thought brought me no happiness, only more unease. I imagined her and imagined her until I fell asleep, far too early.

Those nights, I woke in the middle of the night, all activity in my apartment long extinguished, to the sound of the old man shuffling back and forth in front of my building. My disordered sleep schedule had made me aware of his habit, which had likely long preexisted my tenancy in the apartment, of pacing very slowly on the sidewalk between the hours of two and four in the morning. He seemed to have some kind of handicap, certainly a limp, and it was clear that it was difficult for him to move at all. The walking was work, perhaps mandated by a doctor, or simply by himself, a nightly test. He walked between the two tall streetlamps, bathed in their orange light, face hidden under a large black hat. The first time I heard him down there I went to my window and watched him for what felt like an hour.

After a few weeks of encounters with Juliet and Fabian, I began developing a physical reaction to Juliet. Whenever I saw her, my neck ached. The pain, not at all romantic, functioned in place of a poetic sensation like a prickling scalp or sweaty palms. Although we lived in an enormous city with millions of inhabitants, she and Fabian seemed to be everywhere I went, peeking out from behind scaffolding, appearing silently beside me on the U-Bahn platform, slipping into stride next to me in streets near my apartment building. Juliet's body was long beneath her ugly clothes.

I thought of them when I was not with them. Their image came unbidden, the two of them together at the center of the university, looking happily up into the sky, arms linked. This was right and good, the way things should be. But then my mind performed a strange telescoping and sent the two of them careening together, like pendulums on a grand clock, and Juliet knocked Fabian away. She stood there alone, staring, at the center of my thoughts. I blinked away from her face, ashamed. This happened more and more to me when I was just standing somewhere trying to think about something, anything else. And then, one day at the end of November, just after I saw Fabian swept away for the hundredth time, my neck began to sort of crumble, an inside corrosion. And Juliet appeared, swinging her arms as she rounded the bend and came toward me.

It was later than we normally saw each other—I had stayed on at work reading a novel, not wanting to go home to my vast empty apartment. The deserted office was calm. Snow fell outside, the first of the season. I pulled my chair alongside the largest window in the office and pressed my cheek against the glass, thrilled by the cold. It was quite dark by the time I left the building, the golden glow of the streetlamps amplifying the sound of the snow under my feet. I stopped at the small store on the corner, as I often did, to buy a beer to drink at home. The woman behind the counter at the store insisted on being paid in exact change, and it made me happy to be able to give her what she wanted.

As I left with my beer, the sight of the U-Bahn tracks above the street struck me. It wasn't that they looked different, although I had never seen them covered in snow before. The framing of the night sky and the warm light from the lamps made the bridge seem more alive, like a creature removed from its natural habitat and set free in a foreign place.

That night Juliet wore a long black down coat and gray workman's boots. She came closer and closer, her expression unchanging, and I began to wonder if perhaps she didn't see me, if the snow had blinded her too. But she dipped closer, and when she reached me she slipped her hand into mine.

"Hi." Juliet had never said this before, had never touched me before.

"Hello!" I said, attempting pushing my voice into Fabian's hearty timbre. "How are you?"

She turned her feet pigeon-toed and gave me a weird smile. "It's nice to see you," she said.

My sore wrist ached and I realized our hands were still together, Juliet's gripping mine tightly. What had seemed like an unusual greeting—I thought maybe it was an American thing—was now clearly handholding. The pain in my neck screamed.

My discomfort must have shown on my face, because Juliet said, "Oh, you must be cold. Come over to my place?"

I walked a few steps behind her, transfixed by the movement of her heavy boots through the thin snow, which liquefied beneath her feet. Our procession towards her apartment felt dimly allusive to me, as if I was reenacting some famous walk. But which one: Eurydice? The wife of Lot? I prayed for Fabian to arrive, bearing Teutonic goodwill. For the first time since I had moved there, Berlin seemed utterly abandoned. The occasional taxi glided by, lights clouded by snow, but otherwise we were alone on the giant street. I wanted the U-Bahn to pass above, but it did not.

Juliet lived in the smallest apartment in Berlin. Every apartment I had visited in that city, all of them inhabited by shiftless young people like myself, was massive, room after room unfolding like nightmares. Juliet's was a single largish closet, with a loft bed above a falling-apart pressboard desk. There were no cupboards, so she had improvised: she had a tiny refrigerator with a microwave and hot plate stacked on top, a freestanding cabinet with a broken door and an overtaxed coat rack. Her clothes were folded in cardboard boxes beneath the tall window beside the bed. She led me in with no disclaimer or warning. I was shocked by the disorder, the rickety coffee table across from the bed that was clearly her dining table as well. The idea that all Americans were rich, which had been lodged in my mind from an early age, began to loosen.

Juliet talked nonstop about the cold weather, the way winter was still special to her, not that she had never seen it before, but in the "culture of her family" (a phrase she kept using) her father's stories of California had embedded themselves in her mind and she felt that she, too, was from San Pedro, a little beach town where it was always summer. She talked and talked, filling a handleless mug with the words WHERE'S THE BEEF? on its side from a liter jug of cheap red wine and swigging recklessly, as if preparing herself for something. After my beer was finished, I began to drink the vinegary wine from her other mug, which was printed with hearts and envelopes.

She said nothing about Fabian. I had assumed they lived together, but there was no trace of him in the small apartment. The place seemed to be hers alone; Juliet had left herself everywhere. If I could spend time there without her, I might be able to examine every artifact. Several of her plastic feathers were spread on the windowsill, glittering in the wet snowlight beside three tall potted plants. The lute leaned against one of the boxes of her clothes, and a bright white hen slumbered in a large cage beneath her desk, content in that small place as any creature could be. I wanted to walk around and pick things up, hold them in my hands, but Juliet kept talking.

"I finished a new bracelet, the third one I've done since the night we met. That bracelet, the one I was making, I sent it to Katie and she liked it a lot. I told her in a letter about you, about our meeting at American Hospitality. Then—the next two I made I sent to my mom because there are women in her office who she thought might like to have them, and now this one is for you." She said it without affect—her

American accent had begun to be replaced by something a little more confusing, a downward tug on her vowels that sounded as if it might be a regional accent from somewhere much closer than San Pedro—but the words rang loudly in my head. I nodded and smiled blankly as she dug it out of her pocket: a thick plait of silver and green thread with an adjustable knot. It wasn't ugly, but I already knew I would never wear it; it looked like something for a teenage surfer on a television show. I thanked her and moved to drop it in the pocket of my coat.

"Oh, aren't you going to wear it?" Juliet asked hopefully, and before I could answer she took my sore wrist in both of her hands and tightened the bracelet around it like a tourniquet. The hurt in my body was constant now. Being alone with Juliet made the pain more difficult to understand. I had thought that it was caused by my attraction to her, by her inaccessibility as Fabian's girlfriend. But now that I was with her, I didn't know what would stop the awkward sensation, the burning in my neck. I was staring at the bracelet, grappling with this, when Juliet wrapped her hands around the back of my head, pulled me towards her, and kissed me.

Her mouth was open. Her tongue darted back and forth from her teeth to mine. Her hands slid up and down my back, rubbing hard. At first it worked, the pain seemed to disappear and I felt immediately better, so I kissed her back, sank my hands into the dark softness of her coat and felt the contours of her body. I welcomed the chance to figure out its true shape. I had been right: she did have a soft stomach, she was thick in the legs. We kissed until she was on her back and her sweatered breasts overflowed the edges of my hands. When I pulled away, afraid she was uncomfortable, she clawed at my hair with her left hand, yanking me back down to her.

I thought we would kiss again but instead she held my face very close to hers and whispered. "When I first met you I thought there was something wrong with me, the way I felt about you. I had never been so attracted to anyone in my life. It was intense and weird. My body ached when I was next to you from wanting to touch you so badly. But then when I kept running into you I knew that there was something there. I knew it wasn't just me. We were supposed to come back here together tonight and be together—" Midway through her mutterings she slipped into English, which she spoke with a gravelly intonation. I kissed her again to stop her from talking. When we pulled apart from that embrace, she stood, shook off her coat, and led me up the ladder to her bed.

She shed her clothes like an onion undressing itself. Before I had even removed my scarf she was nude, bobbling round in the low light. I reached for her oblong breast and noticed its golden hue, saw the lamp in the uncovered window. "Shouldn't we?" I gestured for an imaginary curtain, but there was none. She took my mouth in hers and shook her head, slipping her tongue up around my gums. "I just think you're the most compelling man I've ever met," she whispered, and I was glad her eyes were closed so she couldn't see my expression of incredulity. I tried to conjure the cool, disaffected girl glancing at me from over her coffee, but Juliet rose on her knees and pressed my face into her soft stomach and it was hard to focus on anything but the slightly damp mass of curls tickling my chin.

I tucked my head and pressed my tongue into her pubic hair, searching out the little hard knob that would move time forward. The position was hard on my neck, but the pain wasn't just gone; I could barely remember it as I swabbed her fragrant, parting skin. We stayed like that for a while, but I was too drunk to keep track of her experience, and as her hands rhythmically opened and closed in my hair, I realized that she was, too. I felt out of breath, hopeful that the encounter would end even as I tried to enjoy it, but I turned her on her side and entered her that way, still in most of my clothes, my hands gentle on her head as I pushed inside. Juliet made little gurgling sounds, enjoying herself, I hoped. But I couldn't join her, even though I was inside her, pushing at the floor of her stomach, which I allowed my hands to travel down and grope. I thought of pregnant women, I thought of fucking pregnant women, and I saw us up in the lost bed, everything rickety and creaking, I saw the fluid movement of my muscles pushing me towards her body, the cold breath of the window billowing over us. She said my name and I came.

I fell away from her, feeling like I had been in an accident, an incident beyond my control. The room was cold, but the smell of our bodies and the unwashed clothes on the floor and, probably, the chicken in its cage, became rank and full in my nose. I felt exhausted and anxious. Juliet seemed to have fallen asleep beside me. But when I began doing up the fly of my pants, she stirred. "There's more wine down there," she said, limply gesturing to the floor. She turned onto her back and smiled. I realized that her hair had been carefully styled the whole time we had been together. She was like a different person. I had the unsettling thought that the real Juliet, the one I remembered from our encounters, was still out there on the Berlin streets, waiting for Fabian to get off work so that they could go home to their large, clean apartment.

"I've got to go," I said.

"What?"

"I live a far way from here," I lied. "And I have work early in the morning." She wrapped her arms over her breasts. "I can't believe this."

"Sorry," I offered lamely, and descended the ladder. "I want to be on my own for a while." She hung her head over the edge of her bed and stared, tears welling in her eyes. Her chicken clucked anxiously. I opened the door and left.

Out on the street, walking the four blocks to my apartment, I did not think about the bad news or the terrifying future. I felt the cold wind on my cheap clothes and remembered that my mother had moved to California. It seemed I had not had this information before that moment, but of course I had only forgotten it, only willed it away from myself. I felt more present than I had ever been before, stuck in the moment, moored there on the corner before my building.

I tried to imagine California, but only clichés came: palm trees, convertibles, flashing lights. The photographs I had seen showed everything bathed in yellow light. It was never night in California like it was in Berlin. People were never outside in the cold, because it was never cold, and in my mind there were no people in California. It was not like here, where the figure paced in front of my building, a small person in a black hat moving smoothly back and forth on the sidewalk. The man was healed; his limp was gone. He frightened me. I didn't stop to watch. Even when I got up to the safety of my bedroom, I did not go to the window.

Kenya T. Jennings

EPIPHANY

I can see myself sometimes
Through darkened light
Sitting atop
Everything
Everything that was
Before me that I am
Remembering the path but not watching it
Forgetting the bread crumbs
Knowing some dropped purposely or subconsciously
Out of my pocket behind me
I sit there
Atop
Knowing
Denying it was me who laid them there
And saying so with whole heart
Soul
So there must be some truth in it
Sometimes I forget I am not there yet
Remembering only when realizing
I still have bread in my pocket
But I can see myself
Sitting atop
Everything
Everything that is nothing
That is everything
That is me
Here
And there
Sitting atop
And I will be there
I know this with whole heart
Soul
So there must be truth in it

But I won't see me watching me
Through darkened light
Sit atop
But I will know
I was
Here

Julie Marie Wade

GRAMMAR

Here, on the Atlantic, sunrise
the reversed syntax of my Seattle youth:

I marvel, still young, at what
it means to have been *younger*;

to see at last the parent
in *parenthesis*;

to read—for the first time—
whole chapters of my life

as an aside.

Kirk Wilson

THE STORY YOU'VE NEVER HEARD ABOUT
LATTORIAL

I HOOK UP WITH LATTORIAL WHEN
he is just fifteen. I'm trolling the Top 100 lists for the
class of 2001, kids that are still freshmen in high school,
and I can't get past the name. Lattorial Means, Murrah
HS, Jackson, Mississippi. He shows up number three on
ESPN.com and number seven on Rivals. He's the number
one receiver on both of them, and making top ten on
all the other lists besides. I swear to the mother of God
this is all I know. Just like I know one in five of those
kids, maybe, will play a down for Northeast Nowhere
Tech, and one in ten could make Division I, and one in a
hundred will draw a paycheck or two in the NFL. You've
gotta play a pure hunch every so often. You bet a pony
just because you like the way he dances. Am I right or
wrong? Otherwise you turn to stone.

Besides, if you have to know, I don't have that much going on. Jaevon Demmings has just walked on our deal and gone with a hip hop fool that has never scratched anybody's sig on anything besides his balls. So what the hell. I call a guy I know that scouts the SEC. He's seen the name like I have, but he knows diddly except that the in-state schools are watching the kid. I poke around and find some video, not highlights really but a couple plays from the school's first two games some joker has put online. Kid runs like an antelope. You can't tell much but from the catches the hands are big and soft and he's a beanpole. A nice frame though one that could manage forty more pounds of muscle, easy. Things you can say about five hundred baby studs a year. But I'm sitting in my office in L.A., not a lovely place despite the law diploma on the wall, no kind of church, and I feel it, I'm uplifted. I have to stand up and pace around the room. I know.

So what do I do? I hop a flight from Burbank and a couple of connections later I'm at the Enterprise counter in the Jackson airport. It's way too early in the game for that kind of action but the other side of that coin, a kid like that, there are already a dozen guys in his ear, mostly locals probably, selling him the moon. I'm lying if I tell you I don't have second thoughts.

I want a Beemer, a Merc, maybe a Jag, I say. Rag top if you have one.

Milk-faced junior college sweetheart hands me a plastic card with pictures. That's what we got, she says. Her voice rolls out sweet and oily. Cheviz, Fords, Tawotas. Economy, calm-pack, fuuul-size, she says.

I need to make an impression here, I say.

Lady just turned in a Lincoln Town Car, the dude coming in behind her says.

White? Black?

Silva. We'll have to clain it up.

Practice just started. I don't have the time.

I drive over to the high school in a silver Lincoln with a coat of topsoil and an ashtray full of butts with bright red kisses on them. The stadium gates are open. The team is out on the field, full pads, hitting tackling dummies, doing drills with their position coaches. It's the first week of October but still hot. A few guys, parents probably and hangers on, are on the sidelines. They eyeball me in that what's-wrong-with-this-picture kind of way. I sit down in the first row of the stands. A couple of quarterbacks are taking snaps and working passes to receivers running hook routes. There's no question which one he is. Fluid. Graceful. Makes every juke and catch look like a freezeframe on a highlight reel. I'm feeling good about the coin I'll drop on this trip. You have to watch those kinds of feelings.

After practice I approach him as he's walking to the locker room. I notice his parents aren't there.

Lattorial, I say. I stick out my hand and pronounce my name twice. Maybe you've heard of me, I'm saying, but he's saying nada and he doesn't take the hand. He's such a shy kid then, you wouldn't recognize him. Won't look me in the eye. I tell him he looked good out there, that I've come all the way from Hollywood to see him. Really I came from Silver Lake, but I figure Hollywood plays better in Jackson, Mississippi. He takes off his helmet and I get my first look at him up close. Don't starting thinking the wrong things if I tell you his face is beautiful. That's just the right word for it. He would have been pretty even if he was a girl. Butterscotch skin, high cheek bones, green eyes shaped like almonds that I swear came with built-in eyeliner, ladykiller lashes.

I just want to get acquainted is all, I tell him. Come over to the house and meet your folks, that kind of thing. Talk about some ideas I have to help you out. You gotta ride home? He leaves the question in the air for half a minute like he doesn't understand it, then shakes his head in slow-mo. That's great, I say, super good. I'll be waiting for you outside. I'm in the silver Lincoln.

A coach comes up and asks me who I am and what my business is. I say I'm just a friend of Lattorial's, and I walk off. I hear the coach asking the kid what I wanted and turn to see him shrug.

Lattorial ambles out after a while in shabby street clothes and gets in the car, a couple of school books and a notebook in his hand. On the way I try small talk that goes noplace, I ask him if he wants to listen to the radio, he doesn't, so I roll out for him a little teaser about what a guy like me can do for a guy like him, how if he's willing to do the work and walk the walk, which will not be easy and no mistake, I can put him where he deserves to be. Fat contract, rich as a bitch in heat, all the women he can fight off, new brick house for Mama, the whole nine yards plus a couple. That's what I do for my people. If he's impressed you couldn't tell it with a body scan. He's staring through the windshield like there's a circus going on out in the road.

We pull up to his house. It's a little white number, what they call a shotgun down here, that looks like a victim of assault and battery. The paint is rippled up, the roof is undulating, and the porch is falling off one side. There's a Ford pickup from the 'fifties turning into compost on some cinder blocks in the front yard.

I follow the kid inside to a dark, moldy-smelling front room with a sagging couch on a sagging floor, a big teevee, and a rusty red Formica table with chrome legs. There's a baby crying someplace. The first human I meet comes in from the back of the house. I introduce myself and he says his name is Charles. He's in his thirties, maybe, but he's already got the old man shuffle. He's a half foot shorter than Lattorial, moves like there's a river of molasses in the room. No shirt on, and his nipples hang like tits. This is not a blood relative of the kid I just saw running hook routes on the field. Is his Mama at home? She is, and it only takes Charles an hour or so to produce her.

Mama is a tall, strong-looking lady, could have played power forward for the Sparks, and not so bad to look at. She's got the baby on her hip, like a sprouting limb. Up close, you can see where Lattorial's eyes come from, but on her the lids cover half the eyeballs. I do the meet 'n greet, she barely manages a nod. It seems like a good idea to cluck over the baby. It's all curls and Jell-O cheeks and sleepy moon eyes, with tears that have just finished dripping. There's been some kind of baby tragedy. Hey sweetness I say, aren't you the cutest one? Baby wants me out of its face, starts to tune up again. Mama gives it a jiggle and it reconsiders.

I came all the way from Hollywood to meet you and see that boy of yours in person, I tell her. First impressions.

She looks down on me, literally, like I'm a bug. I'm thinking southern hospitality, she offers some sweet tea, we sit around and pass the time of day, but she gets right to it like she's been waiting all her life for me to walk in her front door. What do I have here, Mr. Hollywood?, she says. She lifts her chin a micron higher at the house in general to make sure she doesn't waste too much energy.

I beg her pardon.

I said what do I have here? Take yourself a good look now. I got nothin' but that boy. You want to get rich on his back, you got to pay the fare.

Meanwhile the boy in question is standing right behind her, all six feet two of him that will grow a few inches and a lot of pounds, like a calf on the auction block. From his expression, he could be listening to a conversation about the annual rainfall in Grenada.

Lady goes right to the golden chamber where the gonads are kept. Hold on now, I say. I've just come all this distance out of curiosity, which killed the cat, but that is too obvious to mention. If you wish to conjecture on the subject let me sprinkle in a fine grain of sanity. It will be many moons before that boy makes anybody rich, if indeed he ever does. Were I a betting man, I toss in, I'd take never straight up over ever every time. He's just a freshman in high school for God's sake.

I know what he is, she says, and you know it too. She's examining me like she's thinking about pest control. I've done this dance so many times my soles are holey, but I've never seen a Mama so upfront about the process. Don't think I don't get where she's coming from. I really do. She's got nothing, she wants something, for her and the boy and the baby, et al. I have to remind myself I'm hungry sometimes. They maybe never do.

Here's the thing, I say, I just hope to establish our acquaintance, you know, stay in touch and see what develops, and I show her all my teeth which have only recently been whitewashed by professionals. There's football, sure I tell her, but he's got to keep his grades up, make some SAT scores, find the right place for college ball, all of which my help can assure by the way; it's a long road and only if he clears every single checkpoint will he ever play a down or cash a paycheck in the NFL. Your local yokels and the other practitioners of my trade you'll hear from, and there may be many, will sing the same song but cannot deliver the ultimate prize at the level of yours truly. Ask anybody. I mention a couple of my better known clients, including Jaevon Demmings because I think it unlikely she will have heard he's dumped me. My name, which I repeat for memorability's sake, is a hall pass to the big time.

She's so impressed she looks barely awake. You must be the reason, she says, they say talk is cheap.

Why don't you just keep my card and we can chit chat on his progress over time, I say, make the right decisions for him, and I hold it out but no hand reaches for it. Escalation city. So I say and maybe I could help out with some grocery money in the meantime and I pull the wad of bills I've been holding in my pocket for the purpose, with the hundreds on the outside. I peel off one portrait of Benjamin Franklin in a green frame. I hold it and the card out together.

Mama makes a little noise like half a sneeze and looks disgusted. She's not reaching.

Look we're so early in the game here, I remind, we're not even to the coin toss. If I were to make a substantial investment at this point I would need to be assured that I have exclusive rights in the matter, that there are no other prospectors in the territory, now and going forward. She no doubt knows as well as I do that a contract prior to the exhaustion of college eligibility is meaningless and illegal besides. So, I say, I will require your solemn word. Which, I do not add, is clearly of the selfsame value as my own.

I peel off nine more Benjamins, going slow so she can count. I hold them across with my card and her long fingers wrap around the lot.

This transaction buys me nothing but name awareness. I'm playing odds that the next buyer in the door will be less generous, or foolish, because as long as I'm high bidder I'm the one she'll talk to first on the day it really matters. I don't want you thinking this kind of long shot is my standard business practice. It's nuts but like I tell you, sometimes you just have to play the pretty pony.

Mama and me and this guy Charles say our goodbyes. I wave to the baby, who gives me its version of the bug look. Out on the falling-off porch I hand Lattorial a cell phone and a charger, tell him he can call anyone he wants except another agent. I pay the service so I can see the calls. I tell him the phone is so we can stay in touch. I want him to call me if he's got problems with school, or girls, or his coaches, or if the college recruiters are sniffing around. I'm here to help with anything he needs. I'm his best friend from now on. He just stuffs the phone in his pocket. No thank you and no comment on my bullshit. No expression on his face, looking out in the yard like everything he sees is a figment of his daydream. You have to like him, he's such a kid. You want to take care of him somehow. I'm not kidding.

On the flight home I'm having buyer's remorse like crazy but I tell myself I may still turn out to be a genius. You never know.

I get back to work and forget about Lattorial, pretty much. Of course I send postcards with pictures of Malibu and the Hollywood sign, and Omaha steaks at Christmas. I land a couple new clients, nobody you'll ever see in the headlines but maybe solid guys who can play ten years in the league and make a buck or two if they don't break their necks or scramble up their brains. I'm doing okay, nothing spectacular. I check Lattorial out after the season, the team's gone to bi-district and he's honorable mention All State. Not bad for a frosh. The wolves have gotta be circling. I notice he's not using the phone much. I give him a call.

How was the year? I ask him.

Awright I guess.

You happy with how you played?

Um.

How much you weigh now?

One eighty five almost.

That's up fifteen pounds at least. I'm guessing the school's got a decent weight room.

You get any taller?

A inch.

Anybody come 'round to see you?

Couple ole guys.

Who?

I dunno.

You need anything?

My Mama does.

I'll bet.

What's she need?

Washa drya. She said tell you.

You tell her the Sears truck is on the way.

This kind of stuff goes on his whole high school career. Except he starts needing things too, and the things Mama needs get bigger. And he changes.

Sometime in his junior year he starts going gangsta on me, you can hear it in his voice. He's got a new phone now and he's using it a lot more, or somebody is, but I'm still not finding any agents, at least not any name guys, in the calls. I need a BMW, he tells me one time. I say last year you needed a pickup. He says B-M-W again, like he just learned the letters. You know we can't do that stuff I say. You want to go league someday you got to play in college, you want to play in college we got to keep the NC2A's off your back. I preach patience and the promised land. He can't hear it, and I'm sweating bullets that all the other players on him are quoting the same chapter and verse. I know by now I'm not the only guy he's saying BMW to. Like I say my game is to stay high bidder, top of mind, but the dance is delicate, I gotta keep the profile one hair below the radar. Trust me, there are a lotta ways my investment can go south here. Meanwhile he goes first team All State, his school wins the championship, and he's the number one receiver, number two player overall in a national list for the junior class. He ain't my little secret anymore.

I ask him what colleges you hearing from? This is before the world goes apeshit over texting. Coaches can send old school paper mail and call a certain number of times in certain periods. The rules get broken, but that's what they are.

All of 'em I guess he says. He starts spinning names like he's counting on his fingers. Alabama, Auburn, Ole Miss, State, LSU, Texas, Florida, Oklahoma. He stops with the names and says 'bout a hundred.

That gives me plenty to work with. I have a database of boosters I can talk to at all the big schools. So now it's time for me to earn my first payday. I make some calls, I'm on the plane. It's the first time I've seen Lattorial since his freshman year. He's filled out nice, but all hoodie and shades, hip hop earbuds. Oh my God. Mama claims she won't take less than a hundred large for the amateur experience of a college education. It's steep but do-able. I remind Mama what a critical time we're in, that she'll screw the whole works if she talks to anyone but me. She gives me the exterminator stare. Out at the high school, some of the recruiters put a blindfold on Lattorial and shoot video of how he runs his routes. He doesn't miss a single cut by an inch. This is the God's truth. I've still got the video. The kid goes to auction, and I'm on a tour of Dixie. High bidders turn out to be Auburn and Mississippi State. Mr. Mississippi State sells oil field equipment, has bulldogs all over his office, maroon carpeting, a desk like an aircraft carrier. He says he won't go past a hundred. I take three points on the NFL contract but on an under the table deal like this one I'm looking for twenty, so I go see Mr. Auburn. He's a hotel, food and beverage baron. We have the conversation in his helicopter, chop-chopping over a bayou. He says what does it take to do this deal? Not a man to dicker. I say a hundred twenty gets it done. Mama gets her hundred and I take a small down payment on my return.

I arrange Mama a nice house rent free near the school in Auburn. Lattorial tears 'em up for two years. He's All American, BCS bowl MVP. I can smell a fifty million dollar deal. He's got his BMW, I'm buying him tutors but he's hopeless and the school is doctoring his grades some way to keep him eligible. Then the diarrhea hits the fan. Auburn kills Mississippi State fifty-four to zip and Mr. Oil Field slops a bucket of sour grapes at the NC2A's. Lattorial is a lead item on Sports Center and worse, so am I. He comes out like a rose because he just goes on to the NFL supplemental draft. The school loses scholarships, vacates wins, goes on probation. I go to a grand jury.

Can you say pariah? I squeeze through without doing time, but my days as an agent are over. The California bar pulls my license so I can't fall back on traffic tickets.

Early in the shit storm, while it still looks like I'm in business, I call Lattorial. It's now or never on cashing the chips.

The only good thing in all this, I tell him, is that we can finally sign our deal and get you a job in the league.

I'm on it awlready, he says.

What do you mean?

I'm signed up with Hy Chason.

Hy is just the biggest name in the business, is all.

We have a *relationship*, Latt, I been with you since you were fifteen, I say. I'm sounding so whiny I can't stand it. I even roll out a short accounting of my spend on him and Mama. But he's ice, he's sub-zero.

You got no contract with me.

End of story, except I get to follow his career on the wall of teevees at the sports bar I'm managing in Sacramento. He's playing for the Jets, Super Bowl, All Pro, until his face shows up on Sports Center in the off season. Turns out he tries to pull a Glock on some fools at a bar in Jersey and ends up shooting himself in the thigh. Yes he does. Misses the bones and the arteries but goes to the joint on the gun charge.

I can't help myself, I call him during the trial.

What the hell are you thinking, I ask him.

I guess I'm just a working product, he says.

The phrase is work in progress, I tell him. What's the use?

When he comes out the next year there's footage on all sixteen screens of him and Hy Chason climbing in a limo. Hy's all Armani, but my boy's in the hoodie and the shades. I get a bad feeling. Hy gets him on with the Patriots on a contract a rookie wouldn't like. He has a decent year, but the next summer he's in Miami, God knows, at a strip club all gangsta'd up and some creep's girlfriend takes offense at what he's saying and the creep shoots Lattorial dead.

I couldn't tell you why for a million, but it breaks my heart.

Sam Wilson

MAYBE IN CASPER, WYOMING

MY OLDER BROTHER RICHARD HAS been
the great hope of my family ever since he was fourteen years
old and won the Wind River Reservation Junior Basketball
Championships pretty much single-handedly. That was the
year I skipped eighth grade and joined him as a freshman at
Wyoming Indian High School. Richard started lifting weights
in the mornings and practicing basketball all afternoon. His
shoulders became round heaps of muscle. He wore wrist-
bands and jerseys even to classes, sagged his blue nylon shorts
straight through the winter, and became known on the rez as
our shooter. Now we are seniors, and with tonight's win the
Chiefs varsity basketball team is headed to the semi-finals in
Cheyenne.

"Scouts will be there," Richard tells me as he peels
off his clothes in the locker room.

"You know who?"

"Coach said the scout from United Tribes Technical

College for sure. Maybe others."

Richard fakes a pass and then shoots his jersey into the hamper next to me. I hand him a clean towel from my stack. He says, "Can you imagine playing for U.T. Tech?"

Of course I cannot imagine it. Compared to my brother I'm just another Arapaho doughboy with a nice belt buckle.

"If I went," Richard says, "you'd have to come visit all the time."

"Sure," I say.

"It's colder in North Dakota. I'd need to find a car with a heater."

"With a scholarship, you could buy anything."

"I'd have to learn to cook," he says, shaking his head. "They won't have fry bread or corn fritters in the dorms."

I think Richard is looking for excuses not to go. Either that or he's trying to make me feel better about being left behind. Our high school guidance counselor says with my grades I shouldn't have to stay on the rez and get a job no one wants. She helped me prepare an academic scholarship application to the University of Wyoming, but we all know that good grades on the reservation do not mean much to the outside world. Around here, it's basketball or nothing.

At school the next week, all conversations lead to the upcoming semifinals in Cheyenne. The hallways are blue with banners. The head singer of the Chiefs' drumming circle, Charlie Branam, slings his arm around my neck and tells me, for the hundredth time, that I should have joined the drumming circle this year. Charlie's hair is halfway down his back and he wears it in a thick ponytail which makes him look like an elder. "Hey, you need to learn our ways before it's too late," he says. "Soon you'll be off in the world."

"You sound like my grandmother," I tell him. "Besides, what are you going to do?"

"You really want to know?" Charlie smiles. "I'm going to sneak off the rez with you and keep you from forgetting who you are." He pokes me in the ribs. "Hey, what do you think, Clayton? You want a roommate? We would be good roommates, you know."

There is no point in telling him what I really think. He has the chiseled cheekbones and perfect posture of a true chief, and he can be just as stubborn. Still, whenever I take the motorcycle out past our farm and past the tree line to the water tower, I can't help but think of Charlie. In blue paint on the tower is the image of our school mascot, the face of an Indian Chief painted fifteen feet tall. It is the spitting image of Charlie Branam: high cheekbones, flat cheeks, square chin, long hair, and patient, steady eyes.

Chief Charlie, I call him. My secret name. Chief Charlie, I say, don't forget your drumsticks. Chief Charlie, don't forget the feathers for your hair.

Friday after school, the team makes the long drive to the White Pines Motel in Cheyenne to be rested for their game on Saturday night. My parents are chaperones on the team bus. I wait and catch a ride with a neighbor on Saturday morning, and we arrive in Cheyenne at 3 p.m. Richard and his teammates have been horsing around on an elementary school basketball court, practicing slam dunks on the low hoops. I'm worried that Richard may have sprained a finger hanging from the rim, but he brushes it off.

"It's nothing," he says. "I'll be fine, don't worry." He lets his hands hang loose at the end of his wrists and shakes them. I see him doing this from time to time like a loose-jointed animal, the way a horse might shake his head from side to side, flopping his mane.

Most of the basketball players have crowded into one motel room to watch television. I'm jealous of how comfortable they are with their bodies, how they recline on the beds, some without shirts, the six-packs of their abdominals flexing as they toss a Nerf basketball back and forth or to themselves over and over, straight up in the air. My own stomach is as shapeless as a sack of flour and I have not for many years gone without a shirt in public.

"Clayton," my brother says. "Could you get me a bag of ice?"

"Is it your finger?" I ask, but Richard isn't paying attention to me.

Downstairs the ice machine is next to a vending machine with the candy bars that I try my best to avoid. The fitness of the players has got me down on myself, and when I feel down it sometimes helps to eat. I insert two bills into the machine and select a Butterfinger and a Kit Kat, and then eat the Butterfinger while standing in front of the machine. With the 50¢ change I consider getting a roll of Life Savers, but I think perhaps I've had enough candy for one day, and this small gesture of restraint makes me think more highly of myself. I feed the machine another dollar bill and get a Snickers to reward my restraint.

There are no bags for the ice machine so I hold the bottom seam of my T-shirt out in front of me, fill it with ice, and pin it to my chest.

"I got your ice," I say when Richard opens the door. He looks at my T-shirt.

"You couldn't find a bag, homeboy?" Richard guides me into the bathroom. "It's cool," he says. He takes the plastic bag from the wastebasket and fills it with ice from my T-shirt.

"So," he says. "Did you get a good room?"

"I'm staying with Ma and Dad," I say. "They're out getting dinner."

Richard looks at the room packed with athletes. "You're welcome to hang with us."

Two players are wrestling on the bed, half-naked.

"I think I'll go take a nap," I say.

In the hall I see Norbert and Brian from the drumming circle. They invite me to lunch. Charlie will be there, Norbert says, and they both laugh at some inside joke. I tell them I'm saving room for the fry bread at the game, but when I get to my room I feel like I'm starving. I eat the Kit Kat and the Snickers bar and wrap both candy wrappers in toilet paper before putting them into the wastebasket, so my parents won't see what I have been eating. When I'm done I wonder why I'm in Cheyenne in the first place and not back on the rez, riding my motorcycle out to have a private and personal conversation with my painted Chief Charlie on the water tower.

I have no willpower. I get up and lock the motel door and engage the slide lock that keeps even the maid out, then I turn off the light and take off my shirt and my jeans and my boxers and lie naked on the coarse motel bedspread. I reach down and hold myself, imagining that I am lean and strong on the basketball floor, shooting hoops with the rest of the shirtless players, high fives and snapped towels in the locker room. The overhead fan spins little gusts of air onto my skin. I imagine locker room showers, long bus rides, beers after the games. And then I imagine Charlie.

When I've finished I clean up and dig through the toilet paper in the wastebasket to find the candy wrappers. I suck on the inside of the Snickers wrapper which has on it a thin film of melted chocolate. I am still hungry.

At halftime our Chiefs are down by two to the Cheyenne Thunderbirds. The game has been fierce and two players have already been ejected for fighting. It's not hard to see why. The bleachers are filled with blacks and whites who may sometimes hate each other but who tonight have joined together in their shared hatred of us.

Coach Denny allows me to sit on the players' bench, and each time one of them is called off the floor they come to me first to get their Gatorade and towel. We stay on the bench through the halftime presentation, as Chief Charlie and the five other Indians carry the large buffalo rawhide drum to the center of the basketball court and set it flat on the ground. Before he sits, Charlie smoothes his thick black hair and smiles at me for so long that I have to look away. The Thunderbirds lower a microphone and when the drumming starts the reverberations are amplified many times through the large stadium speakers. Charlie looks at me, and when I smile he catches me completely off guard with a wink.

Later, with the game tied in the fourth quarter, the Arapahos get to their feet and begin chanting my brother's name. Richard pretends he doesn't hear them. He shakes his hands loose and frowns and cocks his head from side to side. He goes on a scoring streak and we win the game by six points. It is decided: we are going to state. As we pour onto the polished basketball floor, Coach Denny is stopped by a white man in a polo shirt and a pair of creased khakis. He is Bobby McAllister, the scout from North Dakota. His pants are held up by a thin braided belt with practically no buckle at all. He and Coach Denny talk and then shake hands.

There is a seat for me on the team bus, but I am filled with the fear that one of the players, maybe even Richard, may have seen Charlie wink at me. The rez might embrace drunks and poverty. Lying, brawling, you name it, the worse it gets the more we know you're part of the tribe. But there are some things for which there is no tolerance at all.

Charlie's dad, Mr. Branam, is driving the drum circle home in the van he normally uses to carry feed and equipment. Charlie nudges me to the back corner and the two of us lie down like the other drummers, our heads sharing my duffel bag.

"Everybody set?" Mr. Branam asks, slurring. "You boys sounded great, I'm so proud of you." He passes us a bottle of Old Granddad whiskey—his second for the night—with only three fingers gone from the top.

We are not the type to pass up free alcohol on a seven-hour drive, even if it is Old Granddad. The drummers and I talk about what we might do if we get off the rez. We always talk about leaving. What is there for us outside, we ask. But also we ask what is left on the rez but alcoholics and high school basketball and running casinos for tourists.

A few hours later I think the other drummers are all asleep. Charlie and I lie on our sides, facing each other in the dark, sharing the duffel bag as a pillow. Charlie says he thinks I will get the scholarship to U-Wyoming. "You're so smart," he says. "There is no way that they could say no."

"There's always a way," I say. "To them I'm just some Indian. You know that."

Charlie says, "Hey, you're more than just some Indian." He closes his eyes for a while and I think maybe he has fallen asleep. I study his face. His long eyelashes curve into a row of perfect tips and I wonder if I could reach out and trace my fingers along them without waking him. With his eyes still closed Charlie says, "When you have gone to a great university, will you still think of me?"

It is a crazy question—how could I forget Charlie? But I don't know how to answer so I close my eyes and pretend I am asleep. Charlie doesn't say anything for a long time and I think maybe we have gone to sleep for real. But then the van hits a pothole and somehow Charlie is jostled even closer to me. I can feel each of his warm whiskey breaths on my face and one of his legs has landed on top of one of mine. I stay very still, neither moving closer nor farther away, exactly as though I was asleep. I let the weight of Charlie's leg hold me in place. My heart pounds. I think perhaps he has fallen asleep, and when I lift my eyelids the tiniest bit to see what he looks like in front of me, face to face, my friend Charlie smiles and kisses me on the lips.

Wednesday afternoon I receive a letter from the University of Wyoming. They appreciate my interest, but they are unable to offer me a scholarship. It is the response I had expected, the response I told everyone to expect, but I had been guarding a small hope and the letter instantly dissolves the secret future I had built in my mind.

The next morning Richard and I are gathering stones from the dry riverbank and throwing them in the back of our father's Ford pickup. That evening, the team will enter the sweat lodge on Coach Denny's farm. We have to establish the fire by noon to make sure the stones will be hot enough by sunset.

"Did the scout say you'd get the scholarship?" I ask.

"He said maybe. He is only the scout." Richard pauses to take a drag off of his clove cigarette. "It depends on what the head coach sees at state."

Richard started smoking only this year. I keep telling him that it is bad for his running, that he is risking the one chance any of us have to get off the rez. He ignores me, and on the court he seems fast as ever.

"You know Ma is already looking to find a room for you in North Dakota," I say.

"Coach Denny, too." Richard throws the cigarette far away from us. "The whole rez is hoping, I guess." He picks up a stone the size of a cow pie and heaves it into the truck. "But what if I don't like college? What if I don't want to go? I'm barely passing classes as it is."

When I look at my brother I see, for an instant, something that looks like fear. "I'll help you," I say. "You'll write me letters and I'll tell you what to do, no problem."

"Sometimes I think maybe the rez is the right place for me," Richard says. "This is where I fit in. Don't you ever feel like that?"

I look out over the cracked plains, the rundown houses surrounded by burnt trash heaps, dirt roads and broken vehicles. I think of the basketball players hugging each other's slick bodies and lifting my brother above their heads. I think of Charlie and the drumming circle, beating their taut drums with their eyes half closed. I have never fit in anywhere.

"I don't know," I say to my brother. "Maybe so."

Back on Coach Denny's farm, we lay newspapers and twigs over a scorched area the size of a basketball key. On top of the kindling we balance layers of oak branches and stones. My brother and I light the newspapers and before long we have a bonfire that will heat the stones until they are red hot and ready for the lodge.

Coach Denny's sweat lodge is a dome made of arched oak boughs covered in animal skins. In the late afternoon he uses a pitchfork to carry each red-hot stone to the pit at the center of the lodge. He sprinkles water onto the glowing stones from a hollow buffalo horn. When the steam is so thick that you can barely see from one side of the lodge to the other, he exits and stands at the front flap wearing only a towel around his waist.

The players arrive at sunset and strip to their underwear. They stretch their legs and arms, and take deep breaths of the cool evening air before ducking into the lodge. This sweat is a chance to clear their minds of confusion before the state finals at the Casper Event Center, and more than anything I would like to join the boys in the lodge. But my father has arranged for me to have a job interview at the Indian Health Services building, and I must hurry to be there on time.

The building is white and built low to the ground with a red shingle roof. A woman with freckles and curly blonde hair greets me. "You must be Clayton!" she says. "I'm Denise. Your dad has told me so much about you!"

"There is not much to tell," I say.

Denise shows me the copy room, the mailroom, the cubicles. She shows me how forms get filed or mailed to other departments and has me prove that I know how to type. If I want the job, she says, I can work afternoons until high school ends, and then work full time.

I look around the room and out the window which opens onto a chain-link fence. The fence is rusty and sagging. But beyond the fence, I can see the scrub brush on the plains and the buttes in the distance.

"Okay," I say to Denise and I shake her freckled hand.

I have not seen Charlie all week, and have been relieved not to discuss the night in the van. Charlie and I had been drunk was the easy thing to say, but it was not the true thing, or at least it was not the only true thing. I had wanted to be in the van with Charlie. Part of me wanted to be there again, and more than once during the week I rode out past the tree line to stare at the face on the water tower and wonder how my own face might look alongside it.

Saturday morning Richard leaves early with the team bus, and later I follow with my parents and my grandmother in the pickup truck. There is barely enough room for the three of them in the cab, so I lie in the pickup bed wrapped in a wool blanket. It is not that cold. We arrive and park at the Event Center in Casper, a city with twice as many people as our entire reservation. This time there is no small swath of Indians in the stands. Every man, woman, and child within ten thousand acres of Wyoming Indian High School has found a ride into Casper to watch the game against the Riverside Rebels.

The starters take the floor. I look out at the basketball court: two hoops and a wooden floor with some painted lines. There is an illusion of simplicity. Richard loses the jump ball and the Rebels score the first basket. They steal his inbound pass and score again. From then on, we are fighting just to keep up.

Midway through the second quarter, my brother takes the bench for his only break of the game.

"Hey, do you see them?" Richard asks.

"Who?" I hand him a cup of Gatorade.

"The scouts from United Tech. Bobby McAllister and the head coach. He said the coach was going to be here."

I look at all the polo shirts in the crowd. This is the largest stadium we have been in all year.

"They could be anywhere," I say. "Don't worry about it. Keep your head in the game."

Richard stares at the ground, his elbows on his knees, knocking his knuckles together as though he is keeping time. Coach Denny stops in front of us.

"I need you back in there," he says.

My brother runs off without saying another word.

I have to use the bathroom. I fill a few cups with Gatorade and leave them on top of the cooler for the players, then I jog along the sidelines and into the underground locker room. I can't remember the last time I jogged, but it's reassuring to feel the impact in my bones. It reminds me that there is something solid inside of me.

In the bathroom I surprise Charlie who is licking his fingertips in front of the mirror and smoothing each of his eyebrows away from his eyes.

"What are you doing?" I ask.

"Getting ready for the show," he says. "What does it look like?"

I walk to the urinals. Charlie and I have been friends for a long time, but trapped in the bathroom I feel awkward. I stand at the urinal farthest from the mirrors. Charlie smiles at me.

"Hey, how you getting home tonight?" he says. "I'm pretty sure we've got another bottle of Old Granddad."

I zip up and walk back to the mirrors.

"I think I'm supposed to ride home with my parents," I say. I feel like I owe Charlie a better explanation, but I don't know what else to tell him.

"You sure?" He puts a hand on my elbow.

"No," I say and it's true. I'm not sure about anything yet. I take his hand from my arm and hold it for a moment between my own two hands, and somehow this layering of skin feels more intimate than anything else we have done.

On the basketball court, the Rebels are playing rough and the referees aren't calling the fouls. Richard takes it personally. He stomps around the court and bucks his head in defiance of the refs. I know what he is thinking. He is thinking they are making him look bad in front of the scouts.

When the halftime buzzer sounds we are down eight points. Coach Denny takes the team into the locker room and I stay behind to watch the halftime show. But once they leave I decide I don't want to see the drummers after all. There is a tension inside me, as though my body is stretched tight even while I am sitting still. I walk out the stadium exit next to the locker room and look out at the horizon.

It is that time after sunset where there is no sun but there is still light left in the sky. I start jogging around the stadium to feel the solidness inside me and to clear my mind. I do a full lap before dropping my jacket on the ground. I run a second lap and peel off my T-shirt which is soaked with sweat through the pits and the chest. I throw it on top of my jacket and keep running. My knees ache. Each time I pass one of the stadium exits, I can hear the reverberations of Charlie's drum throbbing like a heartbeat, as if the stadium itself were alive. Charlie and I cannot do what we have done, not on the rez where everyone knows everyone. But it occurs to me that my whole life is contained inside the stadium I am circling. My family, my brother, all our cousins and friends. Chief Charlie. Outside the stadium in the large city of Casper everyone is a stranger. Maybe in Casper, I think, things could be different.

When I get back into the stadium, the halftime shows are over. The players jog back onto the court and I take my seat next to the cooler. I pour myself a cup of Gatorade, and then another.

The Chiefs rally against the Rebels through the third quarter and the refs make several bad calls against us. There is a fight in the stands between Edgar Cook's dad and somebody in a Rebels T-shirt, a fight that ends in a broken bottle and a security guard with a stun gun. This is not the way it was meant to happen, but by the beginning of the fourth quarter we are only two points behind.

Richard is still mad, still bucking his head and cursing into his hand. The Rebels double-team him, they screen him, they make it impossible for him to score. With one minute left in the game, Richard goes for a lay-up that would put us in the lead, and the Rebels' point guard knocks him to the ground. The refs don't call the foul. Richard gets up and pushes the guard squarely in the chest. The guard pushes back.

I watch what happens next as if it were in slow motion, as if it were happening underwater. My brother locks his jaw. The point guard steps toward him. Behind them, the basketball rolls to the sidelines and one of the refs bends over to retrieve it. Richard shrinks down and for a moment I think it is over. I feel the cool wash of relief, the ebbing of a surge of adrenaline. But then Richard unleashes a right hook and hits the Rebel on the temple. The player drops onto the court, unconscious. The crowd howls. Richard is restrained by his teammates and thrown out of the game.

We lose, but the point guard from the Rebels recovers. The stands are wild after the final buzzer, and the police are called onto the stadium floor to keep the rival teams and fans from hurting each other. I look in the stands but do not see Bobby McAllister anywhere.

"They won't base everything on one game," our father tells Richard as we walk back to his pickup. "You played a good game, you shouldn't worry," he says. Grandmother fingers her necklace and says nothing. "We brought a blanket, anyway," our father says. "You can ride in the back with Clay."

The drive home does not seem as long as the drive to the game. At first,

Richard doesn't talk at all, but eventually he asks me about the Indian Health Services building, the type of jobs they have and how much they pay. I tell him I will teach him the secret to typing fast. I learned it from our father, I say, trying to make a joke. And he learned it from his father. And he learned it from his father. These are the ways of our people.

Richard doesn't laugh, but he shows me his knuckles which are swollen and purple from hitting the other boy's head. He lights a clove cigarette and offers one to me. At first I say no. If it wasn't for smoking, maybe Richard would have scored a few more points. Maybe we could have won. Maybe he'd still be going to North Dakota. I change my mind and take a cigarette.

My brother and I smoke together, looking at the stars. Richard points at a constellation. "Orion," he says. "Remember?"

Of course I remember. When we were boys, we liked Orion best because he was the only constellation with a respectable belt. I puff on the clove cigarette, just bringing the smoke into my mouth to taste its sweetness. I exhale and look at Richard. He seems relieved, his face clean and shining as he looks at the stars.

"Richard," I say. And I stop, unsure of what it is I mean to tell him.

He looks at me, his familiar face a version of who I might have become. "It's okay," he says. "What is it, girl trouble? I can tell you all about girls."

We pull off the highway into a gas station. I wonder what it will be like to tell my brother about Chief Charlie. An image flashes in my head of Richard beating me into a pulp that spreads across the pickup bed like red river rocks. But maybe, I think, he would understand.

When the truck stops at the gas pump I see, of all things, Mr. Branam's van pulling into the same gas station. He stops beside us.

"Hey, watch out," he says. "There's Indians on the road tonight."

Mr. Branam might be a little drunk, but no worse than usual. The sliding van door opens and Charlie is sitting there with the other drummers, a half empty bottle of Old Granddad nearly hidden between two duffel bags. Charlie grins at me and what can I say? I grin right back.

"Hooey!" Mr. Branam says to me and Richard. "You boys coming to the forty-nine tonight?"

"Not in the mood for a party," Richard says.

I ask, "Is it at your place?"

"On the farm," Chief Charlie says. "Hey, you should come." Charlie clears a space for me in the van. "Plenty of room here. Want to ride home with us?"

I look at my brother who is squinting at me as if he's trying to see something through a glare. I climb out of the pickup and stand there for a moment, my hand on the tailgate. "I'll see you tomorrow," I say to my brother and to my dad who is pumping the gas. "I'll see you later, okay?"

Richard watches me climb into the van next to Charlie. He takes a long drag on his cigarette, and then nods. Mr. Branam closes the van door and it takes a few moments for my eyes to adjust to the lack of light.

"Hey, you cold?" Charlie says. The drummers are all huddled under blankets. I nod and he unfolds his blanket to cover both of us. I scoot even closer to Charlie.

"Sorry about your brother," Norbert says. "Will he still go to United Tech?"

"Screw United Tech," Brian says. "If I ever get off the rez I'm going to Laramie, for sure. Either that or Seattle."

"I don't know what Richard is going to do," I say. Mr. Branam fires up the van and makes a big U-turn that leans Charlie into me. I soften up and let him sink right in.

Norbert says, "My cousin visited Seattle once. Rain, rain, rain was all he had to say about Seattle." Norbert takes a swallow from the bottle of Old Granddad and passes it to me. "I heard you applied to U-Wyoming."

"I applied," I say. "I didn't get in. They're all filled up with Indians this year."

"So you're staying on the rez?" Charlie says.

"For now," I say. "I think I got a job. But I've been thinking..." I take a swig from the bottle and hold the whiskey in my mouth to feel the burn. "I've been thinking about moving to Casper, maybe going to the community college," I say. And Charlie says, "Hey, I can see you in Casper. You could get one of those apartments near Meadow Park," and he nods at me like he is actually imagining it as we speak. He says, "You know, I was serious about being your roommate."

The truck bounces along. It occurs to me that this new secret future is already starting to take shape in our minds. Charlie and I, we might have a chance in Casper. I hold the whiskey out to him, and when he grabs it I don't let go. I wait an extra second with both our hands on the bottle, just long enough for us to feel each other's pull.

Elaine Zimmerman

THE FLOOR RATTLED WITH US

Two cobalt vases, the size of urns, on the dresser.
Swirled gold and one cracked lip at the rim where

a large tulip might rest a stem, caught in the crack.
You are on the phone. The dog sleeps on the pillow.

A cigarette in the plastic ashtray, smoke coming out
at a slant. Light pours in through chenille drapes.

Papers strewn about. Some crumpled on the carpet.
Others piled high, held down by paperweights.

When Joey Gallo calls, the room is still. When he threatens,
the room turns. When you refuse him, we all turn around.

Now there are cops at the door, following us to school.
No one is to take candy from strangers. Oh give me

a stranger, just a plain stranger. Not someone blowing up
the house or shooting me down on the living room carpet.

I let him in. Didn't know the difference between the oil man
who came the day before and the one who pretended to be

delivering us heat for winter. Good thing the tank was full.
It blew Joey's cover. Smart as he was. And then the neighbor

says I am her child and I know, just know somehow to keep
my mouth shut. What we see at the door in the nice delivery

hat and outfit is like Halloween. Not real, but coming
for something. A trick. Skeletal and lurking.

For years we feared turning corners, unknown guests,
tree boughs too close to the window, the sound of trains

speeding through night. The floor rattled with us.
Death was loud every day, if there is such a thing as loud

in threats you cannot see. Loud in the kitchen, walking home,
jumping rope. Even in the backyard with the daylilies rising.

No place to hide. Though we did, in our own family ways.
Crazy Joe was gunned down at his birthday dinner.

Two hitmen, five shots. Little Italy sounded like firecrackers.
Nine years of dread turned over like a black jack.

Couples walk Mulberry Street arm in arm. Women wear
felt hats with white peonies, though Easter is weeks away.

At Umberto's, the pasta's so hot, it clouds the mirrors.
Couples share cannolis; Sinatra sings, *Anything Goes.*

Shahé Mankerian

THE MOSAIC OF THE MISSING

We found the doll's head
rolled under the chassis
of the charred Mercedes,

then one plastic sandal
on the cracked manhole.
Her mother fell

on the sidewalk, staring
at the feet of the crowd
that circled the bomb crater

like crows. They found
her braided pigtail twisted
around the telephone wire.

We heard the choked whisper
of the mother get louder,
"Ya, Souraia, stay home

and dress your doll.
We'll have the damn okra
without bread." We mistook

shards of glass for fingernails.

The three o'clock chimes

of the clock tower muffled

the siren of the ambulance.

The corner grocer needed

help behind the counter,

but his son was busy sifting

through bones and limbs

as if searching for souvenirs.

Greta Schuler

WITCHCRAFT

THE ONE-LEGGED ALBINO'S HOME SITS
beneath five burnt orange boulders balanced precariously on
top of one another. Several village men built the mud hut for
her, working for two liters of Chibuku beer a day and long
breaks in the shade. The only baobab tree in Nharira grows
in the old albino's yard, so the villagers cannot sell baskets
made from its bark or sweets made from its fruit as they do
farther down the paved road to Bulawayo. Years ago a local
chief joked that the people here were so poor they tried to
sell stones from the ground. Now they do. Twenty kilometers
southwest is Chiadzwa, where police use Soviet rifles and dogs
to keep a cut of the diamond fields for Zimbabwe's elite.
Eighty kilometers the other way is the city of Mutare, where
one can buy a diamond for a couple hundred U.S. dollars or,
if one is lucky, buy bread for millions of Zimbabwean dollars.

Tall dead grass and dried-stiff corn stalks hide the village footpaths from the paved road. The orphanage washerwoman, Tambudzai, huffs along a worn path with the American girl, Jill, stumbling behind her.

Jill tries to count the flies on Tambudzai's back, chew on her stalk of sugar-cane, and watch the road for goat shit all at the same time, but the sand keeps slipping into her sneakers and the sun is burning her shoulders. She trips.

Tambudzai doesn't listen to the American girl's complaints but instead thinks about the three scrawny goats left in her kraal. One goat has died each week for the last three weeks—always on the day Auntie Eleanor pays her for doing the laundry at Nharira Mission Orphanage. Tambudzai mumbles her disbelief, *Aya maninji chaiwo.*

"English, please," Jill calls out, not wanting to miss anything about the visit to the witchdoctor. She wonders how Tambudzai, who's older and fatter than she, can walk so fast in the sand. Over the tips of the thorny fruit trees, a trickle of smoke floats into the afternoon sky. That's the witchdoctor's house, Jill thinks. Shouldn't there be drums?

Inside the dark hut, Tambudzai and the albino witchdoctor crouch by the cast iron pot while Jill taps her toe. The long Shona greeting, the traditional clapping that never ends, annoys Jill more than usual. She came for one reason: diamonds. Of course she came to her Aunt's mission orphanage to play with children and pad her college applications, but she didn't know then that Aunt Eleanor had chosen to build her orphanage next door to Chiadzwa, home of the biggest diamond fields in the world. The welder who came to fix the doors at the mission told Jill that the ground in Chiadzwa sparkles brighter than the starlight-soaked sky.

Tambudzai and the one-legged albino talk so softly that Jill can hear the chickens' claws scratching the dirt floor. "In English, please," Jill says, suspicious that Tambudzai also wants help from the witchdoctor to go to the diamond fields. The welder told Jill that this old albino can command lightning bolts and cast spells to protect villagers sneaking into the diamond fields. If Jill wants a diamond, she must get protection from this witch doctor, the welder said, or else the soldiers' bullets and dogs will "find" her. Jill doesn't believe in witchcraft, but perhaps she should learn.

"English, please!" Jill repeats.

"Auntie Jill, I was only asking this traditional healer about my goats," Tambudzai says.

"Goats?" Jill squints, trying to see Tambudzai through the smoke.

"Eh-he. My herd is dying, goat by goat. Someone is using magic against me. This healer can help reverse the magic. But please, Auntie, she hears only Shona."

Tambudzai's heavy cheeks make her seem serious enough, so Jill sighs in agreement. Her eyes scan the dark hut for signs of witchcraft or diamonds. Jill doesn't understand how these circular huts stay so cool while people outside gleam with sweat. Mosquitoes swarm around the grass thatching of the hut's conical heights—they must think it's always night.

Something shiny in the old albino's mouth catches the light from the flames flickering around the pot. Jill cranes her neck to see, but the small cooking hut is too dark. The Zimbabwean women continue to whisper even though Jill can't understand their Shona. Tambudzai told Jill that the old albino would not be happy to see a white girl—only Tambudzai said *murungu*, not *white girl*. But Jill begged to go. She even threatened that she would hide the sun-dried linen and tell Aunt Eleanor, Tambudzai's boss, that Tambudzai skipped ironing the underwear to visit the witch doctor. (Aunt Eleanor always insists that Tambudzai iron the underwear to kill the parasites that swim in the laundry water, and Aunt Eleanor hates sorcery.) Tambudzai had no choice.

Jill leans her elbows on her thighs and tries to look the old albino in the face from across the fire. This is the woman the miners come to before venturing into the fields. The albino balances on one bent leg and one stump, which leans against a worn book. A book of spells? Blisters and boils cover the albino's pink skin. Jill aches from squatting. She stands up again and wonders where the African drums are. Shouldn't there be drums this far in the bush? Pa-dum. Pa-dum. Pa-pa-pum, she taps out on the dirt floor. Pa-rump-pah-pah-pum. That's not right.

If only she had known before she left Missouri that she was going to the largest diamond find of the century, she would have brought a shovel or done some research. Who needs financial aid with pockets full of diamonds? Why would she need college at all? But no one had told her about the Chiadzwa diamond fields. She might have spent the whole summer chasing after a soccer ball with the orphans in the dirt yard if Aunt Eleanor's door hadn't broken. While fixing the old hinges on the cheap plywood door, the welder told Jill about Chiadzwa, the fierce police dogs, the soldiers with rifles, and the large diamonds, which Jill imaged to be brilliant blue with dainty points, radiating white light. Aunt Eleanor had to know, or perhaps Chiadzwa was the reason she stayed in Africa. Why had no one told her? Jill suspected her mother had mentioned the incident at South County Mall and the psychiatrist visit and the impulse control disorder bullshit.

The old albino suddenly begins to laugh, or maybe to shout; Tambudzai doesn't seem amused, her heavy cheeks hanging low and lifeless. With the noisy outburst, the albino throws her head back and opens her mouth wide. The firelight reflects off the same spot in her mouth. The sparkle is in her lower left molar, Jill is certain. Jill juts out her chin and squints, poised for another glimpse of that twinkle just bright enough to make her mind turn to diamonds. The Chiadzwa fields are only twenty kilometers away, the welder said. How many miles is that? Can't be many. Jill stares, but the old wood door is closed and the smoke stings her eyes.

The albino lifts the cast iron lid with her bare hands; boiling water bubbles over the sides of the pot and sizzles down to the fire. Jill rubs her arm, conscious of her sleeveless shirt. The welder also told her that the old albino poured boiling water over the carpenter's arm so the soldiers' bullets would not find him in the diamond fields. Is that how the albino got those red sores? Jill's sticky fingers catch on the hairs of her arm—her hands still carry bits of sap from the sugar cane she sucked during her walk from the mission. Last night, Jill wondered what color a black albino's hair would be, but a dark scarf wrapped around the pink head hides the mysterious scalp. The old albino wears a worn velvet gown, torn around the bottom with puffy short sleeves, maybe turquoise in color. Jill can't tell—even Tambudzai's faded T-shirt looks midnight blue in the hut.

Tambudzai whispers a little prayer of thanks for Auntie Jill's silence. She warned her on the walk from the mission: "Say nothing. The old woman hates murungu. She will curse you." That scared her, Tambudzai thinks. But she notices that Auntie Jill is staring at the old albino's mouth. Like the rest of her flesh, the albino's lips are chapped from the sun. The same sun took the albino's leg. "Cancer," the women at the borehole told Tambudzai, but some of the villagers blamed the missionaries. Cancer is an English word, not a Shona one, and, to Tambudzai, it seems mysterious, like the life of this one-legged albino. How does she fetch her water and firewood and lift the heavy pot to sear the skin of those going to the diamond fields? She has powers and was probably the one who put a curse on Tambudzai's goats because some vengeful woman had paid her some mangos to do it.

"Someone is jealous of me," Tambudzai confides to the albino. She begs the albino to put a curse on the perpetrator or do something to protect her goats. If they die, she will have nothing. With inflation, not even a trillion dollars buys a loaf of bread.

Tsvaru akabara tiu, the albino says, reminding Tambudzai that provocation gave birth to retaliation. Tambudzai begins to pull nervously at the frayed edges of her jean skirt because Auntie Jill is standing over them again. Why did she have to come? Just to see this traditional healer? The albino is only a woman, though Tambudzai must admit that she looks ghostly in the firelight—as if one of the dead chiefs tore through his cowhide bindings, pushed off his burial stones, and came down Nharira Mountain to sit by this fire. While the blood beneath her red sores proves she is not a ghost, no one knows where the old albino lived before she came to the village. She claims her family farmed here for years, but not even the oldest headman knows her surname or recognizes her totem. The crocodile is a family symbol of people in the north, people in Mashonaland; no one in Nharira inherited the crocodile as his family's totem. The old albino came to the village months ago when the price of mealie meal jumped to fifty million Zimbabwean dollars a kilogram.

The boiling water beating against the pot's iron lid creates a chaotic rumble over the beat of Jill's tapping foot. Jill reasons that, with magic, the old albino can go to the diamond fields without getting shot by the soldiers. The albino might have so many diamonds that she can put them in her teeth. Jill stares hard at the ghostly woman. Bits of firelight make the old albino's translucent eyelashes glow. Can she keep Jill safe from bullets, too? Jill squats down again, hoping to catch words like diamonds or Chiadzwa or police dogs. Tambudzai might be here because she wants to go to the diamond fields, and the goat story is a decoy. She would only need to scoop up dirt from the Chiadzwa earth and run, that's what the welder said: rich with one handful, diamonds just sitting on the ground waiting to be taken. Jill feels faint from the thought and the fire and the ache in her legs from squatting, and she falls backward. A small cloud of dust puffs up around her, and the chickens flee to the shadows by the wall.

The white albino grumbles and readjusts her half-leg against the book.

Millicent knows she's getting anxious because her stump won't stay still against her copy of *Riverside*. "Shit," she says as the tip of her amputated leg slides the book away again.

Tambudzai cocks her head, not hearing exactly what the old albino just said. The albino seems distracted by Jill, and Tambudzai wishes it were only the two of them. The albino regains her balance with her half-leg against the heavy book and quickly tells Tambudzai in Shona that no one has asked her to put a curse on her goats but perhaps someone is poisoning her borehole.

Di-dum. Di-dum. That sounds more African, Jill thinks, kicking her tennis shoe against the rusty stand holding the pot over the fire. Her heart beats faster; she shouldn't have sucked so much sugar cane. Twenty kilometers to *Chiadzwa*. That can't be more than twenty miles. Jill will have to steal Aunt Eleanor's car. Di-di-dum. She can hear the drums beating in time with her footsteps on that ground glowing with gems.

The old albino pulls the iron lid off the pot again. The boiling water pushes up and over, hissing at them. She is going to burn Tambudzai, Jill thinks, so she can go to Chiadzwa. Diamonds just sitting in the dirt. Fields and fields of that red, sandy earth tiled with glowing gems. Chiadzwa must look like fire—a valley of sparkle made even more brilliant by that African sun, which, in truth, Jill hasn't found too different from the American sun, but she knows the diamonds of Chiadzwa must make the sun burn brighter there. Sun and stars and celestial bodies beaming up from the ground, waiting to be plucked from a shining, dry sea. Pa-dum, pa-dum. The drumbeat quickens. She feels suddenly blinded by the intense brilliance of millions of diamonds piled in a valley waiting for her.

"I want to go!" Jill blurts out, unable to bear the thought of Tambudzai scooping up hot dirt and diamonds without her.

"Hush," Tambudzai hisses like the water falling on the fire. The old albino looks curious. Perhaps she cannot understand English. Tambudzai wonders if this albino didn't go to school for very long. Maybe her family village is even more rural than Nharira. "Ignore the white girl. She doesn't know any better," Tambudzai apologizes in Shona.

Jill cautiously watches the old albino drop three sweet potatoes in the boiling water and replace the lid on the pot. Maybe Tambudzai isn't going to the diamond fields. Jill snorts and stares at the old albino through the bits of steam still easing up from the crack around the pot's lid. If Jill could get the diamond out of the old albino's mouth, then she wouldn't have to go to Chiadzwa at all. That stone must be huge to catch the light from the back of the albino's mouth. The old albino suddenly slaps at a mosquito on her neck—rather too violently, it seems to Jill.

Tambudzai continues to beg in Shona, moving closer to the old albino, pleading with her. Someone is jealous of her. Someone is killing her goats.

Jill leans toward them, near the fire, and purses her lips as if considering Tambudzai's case. Whatever it is, Tambudzai looks desperate. Must be diamonds. The old albino responds, but moves her mouth too quickly for Jill to see inside it.

Tambudzai continues to insist that the old albino can help her, or at the very least name the person who is killing her goats. Affronted, the albino's jaw drops to show her displeasure, and she lets out a "ha."

There. Jills sees it clearly. The diamond is almost as big as half a peanut and is not set in a tooth at all but rests in the tooth's place. Jill could easily rip it out of her gums. Gums are soft. The hut is hot now—no, Jill is leaning much too close to the boiling pot, her T-shirt hanging over the fire. She pulls back, her head feeling light as though she has stared at the sun for too long. Does Tambudzai know about the diamond in the albino's mouth? Jill wishes she knew Shona and could understand their argument. If Tambudzai is after the diamond, Jill must get at it before her. She looks up at the buzzing mosquitoes—the top point of the thatched roof is about fifteen feet high. No windows. She can hear the chickens pecking and scratching, but they are only faint sounds in the shadows by the wall. The door is her only way out. Pushing herself up, she struggles for a minute, then stands tall above the other two. She casually strolls to a picture by the door, something torn out of a textbook: "Learn English One Two Three."

"Mind if I let in some air?" Jill calls over her shoulder. The two women carry on their strained discussion but jump as the rotting wood door lurches open. The rusty wire on the door screeches against the half hinge holding it to the hut. Bits of sunset stream in; the chickens scramble out the door. Tambudzai sighs, "Stupid murungu," and the albino groans.

Millicent groans not because she will have to chase her chickens but because she hates the word murungu. Since she moved to the rural area, murungu has crept into her vocabulary. And here the villagers mistake "white" for "master." Why keep making white people special, set apart or above or wherever these villagers place them? However, Millicent muses, something about how they use the word here—as master—does capture that sense of pillaging, the contagious thievery: the British in 1888 pirating the mines, President Mugabe's thugs in 2000 taking back the farms, the foreigners lurking around Mutare's few sit-down restaurants to buy Chiadzwa diamonds. Millicent feels sorry for this poor, fat village woman whose goats keep dying. This drought is probably to blame. The goats are starving as everyone else is, but this woman seems to think that by promising Millicent a few pairs of underwear stolen from the missionaries that her goats will be saved. Millicent feels uncomfortable convincing the villagers that she knows magic—taking a little bit of food here and there in exchange for "witchcraft"—but her PhD in British literature is no good now that teachers earn a few million dollars a week while a Coke costs a billion and you have to return the glass bottle to the clerk before you leave the store. In Harare she isn't safe, not after her comment about President Mugabe during her King Lear lecture. Yes, she is glad she took that diamond for the "curse" she put on that soldier. If only she had thought of a better hiding place for it when these two women came, she wouldn't have to be so careful about her tongue pushing the stone from the crater in her gums. If she had buried it in the yard, she could have yelled at this murungu to catch the chickens and at this village woman to go feed her goats. But the harvest is bad again this year like the years before, and there is nothing. Millicent knows that Tambudzai's goats will all die. Now her own chickens are running around the yard for any hungry child to steal.

"Sorry, thought we needed some fresh air," Jill murmurs, trying to hide her smile. A getaway. Her heartbeats come back strong in anticipation of her escape—pa-dum, pa-dum—no African drums, just her, the diamond, and, soon, her two feet pounding against the dry earth.

Tambudzai wishes Jill would sit down again. Her body moving around the small hut is too much. Tambudzai can tell the old albino is annoyed and now less likely to help her, so she stares at Jill like a bull, her "Mugabe face" as her husband says when he comes home tipsy from Chibuku. Jill whistles; her eyes seem fixed on a spider falling from the shadows on invisible thread. Sit, murungu, Tambudzai sighs. The murungu ruins everything. The old albino is losing interest or is set against her, Tambudzai worries. Maybe the goat killer paid the albino more than some dirty missionary laundry. But paid her what? This old albino has nothing but two pots, a blanket, a large book, and some boiled sweet potatoes. Not even cooking oil! Her torn dress looks as blue as the sky beneath the strips of light coming in through the door.

Tambudzai gasps.

A white arm flashes like lightening toward the albino's pink face. Tambudzai's eyes open wide trying to take in the sight of Auntie Jill reaching into the old albino's mouth. One of Auntie Jill's hands pushes hard against the albino's boiled forehead, the other hand pushes past the worn teeth. Auntie Jill pulls her hand away, ripping something from the back of the albino's throat—a tooth?—and Auntie Jill almost knocks over the pot, plowing toward the door. While Tambudzai shrieks, the old albino rises from the ground, bringing the heavy book with her. Balanced on one foot, she flings the book at the back of Auntie Jill, who races toward the fiery sun. The book hits her head, and Auntie Jill clunks to the hard ground that has been swept to rock. Tambudzai rushes outside to her.

Dazed but conscious, Jill sees the roots of the baobab tree next to her face. Late afternoon shadows streak the ground, and she can make out "Shakespeare" on the book's binding. A pair of shiny red boots stand nearby. The old albino hobbles out of the hut on a stick in time to watch with Tambudzai as a policeman nudges Jill onto her back with his freshly polished boot.

He must have heard me scream from the road, Tambudzai thinks.

He'll take my diamond, Millicent worries, clutching her throbbing jaw.

Jill feels the unevenness of the stone ground beneath her aching body. The earth seems to be pounding against her head, pa-dum, pa-dum.

"*Zvakanaka, mbuya*; good work, grandmother. You may have killed a murungu!" The policeman laughs, scrunching his whole face until his eyes—set close together and low on his face—disappear. A small olive cap sits on the very tip of his narrow head, and his police sweater hangs loosely on his body.

"She took mbuya's tooth!" Tambudzai says, unsure of whom she should protect.

"Ah. You should be more careful than to let a white person into your home. They will rob you blind, mbuya," the policeman says.

Millicent's nose twitches. She hates when people call her "mbuya," grandmother, even more than when they say "the one-legged albino." She would have been a senior professor at the University of Zimbabwe this year if the economy had not crumbled.

Tambudzai wants to go hide in *Buwe Rimwe* cave and wait for the spirits to steal her away; she cannot return to the orphanage. Auntie Jill will tell Auntie Eleanor, and she will lose her job. And her goats will continue to die one by one until her kraal is as empty as her stomach.

"*Chi?*" The policeman questions, leaning down to examine the white girl's hand streaked with red. "What is this young murungu holding?" With the muzzle of his AK-47, he pries open her fingers and sees a rough diamond in a shallow palm of blood. "Ah. Someone has been mining in Chiadzwa. Illegally." He smiles, showing little teeth, which Millicent finds dull in color and perhaps too sharp at the tips. "Show me into your home, mbuya. Let's see what else we can find!"

Walking toward the hut, he picks up a *mawuyu* that fell from the baobab tree. He slams the hard shell against the swept rock and bites into the chalky fruit.

Allison Alsup

A GOOD LIKENESS

OLD L. SAYS MY FATHER'S LINES ARE very
fine. It pleases me to hear the fortune teller say such things
since he has gone to school for many years and is a real scholar
with a jewel in his hat and a silk padded jacket. Mother tells
the letter writer that my father had eleven years of schooling
in his village back in Sunning County. I think I am eleven and
this is a lot of years. Then I remind the fortune teller that the
fish factory in Washington closed and so my father is now east
of the Sierra, in Bodie, where he chops wood for the gold
mills.

Old L. nods. Show me your fingers, he says, turning
his wide hand, his fingertips and nails blue with ink. I am glad
Old L. does not send his clothes to Sing Lee. It would be hard
to wash out all the stains.

Old L. explains that with hands like mine, I will
always be able to make my way. I will not work at a laundry forever. He can see the future in the rivers of my palm.

Someday, I too will make my way from Chinatown and travel like my father. When Old L. talks like this, my mother frowns.

Still, she will bring Baba's letters to no one but Old L., who is not even old enough to have grey hair, but must be called so since he has already learned more than men twice his age. He has mastered the five desires and does not eat meat and sleeps on a straw mat even when he can afford a feather mattress. He prays for hours at the temple, and has forbidden himself wealth. He does not pay to lie with legs-in-the-air girls or use his learning like other scholars, to predict *jiri*, lucky days for gamblers. Other fortune tellers have banners and storefronts, carved chairs and boys to bring tea and copy fortunes. But Old L. does not have show-off things and so I think he is cheap and that it is this last reason and not all the others, why my mother brings Baba's letters here.

What Old L. has is a sidewalk table with ink pots and a white dog whose hair sprouts like wild weeds. It sleeps on a dirty pillow and waits for Old L. to finish cracking his peanuts and to sweep the shells from the table with the wide cuff of his jacket. When the shells fall, the white dog stands and licks the bits from the sidewalk. It sucks on the salt and spits out the dark nest like tobacco. Then the dog goes back to sleep and does not open its eyes, even when I pet it.

I think Old L. must care for the dog very much. He has tied a red silk cord around the dog's neck; a copper fish pendant lies against its rough fur. Uncle and Auntie Boss have given me and their daughter Lan necklaces very much like this one. Auntie Boss says the pendant will bring good fortune as the symbol for fish and profit sound so alike. Uncle Boss says the carp is a reminder that I must jump over obstacles to reach success. My mother says I am not to think about getting a dog; the landlord will never allow it.

This dog is even older than I am, Old L. says. Do you know your numbers?

I nod. I have been practicing with Uncle Boss who says any future man of business must know his tables or be robbed with every transaction. He makes Lan practice too, even though she will never be a man of business. He tells us about laborers who cannot figure if they have been paid fairly for a day's work.

This dog is fourteen, Old L. raises a finger, but each year a dog lives must be counted seven times. So what is the age of this dog?

I pause. Uncle Boss' questions only go up to twelve. I have never practiced fourteen times anything.

If I don't answer right Old L. will see no longer see good things in the rivers of my hands. Wait, I tell him, I know.

He cracks a shell and taps the nut out. If you do, you can save your mother ten cents.

Mother looks hard at me. So I think that seven twelves is eighty four and then add fourteen more.

Ninety-eight, I say.

My mother looks to Old L.; I can tell she does not know the answer. The letter writer smiles, says I am a smart boy and scoots some peanuts towards me. As I snap the shells, he clicks his long nails on his wood table. I try to think of how many letters Old L. has written and read. In truth, there is no way to know and even if I did, it is more than I can count. He says I can give the dog the new shells and I sweep the small pile with the cuff of my jacket. The old dog stands and chews, its copper pendant tapping against the sidewalk.

Anything else today? the fortune teller asks my mother. Writing? Dreams? She hands him the envelope from my father. She has already opened it and removed the check. She never asks Old L. to explain her dreams. I do not think she has any.

When I wake, my mother tells me to bring her the brush. We are not going to Sing Lee now, she says. First, we must see the photographers as my father has written. She oils my hair and smoothes it and weaves a strip of red cotton through the strands so that the braid will hang long and thick. She says I must keep my braid over my shoulder so that the red fabric hangs down the front of my shirt. I must stand tall and look serious like a good son. She explains it is important that my father like the photograph so that he will send money and not gamble it away. I remind her of what he wrote, that the money for the photograph was from winning at *fan-tan*.

And if he won all the time, she scolds, we would sit for a photograph every week.

We climb the stairs to the studio, and I occupy myself with the prints on the walls while my mother argues with the owner Mr. Yu and his wife over the price for three copies, one for my father, one for us and one for my grandparents in Sunning County whom I have never met.

There are dozens of pictures, each framed by cardboard printed with scrolled lines in black and gold that make each person look expensive and important. Most are merchant families in gardens, one with three sons. The boys wear black caps and white silk jackets with horse-hoof sleeves as long as their knees. I would be useless if I wore such jackets to Sing Lee. But of course rich sons don't wash and iron.

On another wall are American photographs. There are no Americans here now, and so I can study their faces in a way my mother forbids when they pass through Chinatown. She does not like it when Americans stop us to take my picture. They get angry when she rubs her fingers together for a coin. I stare at a clear-eyed man with a yellow mustache and short hair that rolls over his head in polished waves. Even if it were cut short and greased, my hair would never make waves. My hair is a flat sea. The American wears a tight suit, and with one hand pulls back his coat to reveal a gold pocket watch. His other fingers rest on top of a globe and behind him are rows of books that rise to the ceiling. I do not doubt he has read every one of them, perhaps even ridden on an Indian camel. I think the photographer must be very good to make an American look so handsome. It is hard not to look at his face, his clear eyes. For a moment, I think that if I were this rich man's son, he could take me with him. Then I am ashamed.

Finally, my mother agrees to a price. She tells Mr. Yu that we have someplace to go as if we are meeting an important person, not rushing back to the bleaching vats.

He says it will take just a few minutes to set up. He pulls a black cape from his camera. It is an expensive thing propped up on polished wooden legs and I know not to step near it. So I watch Yu's wife. She is a small round woman with a wide face and hair pulled tightly in a knot. Even though her clothes are cotton, I can tell her husband is successful. Yu's wife is rich around the edges: embroidered silk slippers, jade bracelets and gold earrings that swing from her ears.

She pulls on a small black cord hanging from the ceiling. A wide shade rolls down and suddenly, the rows of books from the rich American's photograph appear. But the books are not real, only painted. The photographer calls out to his wife, no, no and she pulls on the cord and the shade rolls back up. She tugs on another cord and this time it is a garden scene, with a curved bridge and mountains, the same garden as the merchant family on the wall. I have never seen a garden like this in Chinatown.

Americans, she tells us, do not like the garden. Always they want columns or books.

Ai-yah, the photographer says, no one cares. Get the screen.

From a stack in the corner, Yu's wife unfolds three panels painted with a red pagoda. Then she pulls a carved chair so that the legs cover four spots marked with tape on the floor and slides a little bamboo table beside the chair. She disappears into the back room and returns with a small crate. She lifts out a bowl of oranges and sets them on the little table. The oranges are made of clay and glued together. Then she unfolds two silk jackets, one for me and one for my mother. I laugh because the jacket is so large. I tell my mother she looks like a little girl. She says I look no better. Yu calls out that we must stop our squabbling or the camera will show our anger. His wife fastens the back of the jackets with clothes pins so that from the front, they look custom, made just for us. I think this is why photographs show only the front. If they showed our backs, we would not appear with oranges and silk but as we really are in plain cotton and rough edges.

Yu's wife smoothes my mother's hair with a brush, then carefully lifts out a beaded headdress from the crate. She tells my mother to be still as she lowers the rustling tassels.

Are they real? I ask.

Real enough, Yu's wife says.

I have never seen my mother with bangs of gold, jade and pearls thick across her forehead and I think that if she always wore silk jackets and beads, if her hair was always smoothed and if she was to sit here in the cool air where her face did not turn red from lye and steam, she would be pretty. I think my father will like seeing my mother this way and that anyone who sees our photograph will think we are rich like the merchants on the wall. We sit in the same garden, my mother on the same chair as a *nei ren*, the wife of a successful man, not like a woman who must fetch her own greens from the market. Even if these things are not really true, they will be in this photograph. This is what I think Yu's wife means by real enough.

She tells my mother not to move, then takes a final item from the crate. Mrs. Yu flicks her wrist and a large silk fan drops open. Branches heavy with yellow orchids spread their flowers. My mother reaches for the fan slowly. Like all things expensive, everyone can see its cost. This fan will not move the air any more than the ones she keeps, but her fans are paper and quick to rip and the handles are not carved ivory or tasseled with jewels. She forgets the woman's warning to hold still. The studded bangs of her borrowed headdress go tap, tap, tap as she waves the fan. The photographer's wife gripes and readjusts a tassel.

Then from the shelf, Yu's wife takes a thick book with gold pages and hands it to me. Inside there are pictures of ships but mostly many words. It is in English; I remember a few of the small words, but not the long ones and each sentence is full of long ones.

I cannot read it, I say quietly.

My mother groans.

The photographer laughs. Ai-yah, you do not need to read it. Just hold it.

He steps over and turns the leather cover to face the camera. So I hold the book even though it makes me feel foolish for pretending it is mine. If I were still in school, I would not be reading the little primer my mother hid when I started at the laundry. By now I would be able to read any word in any book, even a thick book with gold pages and we wouldn't have to pay Old L. to write our letters. But I try to put these thoughts away or my anger will show on our picture. I remind myself that the photograph is for my father, so that he will remember family. I think that when he comes home and learns that I am not in school, he will be angry, but I can already hear my mother's voice: when Baba comes home and there is only one rent and all the money he earns stays with us, I will go back to school and so it will not be a lie anymore.

Yu's wife places my free hand on the back of the chair where my mother sits. Now everyone will see the son and mother connected, she says. A loyal son.

As I grip the chair, I tell myself that when my father returns from Bodie, we will take another picture. I will stand between two chairs then, one hand behind my mother and the other behind my father. That photograph will not be a pretend, just-for-getting-money picture, but the true one that shows us as we really are.

Ready! Yu calls out and covers his head with the black cape.

His wife steps back to inspect us a final time as if we are people of great importance and we stare back as if we do nothing all day but eat sweet fruit and call out to servants. The photographer says not to smile or blink or even breathe. He holds the shutter and says to think of our family in China. But I cannot think of people I have never seen. What I think is, *Come back.*

The photographer lifts his cape and says it will be a good likeness. It is then that I remember my braid. Because I have stood behind her, my mother does not know I have forgotten to put my hair over my shoulder. Now it's too late.

The photographer's wife packs up the clay oranges in the crate. She lifts the beaded headband from my mother's hair, then holds out her hand for the book. She unfastens the pins and slips off the silk jackets. The chair is pushed aside, the screen folded, the backdrop rolled up. The photographer pulls the film, steps to the front desk and writes a receipt. Voices rise from the stairs.

Somehow my mother is still holding the fan. When Yu's wife asks for it, my mother hesitates. Several strands of her hair have come loose from their knot. She does not look like a nei ren anymore but as she always does.

It is very beautiful, she says quietly. She traces a finger over the jeweled tassel.

It belonged to my mother, Yu's wife explains. A gift from my father when they were engaged. When I come over on the boat, she says that I can sell it. But I keep it. Even if things go bad, I will never sell it.

My mother nods, but she is looking at the fan. She does not see Yu's wife's press her lips together until they look like dried mushrooms. I can tell Yu's wife wants us to leave. My mother almost smiles, then hands the fan back.

The voices come through the door—two men in plain black jackets and pants, wide brimmed hats, laborers like any other. One of them looks at my mother in a way he should not. The other hands me a nickel and tells me to buy a sweet bun or a balloon. Yu says to come back next week. His wife calls to the men to step forward. She reaches for the cord and the garden comes down again.

My mother taps my head. *Ai-yah*, stop dreaming. We are late.

I ask my mother why father cannot come back to *dai fou* and work in the laundry with us.

It is not so simple, she says. She rinses rice in the corner sink and sets it on the stove. When the metal pot whistles, she says I am to pour water for tea.

Why can't he work at Sing Lee? I ask again.

The laundry is full; there is not space for another. Besides, your father will never wash and fold other people's clothes.

Why not?

Too much like a woman.

I am not a girl.

That is different, she says. You are young.

We sit in silence for a minute until the water boils. Outside two men yell back and forth. She shuts the balcony window.

Other men work in laundries. Uncle Boss, I tell her as I scoop the black tea from the tin.

He is the owner. Different.

Old Uncle.

He delivers.

Father could buy a wagon.

And what about Old Uncle? Besides, your father does not like to stay in one place. He does not like, she waves a hand, small rooms.

Then he can find another place and we will all work there. He can bring us.

Yes. Maybe.

She checks the rice, adds bamboo shoots and mustard greens. She unwraps a small package from the butcher. When my father sends money, there is pork.

My mother hands me the photograph. The decorated woman staring from the paper is her. The jacket and book make me look older, serious, and this is good, but my face is ugly - too narrow and a chin that gives up.

Ai-yah, my mother says and slaps my shoulder. Your forgot to show your braid.

You like or no? Yu asks.

When people see this picture, Yu's wife tells my mother, they see success.

It is good, my mother says.

No one is blurry. Your husband will be happy.

Yes, good.

Yu's wife returns to arranging her crate. The shade with the fake books is down. I stare at the yellow-haired man on the American wall. It is a test to see if he is still handsome even if the books behind him are fake. He is still handsome.

My mother pays. She says that after work, we will see Old L. and send my father and grandparents letters in envelopes big enough to hold the photographs. But there is not time to go back to our room now, so she must bring the pictures to Sing Lee. As soon as we are through the door, Auntie Boss asks what is under my mother's arm. They all want to see the photograph, even Old Uncle comes down from his wagon. Mother makes everyone wipe their hands and move away from the vats, then unfolds the brown wrapping paper.

So pretty, says Mei who comes when there is extra work. Mei is very plain, plainer than Lan, and her ears do not match. Mei does not sound jealous, only surprised. Perhaps she is thinking that she too can take a photograph and be as pretty as my mother.

Yes, says Old Uncle. Very lovely and you, he taps my head. Smart-looking. Auntie Boss elbows my mother. Rich family.

Everyone laughs and agrees it is a good likeness and that my father will be pleased. My mother almost smiles. I like the photograph again and think it shows us as we really are on the inside, not our just-for-now, pretend life until my father returns.

But Lan stares as if I have stolen something from her. Where did you get that book? I don't answer.

Is it yours? She crosses her arms. She is imitating her fat mother, trying to look the boss.

My mother slides the photographs back into the brown paper. Tell her, she says.

But I don't tell Lan. Old Uncle looks away. He knows the book isn't mine. Everyone knows.

Lan turns to my mother. Auntie, your fan is very beautiful. Where did you buy it?

Ai-yah, Auntie Boss slaps her daughter's shoulder. Stop asking stupid questions. Back to work. She tells my mother to put the photographs on the shelf where they will be safe.

Lan waits until we are alone in the back.

I know those things aren't yours, she says.

Our sleeves are rolled and we stir the bleaching vats with our poles, pushing down the white clothes as each rises to the boiling surface. The steam lifts the stray hairs from Lan's braids. None of those things are yours, she says.

No. The fan, I tell her. My father gave it to her. She will never sell it.

That's a lie.

Ask her.

Lan holds a petticoat under the boiling water. I can tell she isn't sure if she should believe me. I silently promise to save my New Year's money and my numbers money and my share of the change-left-in-pockets jar and buy my mother a painted silk fan. Then it won't be a lie anymore.

But then Lan turns from the vat and walks into the front room.

Auntie, she calls.

I drop my pole.

Wait, I say, ready to confess. My mother will make a point of shaming me. But if Lan hears, she does not stop.

Auntie, I keep thinking about your beautiful fan, Lan says, her voice falsely sweet.

My mother looks up from the counter where she is wrapping clean shirts and blouses with brown paper. Auntie Boss and Mei pretend not to hear Lan's words. Mei drops a nickel left in a pants pocket into the change jar.

Bao told me that your fan was a gift from your husband, Lan says.

My mother looks over Lan's shoulder at me, then swipes at the roll of twine with her blade, knots the package and attaches the tag Auntie Boss gives her. As soon as she is done, she pulls out more brown paper and Auntie Boss stacks three more ironed shirts on the counter.

The fan? Lan asks. Is it true you will always keep it, Auntie?

Ai-yah, a gift, my mother says, sliding a sheet of paper under the shirts. Too precious to sell.

Lan looks at her mother, but Auntie Boss yells at both of us for leaving the vats. You can't read that book, Lan says once we are in the back again. She lifts a dripping blouse from the boiling water and drops it into the rinsing tub. So don't even say you can.

There's no point in arguing. We both know when I stopped school—a year after she did.

At lunch, my mother whispers to let Lan win at numbers. I have won three times in a row, she explains, no more showing off. I think that my mother says this not because I have won three times but because our photograph is too good and because we lied about the fan. I do not see what these things have to with practicing numbers, only that in my mother's mind, they are connected. But I do not forgive Lan and when the clock says two and Uncle Boss calls out numbers from his stool, I hold the jumping fish at my neck and close my eyes. I answer faster than ever, so fast that when I look again, Uncle Boss is shaking his head at his daughter. Lan runs up the stairs to their apartment and Auntie Boss must go after her. My mother glares as Uncle Boss hands me the coin.

After work, my mother does not take me to see Old L. and his dog, so I do not get to see the large envelopes sent to my father and my grandparents in China. She does not stop by the bakery and even at dinner, we do not speak. She does not unwrap our copy of the photograph from the brown paper or set it on the mantle. When dinner is over, she opens her trunk. She pulls out several bundles of my father's letters and things from when she was a girl, things that I am not allowed to touch. She places the wrapped photograph at the bottom of the trunk, then puts everything else on top and closes the lid.

Old L. folds Baba's letter back into its envelope, then asks how long my father has been on Gold Mountain.

Long time, my mother says. I pet the dog as she explains that my father was sixteen when he came to Gold Mountain with his father. My grandfather mined gold, then later worked the railroads, then was chosen by his village to return for a third time and it was on this third time that my father came with him. My grandfather was to fulfill a *jup seen yu*, a final task, to retrieve the bodies of five men, track layers, still buried east of the Sierra. It was my grandfather's duty to see that these men were returned to the village. But the task was too much for one man and my father was sent as well. It is a story I know. It is the reason we live on Gold Mountain and not in my father's village.

Important man to be chosen for such a task, Old L. tells me.

I do not know if he means my father or grandfather.

And did they find the bodies? Old L. asks.

Four, my mother says. One man's grave was empty. No one knows what happened to the fifth man.

I do not understand, Old L. says and brushes the peanut shells off his table with his cuff. The old dog stands and moves towards the fallen husks. Your husband came and saw all this and did not go back with his father to his village?

No.

And now your husband has returned east of the mountains again?

My mother looks at her feet. A small, nervous-looking man has come up to the table. The man twists the ends of his jacket and says he needs a letter written. Old L. tells him to wait across the street.

I am sorry, Old L. says to my mother, it is not my business.

No, my mother shakes her head. They argued. My husband and his father. It is why my husband did not return. That is all.

Old L. nods. I wait for more. No one has ever said there was a fight. No one has ever said we are here because of an argument. I hold out a shell to the dog. Inside my head, I beg Old L. to ask another question, to ask why they fought, to ask if my grandfather is still angry. If I ask, my mother will not answer. But if Old L. asks, she will have to.

But Old L. only reaches for another peanut and my mother says we must be going.

Am I American? I am careful to ask in the right way, as if I do not care, as if I am more interested in sweeping the floor of our room than in her answer.

She says no. Born here. I have papers, so they can't send me back. But not real American. Chinese born here. Different.

I rest the broom against the wall, then reach for the old picture magazines she keeps instead of buying a dust pan. A mouse has chewed the corner of the pages. I ask her where our village is.

Sunning County.

I know that, I say and brush the dirt into the paper. Where?

You would not like it.

Have you seen it?

All the same: no good.

But I don't believe her. If it was bad, father wouldn't want us to go back. I remind her of what he wrote in his last letter, how he was letting his short hair grow long enough to braid again, how he reminded us of the old saying: falling leaves return to their roots.

Talk, she says. He's Gold Mountain now. *Guamshanke*. Don't think he means what he says. He won't go back.

I want to see it, I tell her.

See what? she asks.

Our village.

We have no village. Our life is here in dai fou.

I want to go with him, I say.

Stop dreaming. The past is over. Think about it and you never move forward.

But what if the village is our future?

She waves her hand. The future is a meal that hasn't been cooked. Sit at that table and you go hungry. Now is what matters.

You don't know anything, I tell her. I remind her of what Old L. said: I am like Baba and have rivers in my palm.

Ha! You think you know? If it's so good there, why does everyone pay to come here? This is your village: small and muddy. No noodle house, no candy shop, no balloon man. Sometimes people starve. Sometimes bandits attack. You like to sit on the balcony and watch the streets. But in your village, there's no balcony, no sidewalk, nothing to see but chickens and dirt. You think strangers give you money for candy in the village? No. Here, not enough children, but in the village, there are many, too many to feed. Children get sold, work as slaves. That is your village.

She is breathing hard; her chest moves under her grey jacket. She stares back, her lips bunched. It is the most she has ever said at once.

It is because of you that Baba leaves us, I tell her.

She raises her hand and I tell myself I will not cry or close my eyes when she hits me. But she does not touch me. Instead she flings open the window and steps outside onto the balcony. There is no other room, no other place to go.

That is not his village, I shout through the open window. You don't know it. You don't know anything.

She says nothing. She stares up the alley, her fingers gripped around the rail.

When he comes home, I am going with him on the boat, I yell at her. I am going back!

She waves a hand towards the top of the alley. Go then.

There is nothing about returning to our village in my father's next letter, nothing about how long his hair has grown, only about the cold. There is also no check; most of his pay has had to go to a thick coat and waxed boots. We are to be careful with our money as the snow will soon block the roads and the mail wagons. When Old L. finishes reading, he slides the letter back into the envelope and asks my mother to tell him her dreams.

She shakes her head.

He holds up a hand. No charge.

She nods. It is strange to think that she lives in images I cannot see. Of course I dream and do not tell her. I have had three dreams about the American man on Yu's wall. I have touched his yellow hair, felt his mustache on my thigh. I have been careful to cover my sheets. Still, I do not like her keeping secrets.

She hesitates, then lowers her voice so that none of the men shuffling by can hear. She has dreams of sucking on dark seeds, sometimes very large.

Sweet seeds. Like a plum? Old L. asks.

My mother shakes her head. Bitter. Dirt.

Old L. brushes a pile of peanut shells to the ground and the dog stands. It sniffs as if this pile may be different, then licks the salty husks. The fortune teller says that the seeds are anger, large because the anger has already grown. She must spit out the black things before she wakes. As if to prove its master's point, the old dog yacks up the peanut shells, then goes back to sleep on its worn pillow.

Be careful, Old L. warns her. As dark thoughts grow, they sink roots. He twists his blue-tipped fingers. The shoots will wrap her bones tighter and tighter until her heart turns black.

She flips through a magazine. It does not matter that she cannot read the words, she makes up stories to fit the pictures. She has taken our photograph from the trunk, unwrapped it and set it on the mantle. I wonder if our grandparents have done the same, propping up our picture or pinning it to the wall. I wonder if they believe we are really the people in the picture. Already I look at our photograph and see strangers staring back.

I sit on the balcony and look up the alley to where it meets Jackson Avenue and men crowd the cobblestones dimly lit by red lanterns. Workers shuffle past in black hats and black jackets, black braids swinging. They call out to each other on their way to Spanish Alley to gamble, to visit women and smoke in the dens. They are a slow loud river, dark currents rising and falling, pushing between the buildings. I have never seen a real river.

It has been a month since we have brought a letter from Baba to Old L. At first we returned the fortune teller's wave when we walked by his table. But since no new letter has come, we walk a different block and it is like when I started at the laundry and my mother took the long way so that we would not pass the school yard and I would not be reminded of what I had before Sing Lee.

I run my hand over the copper fish at my neck. When my father comes home, it will not be on the ocean steamer like a newcomer, but like a Gumshanke, a Gold Mountaineer—on the ferry and from the east. He will take the train to Oakland and then a little boat across the bay, his things bundled in a sheet or carried in a tall basket strapped to his shoulders. To most, he will look no different from other men. But he will be different because he will not stop for gambling or women or the pipe. He will not stop for anything. He will walk up Sacramento Street, past the boarding houses where new men sleep in bunks stacked as close as dishes, then turn and make his way along the vegetable stands lining Dupont. He will turn again on Jackson and then at our alley. I will be the first to see him through the balcony rails, the drying shirts, the hanging ferns, the birdcages and lanterns. I will be the first to pick out his new coat and boots from the others, the first to run down the stairs and call his name.

Soma Mei Sheng Frazier

THE DEEPEST HOURS

Sometimes my infant daughter
wakes in the middle of the night
irrepressibly happy.

My husband and I lull her back
to sleep with our various
Shaolin techniques:

His trick is to stroke her ears and mine, to
put the radio on static and
dance slowly.

These things work like hypnosis, like
narcotics, like prayer:
hit or miss.

Sometimes our desperate trying
reminds me of all the stops
my mother pulled out, years ago

to try and cheer herself up
about life: liquor, crystals, seminars, triathlons
and legal drugs that made her hair fall out.

I remember driving home late

a senior in high school

and seeing her dart

across the road in front of our house

barefoot, eyes wide. I slammed

on the brakes and

when the car stopped

inches short of her

she met my eyes.

We stared

through the windshield and

my mind kept trying to turn her into a deer.

Like a doe she darted off wildly

over the dirt shoulder and into

the dark door of the forest.

My father was waiting at home.

I don't know what to do, he croaked, and

it was the only time in his whole macho life

that he ever admitted as much to me, so

although he was an abusive bastard

I took him in my arms

and swayed.

Sometimes

in the deepest hours

I sway that way with my daughter

to sedate her.

Other times

I remember how

my mother slept

still as a stone, for days and days

when she finally came home.

It was like

she wanted to forget

her husband, her house

her thoughts and me and

recapture the darkness of the woods.

Those nights I

set my daughter on my stomach

facing me, wobbly

and we talk.

Her words rattle up from her little chest

and straighten out into

rapturous ooohs and aaahs.

I tell her

all of my secrets and

sometimes

we stay awake

for hours.

Marcia Popp

when she died she took all her best stories with her

not the ones she repeatedly told family members about her great-great grandfather james who was killed in the civil war or gran on the other side who lost everything in the war between the states or the ones she told outside the family about the day world war II ended or seeing president kennedy speak at the university when he was still a senator nor were they the stories she told in different forms to everyone about how an earthquake in southern illinois made the telephone poles sway the same year there was snow on easter and the first tornado in a hundred years it was not any one of these stories that she took undelivered to the grave but the ones she had never told anyone which did not seem like stories at all to her but might be cleverly used by a novelist to set a scene develop a character or move the story in an unpredictable direction the ones that were simply what her life was like on a regular basis what she saw when she looked in the mirror which was mostly not pretty or how she feared losing her mind when she floated about the room unexpectedly during especially trying moments or the memory of waking up to the stillness of a world newly whitened with snow and not wanting the sun to melt it away or footprints of any kind to disturb the gentle drifts that stacked softly against the door outside.

William Doreski

CONFESS TO ME

Confess to white slavery.
Confess to armed burglary.
Confess to cooking crystal meth
on your range. Confess to running
over motorcyclists sprawled
in the street. Confess that you hate
priests and nuns. Confess to humming
bombastic Wagner overtures
while shaking hands with rabbis.
I know you more deeply than your many
lovers do. Your eyes turn blue
for some, brown for others, green
for your favorites. The night we drove
to the lake and swam all silver
in the uncensored starlight I spoiled
the moment by naming the gap
between spirit and body, ending
forever your love of the bible.
But you've never trusted books.
When I gave you *Anna Karenina*
you choked on the thick Russian names
and blamed me for rumpling your tongue
and souring your favorite kisses.
Later at the Black and White Ball
we danced like the plastic couple

on wedding cakes. Your rococo gown

swept the floor clean. My white tie

twinkled moth-like, my carnation

suggested a shell-burst. Confess

you liked me a little that night

although you went home with a crowd

of men you hadn't met before.

Confess to harboring symptoms

of benevolent dictatorship.

Confess to pilfering mother lodes

in a dozen African nations.

Confess, confess, confess to me

while we lie in bed and hear robins

trouble over a fallen nestling

and a hawk in the distance whistle

a single explosive note.

Jackie Zollo Brooks

CHINABERRIES

TWO WEEKS BEFORE HE DIED, MY father
began claiming he'd had visions of heaven. This was an
embarrassment to my sister, an avowed atheist, but not to
me with my mixed and ambiguous beliefs, not to mention
my professional interest in all things bizarre and inexplicable
in human nature. My mother took the news with aplomb. At
once she readjusted my father's heavenly visions as she had
readjusted his every choice, every thought, every move, every
necktie. The man was a pawn in her hands. My mother decided
that heaven was probably a resort. If he was determined to
go, my father must show the decency to select a four-star
establishment where she, at some future time, would likely join
him and begin nagging him to death all over again for eternity.

"Yes, Fredo, I can see it all now," she said, crisply,
as though she'd received a brochure in the mail. "Luxurious,
especially the rooms."

"Rooms?" my father said, puzzled. He looked at me

and I shrugged back to show I didn't get the picture either.

The last few days of his life he was confined to a hospital. I couldn't help remembering the primitive days of my childhood when people died at home, mostly in their beds. My father's Italian father died on Christmas Eve, sitting up in his great oak bed, cheating at solitaire. I, the youngest grandchild, came to offer him some of my grandmother's baked oysters and eels from the midnight feast to find him sitting back among his pillows with the fedora he insisted on wearing tipped over his eyes. Two cards from the marked deck were still in his hand. But, as I say, that was in another time. These days we leave home behind before we die, we pack our bags or someone else packs them for us, and if we are lucky we get to wear our own pajamas in the hospital as we lie dying.

I came each day directly after rehearsal, flying in from New Haven where we were opening out of town as was the custom in those days with shows headed for New York. Neither my mother nor sister met me at Logan because both of them had unofficially certified themselves as full-time hospital caregivers, although understandably neither of them could actually be there full-time. Eventually, my mother buckled under the strain of daily devotion and she contracted the flu—or so she said. She took to her bed for the duration when presumably my father would finally finish off his ramblings about heaven and God, and die. In the last days then, all bedside vigils were left to my sister and me. My sister, though, was not one to sit by quietly.

It was a very nice hospital as hospitals go. It was the smaller of two in town, the one nearer my parents' home. The low two-story ivy-covered buildings were surrounded by the most wonderful shrubs and at the head of the drive to the visitors' parking lot was a row of what my sister identified as chinaberry trees since they were covered with bright red berries in winter, but were too tall to be holly. I think chinaberry trees only grow in the south with yellow berries so I'm not sure what they were, but it was never wise to contradict Clara. Thick Douglas firs clustered in a sort of fat embrace at the rear of the hospital, just outside the windows to my father's room; they stood watch over him, seeming to nod and consult by layering their branches in each other's arms. Even the brisk moist winds of January couldn't penetrate their solidarity.

My sister, who had made a mid-career change from physical education teacher to registered nurse in an allergist's office, was now virtually running the hospital. When I came to Dad's room she was wearing an apron and rubber gloves.

"You cannot begin to guess what I've been through," she said, an unruly lock of dark hair – my sister never went grey in her lifetime—fell in her eye. With a terrific huff she sent the disobedient hair flying back up on her head.

"What's wrong?" I said. I tucked my script deep in the pocket of my winter coat so she would not think I was going to be frivolous in my intentions to minister to my father.

"Alicia!" My father called to me from his bed. His voice, not as strong as it once was, still had the rich melodic tone of an Italian tenor.

I went to his side. They had put up the side rails on my father's hospital bed so he was like a baby in his crib. He was nicely tucked in, wearing his own blue cotton pajamas, with his beautiful hands folded on his chest. He looked, in a word, like an angel.

"You've got to listen to me!" my sister, Clara said in a strangled voice that muffled a shriek.

"What is it, Clara?" I asked. I was standing by the bed now, holding my dad's hand which he'd extended through the railings.

"Don't listen to her," my father whispered to me before she got closer. "She's gone completely nuts."

"I heard that, Dad," Clara said crossly. "They came finally, after God knows how many hours, to put a new mattress on Dad's bed and when they lifted the old one off, good God! the bed underneath was filthy, absolutely filthy. I had to get down on my hands and knees to scrub around the legs and the wire things. Look at my hands," she said, holding out her rubber-gloved hands as though I could see the knuckles on her fingers.

"Crazy," Dad said, shaking his head a little. "I told her not to bother, Alicia. I didn't even want the new mattress, the old one was fine with me...."

"You were in pain!" Clara cried in a high shrill voice that made my father wince.

I tried to comfort Clara, a lifelong task, and I'd mostly failed. She put her head on my shoulder and began to cry.

My father turned his head on his pillow and looked out the window at his companions the Douglas firs, bending toward him now in the wind to scratch at the glass. A storm was gathering. I'd already noticed the swollen grey clouds dragging themselves across a dark sky when I drove the rented car to the hospital. I was worried about getting the flight back to New Haven.

"It's going to snow," Dad said. He pulled his sheets up to his chin and gave a happy little sigh. "It's going to be just beautiful."

"Oh, god," Clara moaned, "his feet are turning black. I can't do everything."

I took my sister by her thin shoulders and steered her toward the door.

"You go right down to the cafeteria and get yourself a pot of hot tea," I said. "Did you eat any lunch?"

Clara was looking desperately over her shoulder like a child being dragged away from the Christmas tree. "Do you think I really should? I've been here since noon."

"That's ridiculous, Clara," I said. "That's what the nurses are for."

"Well, they don't do anything," she said, untying her apron.

"Give me that," I said, "and don't come back for at least an hour. In fact I think you should be getting home."

Clara peeled off her gloves and set them in my hand. She ran her hands through her hair, picked up her purse and went down the hall, stopping once to look back and call loudly,

"Come down and get me if anything happens."

I nodded yes but, of course, that would not suffice.

"You promise?" she shouted.

"Yes," I shouted back and went back in the room to sit with my father.

I drew a little wooden chair over beside his bed and sat down. My father reached his hand through the railings again and took my hand. This time he squeezed my hand a little. Then he put my hand over his heart. And we sat there like that.

After a while Dad said, "Your poor mother has the flu. I wish I could be there to help her."

"She wouldn't want you to worry, Dad," I said.

"Are you kidding?" Dad said, "She'd love me to worry. She'd like nothing better than to know I was over here fretting my head off about her. She'll be jealous if she finds out how happy I am with my lot. Breakfast in bed and a big window to look through. Oh, look!" he cried, dropping my hand to point to the window. "How beautiful. It's starting to snow. Big, soft flakes, aren't they? I love that kind of snow, don't you? The snowflakes are like big soft flowers. When we're in here safe and warm, they don't even look like they'd be cold and wet, do they?"

I got up from my chair and leaned in over the railing and kissed my father's forehead. He smiled up at me in the gathering twilight and shook his head no when I wanted to turn on his light.

"Alicia?" Dad said when I sat back down and he took my hand and put it on his heart again. "I'm not going to talk anymore. I hope you'll understand."

"I do," I said.

"But you could read me your part if you like or recite anything you remember. Remember how you used to recite things for Grandma and Grampa when you were little? You could recite things even before you could read. Well, that's it. That's all I'm going to say. Okay? You know that I love you and all the rest of it."

I couldn't think of anything from Edward Albee that would interest my father. You can't really excerpt things from Albee, not speeches that can stand alone anyway or if there are any I couldn't think of one from the new play we were rehearsing. So I just recited Shakespeare's 29th Sonnet. It came back to me slowly, word for word, from some long ago time when I'd had to recite it, for an audition probably or maybe when I was a guest in Monty's acting class in Manhattan. I don't know exactly when I learned the sonnet but it was part of my repertoire, my bag of tricks, my show-biz treasures. Although, can you really call Shakespeare show-biz? Well, why not? Monty once said Shakespeare was the biggest ham of all. Anyway, I began:

" 'When in disgrace with fortune and men's eyes

I all alone beweep my outcast state

And trouble deaf Heav'n with my bootless cries…'."

"Deaf heaven," my father murmured. He had closed his eyes.

" 'And look upon myself and curse my fate
Wishing me like to one more rich in hope
Featured like him, like him with friends possessed.
Desiring this man's art and that man's scope
With what I most enjoy contented least…' "

I thought perhaps he was asleep but when I paused my father squeezed my hand so I finished:
" 'Yet in these thoughts, myself almost despising—
Haply I think on thee, and then my state
Like to the lark at break of day arising
From sullen earth, sings hymns to Heav'n's gate.
For my sweet love's remembrance such wealth brings
Than then I scorn to change my state with kings.' "
Whether my father was asleep or just letting the words soak in I don't know. We stayed quietly for the rest of my visit. The snow fell and fell with those same big soft flakes my father liked until gradually the Douglas firs looked more like polar bears than trees, and through their branches I could see the sky, a yellowish misty pool filled with yet more snow. Poor Clara must have fallen asleep somewhere for I couldn't find her to say goodnight. And when I checked in at the desk where the night nurse sat under the glare of a green-shaded desk lamp, she told me visiting hours were over long ago but since my father would not be with us that much longer she wasn't going to be strict about them with my sister and me.

"How long do you think it will be?" I asked the nurse.

"No one ever knows these things, dear," the nurse said, taking off her glasses and rubbing her eyes wearily. "We haven't found a specialist yet who can predict a death."

"I'm glad," I said, thinking this nurse might have had her fill of doctors who acted like they knew everything. Stage and film directors could be like that, too. Quashing your every idea when you were working as hard as you could. And really anyone with a position of authority should be careful not to be "drunk with power" as my father liked to say when he watched the politicians talking on television.

"Me, too, dear," said the nurse. "You be careful driving now. Are you really going all the way back to New Haven tonight?"

"Oh, I have to," I said, "it's my job."

"Isn't that the way?" said the nurse, "Even when those we love are dying we have to keep on truckin'. Good night now and you take care. We'll take care of your father at this end. Try not to worry. He's a sweet old dear."

Outside about three inches of snow had already accumulated so after I brushed off the car, I went back into the hospital to call Logan to see if my flight had been cancelled. It was still on schedule so I took off into the snowy night, wondering if I would ever make it back tomorrow and if my father would be alive if I did.

But sure enough, even though I missed a day because all flights were cancelled next afternoon when I was due to fly to Boston, there was my father still alive in his blue pajamas in his crib-like hospital bed. Only this time there was a distinct difference in his condition.

Not so with Clara's. When I arrived at the hospital around six p.m. two days later, Clara had just gotten into a terrific fight with a nurse and was asked to cool off in the lounge at the end of the hall. That same older night nurse from before reported the whole thing to me.

"You see, dear, your sister keeps thinking she can do something. Something we can't do or, according to her, won't do. When, perhaps—you seem more rational—you realize there is nothing anybody can do except keep him comfortable. You'll see, he seems quite happy. When they begin calling out to heaven, you know it's not going to be much longer."

"My dad's been calling out to heaven?"

"Oh, yes, most people do that. Even the lapsed Catholics…in fact," she lowered her voice, "those non-practicing Catholics who refuse the priest when they're first admitted shout to God the loudest."

"My dad isn't a Catholic," I said, "but he is a Mason."

"There you are," said the nurse with satisfaction. "I'll just go down and have a word with your sister…Claire, is it?"

"No, it's Clara. She's terribly upset, is she?"

The nurse looked like she might laugh when I said that. Instead she winked and walked off down the hallway.

The first thing I noticed when I went close to Dad's bed was the glow. There was an actual glowing light around him which I thought at first must be from my eyes adjusting to coming in from the darkness of the parking lot. Then I figured the lamp on his night table might be casting it. But no, the glow emanated from my father himself. He was smiling, looking up at the ceiling. I wondered if he was seeing heaven but when he saw me, he extended his hand through the railings of the bed as before. This time, though, instead of placing my hand on his heart, he put it to his lips. I was afraid my hand might be quite cold but he seemed not to notice and held it there to his lips for a while. Finally, he gave me back my hand and smiled up at me. That's when I noticed that his eyes were intensely bright, very black, glowing, too. I quickly took off my coat and threw it over the back of the chair that I dragged over to the bed.

Just as I sat down, a young doctor entered the room. I hadn't met him. He nodded at me and went to my father and put his hand on Dad's shoulder.

"I'm going to lift you up just a little," the young doctor said, "so I can hear your heart from the back. Is that all right?"

My father simply smiled, still glowing. I wondered if the doctor noticed the glow but I was quiet while with his left arm he supported my father who'd grown very weak and seemed about to topple over in the bed. After the doctor listened with his stethoscope at several places on my father's back, he gently laid him back on his pillows. The doctor stroked my father's cheek.

Then he looked at me. He was such a young doctor and his eyes were a deep brown and capable of expressing the deepest compassion. Almost imperceptibly, the doctor shook his head at me. I took that to mean my father was slowly sinking into death. After the doctor patted my father's shoulder, he put his hand on Dad's head as if he were a priest, then he left. My father went on smiling, reaching for my hand through the railings as I sat back down in the chair.

After a while it came to me what Dad had meant the last time I was here and he said he wasn't going to talk any more. He didn't mean just for that night, my father meant he was through with talking. While we were sitting there, my father suddenly lifted his hands to draw a rectangle in the air with his forefingers. Afterwards he put his hands back on his chest and rested. Then in a few minutes he repeated drawing the rectangle in the air with his fingers. Soon after, he turned his glowing face toward me. His cheeks were as rosy as a child's. The word cherub came to mind. And now he held up one hand with four fingers extended, the thumb folded into his palm.

"Four?" I said. "Do you mean four, Dad?"

He held out his hand with the four fingers again. He was smiling at me as if he were already on a cloud, floating high above me in the sky. Then he rested. For the next half hour, my father alternated drawing rectangles in the air with holding up the four fingers of his right hand.

It occurred to me that maybe the four stood for the four pillows piled under his feet; maybe they needed moving. I got up and went to the foot of the bed but when I tried to adjust a pillow my father shook his head at me. Still smiling, still glowing, but letting me know not to touch the pillows under his feet. That was just as well because my father's feet were black from lack of circulation.

My father pointed to the window now. It had begun snowing again. The Douglas firs which had managed to shake off some of their snow trembled in the wind as though dreading the next onslaught. I wondered if there would be another storm or if these were just flurries. I wasn't worried about traveling as I had been last time because the director had given the cast the week-end off so he could run up to New York and work with Edward Albee on some cuts, especially in Act Two. I am not one to relish unlearning my part but there you have it, that's what we do in late rehearsals; we cut and forget as fast as we can, a last-ditch effort to ensure a successful opening by keeping the audience awake and, more important, in their seats. An actor has to have an old woman's patience that does not come naturally as actors are an impulsive lot. But this discipline of being patient proved to be just what was needed sitting there by my father, observing the gestures he continuously repeated, ritualistically, while darkness fell. The ritual, as a matter of fact, is the earliest form of theater and its gestures are repetitious and symbolic coming from a primordial place within us. I sat thinking about my father who had once been a practical-minded marine engineer, coming now to the end of his life by surrendering to the irrational.

Clara was finally allowed back in the room. I tried to tell her about what our father was doing but just then he held up his four fingers and she went fussing about with the pillows at the foot of his bed which made my father cry out in pain.

"Oh, God!" shouted my sister, the atheist. "What now? You've got to talk to me, Dad. Tell me where the pain is. I'll help you but you've got to tell me."

"I don't think Dad is going to talk to us any more, Clara," I said.

"Oh, you and your drama," my sister said, "you've got to keep a clear head about these things. I bet it's his back. He's been lying on it for five days now. The mattress, even this new one, isn't enough support. I'll get him an egg crate."

My father began drawing his rectangles in the air again.

"Yes, yes, Dad," Clara said, grabbing his hands in both of hers. "I hear you now. I know what you want. You want an egg crate…"

My sister made a dash for the door but I stopped her by asking what she was talking about.

"Oh, you wouldn't know," she said distractedly, trying to get out of the room, "it's what we in the medical profession use on the beds of patients who have bedsores, to relieve their agony."

I said I hadn't noticed that our father had any bedsores.

"Not yet but in another couple of weeks he will and then what? I'm getting the egg crate and don't interfere when you don't know anything about it."

"But, Clara," I said, "Dad's dying."

"Not while I'm around he's not," she said grimly. She came back over to the bed and leaned in to scold my father. "Don't you dare go, Daddy. You hear me? You stay right here. I'm going to get you an egg crate and I'll be right back."

We could hear Clara out in the hallway calling out in a piercing voice for what she wanted from the supply closet.

Part of me wanted my father to die right then before my sister could come back into the room. But now something interesting was happening as my father reached up from his bed for my hand. I leaned over him and he whispered, "Four, four."

"Four," I repeated, holding his hand. I didn't even feel like crying because I was in the face of something distinctly out of the ordinary. My father was having a mystical experience. He went on glowing and smiling, making his rectangles, holding up his four fingers in between times until finally in exhaustion he dropped his arms back at his sides.

"Alicia?" he said in a weak voice.

I leaned over the bed. He smiled up at me with his unearthly, almost unbearable radiance.

"Four men will carry me. Four. Four men. Don't forget," Dad said.

I said I wouldn't forget. Then I sat down; he pulled my hand through the railing and put it on his heart and we sat that way until Clara came tearing back, carrying a long blue plastic mat with rows of the same oval indentations of an empty egg carton. By then my father had gone into a deep sleep and I was able to persuade Clara not to try rolling him over to slide the egg crate under his body until he woke up again.

And so the evening passed. My father woke from time to time, smiling at me, indicating that he wanted my hand in his. He didn't draw his rectangles any more nor did he speak. He lay quiet and serene, waiting to be borne away. Clara in the meantime ran from the room, up and down the halls, looking for this doctor or that nurse until blessedly her husband Blake arrived, wrapped her in her coat and led her away. She sobbed out loud as she clutched his arm and he tried to comfort her as best he could. Poor devil, he had his work cut out for him. Not only did he have Clara to comfort but she had convinced him to stay at my parents' home where my mother would descend on him with a list of complaints a mile long. Luckily, I had already considered what staying in my old room might do to my psyche. I registered at the local hotel where maybe I could dream of my father when he was young, throwing open the front door as he sang snatches from Verdi's operas when we went out for a walk to buy ice cream cones.

As it happened I was so overcome by my father's experience in the hospital that I slept a deep, black dreamless sleep. I awoke refreshed as a baby. I could hardly wait to finish my coffee so I could get back to the hospital to watch the breathtaking transformation of my father's dying.

When I parked the rented car in the hospital parking lot, I noticed the sun had come out at last with the blinding brightness that appears in winter after a storm, spreading its relentless brilliance over the snow until it's like the sheen of boiled icing on a wedding cake.

I remembered I'd brought Dad some flowers so I had to go back to the car and when I turned around I happened to notice the chinaberry trees lining the drive. The berries were glistening in the sun. I took a step toward them and they began to tremble, making a tinkling sound like tiny bells. I stopped. I stood quite still. The chinaberries were pulsating, alight with color, strangely crimson, a blood-red sunset was reflected in each one. I stood deeply transfixed, realizing that my father had died. He had died and his released energy was traveling through the chinaberries with a charge of exquisite reality.

Inside the hospital my sister was crying softly in his room in a chair beside his empty bed.

"He's gone, Alicia," she said looking up at me when I entered. "They took him away before I could get here. The nurse said he woke up this morning and told her he wanted breakfast. She couldn't believe it but she went to get him a tray and when she came back he was sitting up in bed. The nurse said he was still smiling."

Clara buried her face in her hands. I went over to rub her back.

"That's funny, Clara, don't you think?" I said. "That's just how Grampa died."

At the house Clara and Mother had a dreadful row over Dad's funeral. He had told us even before he went to the hospital that he wanted to be cremated and have his ashes scattered out over the Atlantic because he'd made his living as a ship's engineer by going to sea for forty years. But Mother wouldn't hear of it. She had already bought her plot and made sure at the time there was room for her husband. Mother told me she was upset from arguing with Clara right after she'd picked out the most beautiful coffin at the funeral parlor and my sister didn't even admire it. Mother said she was so exhausted she wanted me to pick out my father's clothes for the funeral, leading me to their bedroom.

"Oh, you are never going to have an open casket!" Clara screamed, charging down the hallway to the bedroom doorway. And when Mother said she certainly was, since the entire Masonic Order was coming to the funeral to perform some ritual over Fredo's body, Clara slammed out of my parents' house and did not come back until the funeral.

From his closet I chose a bright red tie to go with my father's blue suit. It still had a price sticker on it, so my mother had probably never allowed him to wear it. The tie had huge white seabirds flying all over it.

At the funeral parlor, my father, stiff as a board, lay in his coffin. The service at the funeral home was blessedly short, concluding with straight-backed old men from the Masonic Lodge, who shuffled slowly around the body saying something about life everlasting and dropping little sprigs of evergreen into the casket.

I rode with my mother in the first long black car to the cemetery. Mother was in high spirits, considering the occasion. Her cheeks were flushed pink with excitement because so many people had shown up for the funeral. Still sulking, Clara rode in the second car with some of my cousins. We stopped at last at the foot of a little knoll where a canopy had been raised over a gaping hole in the ground. My mother pulled on her gloves and laid her hand on my arm.

"Alicia," she said, "I planned for every contingency but I forgot about assigning pallbearers."

As if they'd read her mind, some of my cousins in the car behind us came up and knocked on the glass. Lowering the window, we saw big flakes starting to fall again; they were more like magnolia blossoms than snow. My cousin, Renzo, his hair already covered with snow, stuck his head in the window and said, "Auntie, would you like us to carry Uncle Fredo up the little hill to the grave?"

"Oh, what a coincidence!" said Mother.

"There's just Paolo, Louie, and Nick, but I think we can manage the casket all right."

"Thank you, boys," Mother said, preparing to get out of the car, and having forgotten that my cousins hadn't been boys for twenty five years.

For a minute I sank back against the leather seats. Four of my cousins were going to carry my father up the knoll to his final resting place. Four men would carry my father and the rectangle he had drawn in the air with his fingers.

My mother leaned back in the car for me.

"Alicia, wasn't that a coincidence that your cousins popped up out of nowhere just when I needed them! Come on, darling, why are you sitting there? We must finish up here to make it to your aunt's house for the buffet."

For the longest time I wanted to be able to tell someone what had happened before my father died, and what happened afterwards when my cousins came to carry him. I wanted to be able to tell someone who would not only listen but marvel; no, more than that, I wanted a listener who would be spellbound. I wanted to share all of it with someone who would be transfixed as I was by the rosiness that filled my father's room, by his utter radiance, by the chinaberries that made music and were lighted from within like tiny glowing paper lanterns floating on water at a river festival. I felt isolated from everyone because I couldn't share my experience.

Then one night at the theatre, lingering in the wings to see if the stage manager—waiting for another rise in the applause— would cue us to take a third call, I heard an actor talking softly with his wife who'd come backstage to meet him. He was Alonzo, an Italian actor who had a small part because his English was still accented, fine for movies but not so much for the stage. His wife was American and she was helping him to get rid of every trace of his accent. She was whispering to Alonzo. I couldn't quite hear but it was something about his performance. He interrupted her suddenly, angrily. So the stage manager had to hold up his hand to quiet him although Alonzo wasn't as close to the stage as I was. Still the audience hears just about everything that goes on in the wings.

"You can't know this!" the actor protested to his wife. "There is no way on earth you can know this unless you stand here, in my shoes, in my place, in my heart."

Alonzo's wife put her hands on his shoulders but he shook them off. He started to stride away when the stage manager hissed at him to take his place; he'd decided on another curtain call for us.

We jostled one another in the darkness to get to our places, a bunch of tired, sweating actors whose make-up was beginning to cake or run, whose transcendence was starting to wear off like Novocain; all of us like balloons slowly deflating.

Then the curtains parted with the soft dragging sound of heavy velvet on wood and we came alive. In perfect unison we took our one allotted step forward on our right foot. And we bowed, we held hands and straightened up, we smiled the blinding smiles of radiant stars. The audience applauded with a resounding wave of approval. We squeezed each other's hands to signal one another we'd decided on a last farewell step forward. Then at the count of three we took our final bow, we smiled, we glowed.

And I happened to think as we were falling from great heights to make our way back to earth after our night's work as artists, that we were as much like a row of trembling red chinaberries as any human beings can be.

Mitchell Stocks

WE CHINESE

OLD PEOPLE WEAR TOO MANY COLORS, like peacocks. Not her. Blouse, the black and white pattern of a loon's back, flows to her knees. White slacks, baggy like those of a Vietnamese, flutter with each dignified step. Black leather purse hangs from the bend in her left arm. Eyes glance between plane ticket and the numbers below the overhead luggage bins.

The center seat is open. She smiles and says pardon, waiting for me to stand so she can pass by. I offer her the aisle seat. Thank you, she says, that is very kind.

She tucks her purse neatly under the seat in front of her. White skin merges with silver hair bound tightly to the top of her slender head. She is a cotton swab dabbed with apple-green eyes and maroon lips, the only notable features on her plain, but pleasant, face.

Mostly to help relieve the discomfort one feels when seated too close to a stranger, I say, are you visiting family?

Before answering, she removes her hat and places it on her lap. It is brimless, black, and trimmed with mesh. The kind Audrey Hepburn wore.

My daughter is with me, she says.

Would you like me to change seats with her?

Thank you. No. She prefers to sit alone.

Perhaps it is common for Americans to sit apart. After all, they are famous for their independence.

The captain tells the flight attendants to prepare for takeoff. She reaches for her purse and removes a small book. I am curious, glimpse left and see *The Five People You Meet in Heaven,* by someone named Mitch Albom.

I am a retired translator for the China Youth Daily. I can read English books but find them tedious. I read Chinese books instead. Histories mainly. I wish I had kept my book with me instead of packing it in my suitcase. Anyway, we Chinese don't worry much about heaven which means we also don't worry much about hell. Americans spend too much time thinking about these things and not enough time thinking about each other.

After we are airborne, the flight attendants ask if we would like something to drink. She requests ginger ale and says thank you when they place it on her tray table. I ask for orange juice without ice. She closes her book as the flight attendant reaches past her to hand me a paper cup. I say thank you and try some more small talk.

May I ask where you are going?

I don't know, she says.

Oh. Then it is a surprise.

You could say that. What is your destination?

I am travelling from Beijing to visit my son and his family in Houston.

That's nice. Yes. When we arrived at the boarding gate in Los Angeles, I noticed this plane was bound for Houston.

Do you travel often?

Occasionally. When my daughter wants to.

Then you stay with your daughter? That must be nice.

I had my own home once, but I suppose it's for the best.

We Chinese prefer to live with our family, but I understand. When my son and his family moved to Houston from Chicago six years ago, I had expected an invitation to live with them. The invitation did not come. You see, I don't drive. And in Houston, one cannot go anywhere without driving.

She has closed her eyes. Her back is straight, and her hands clasp her hat as if she is praying. I have the urge to use the toilet, but she looks so peaceful, I do not wish to disturb her. I allow a few minutes to pass.

Excuse me, I say.

She does not hear me. I have no choice but to reach over and touch her right arm. Her skin is clear and thin and soft, the veins and tendons visible like shrimp in a Cantonese dumpling.

Her eyes open.

Excuse me, I say. So sorry to bother you. She is polite and reaches to unbuckle her seat belt, sparing me from having to say more. She uses her left arm to lift herself up. I graze her leg with mine as I step past her.

When I return, I excuse myself again. She smiles and plants her hands on the armrests to lift herself up. We rearrange ourselves to fit in the cramped space.

A younger woman approaches.

Mother, she says. Is everything all right?

Yes. Quite all right.

I smile at the young woman, a much heavier version of her mother. I am pleased to have made your mother's acquaintance, I say.

I'm Ellen, she says, extending her right hand. She likes to travel by herself. It's best for her to have her own aisle seat on these long flights.

I shake her hand firmly, as my son has taught me to do. My name is Eddie, I say. Eddie Zhou.

My real name is Zhou Di. My son told me that in America I should have an American name, and so he gave me this name, 'Ed-di.'

But I don't yet know your mother's good name, I say. Perhaps you could do me the honor of a proper introduction.

Sure, Ellen says. Her name is Mildred. Mildred Sample, but her friends call her Millie.

This is not what I expect. We learned that a proper Western introduction goes something like this: "Mr. Zhou, this is my mother, Mrs. Sample. Mother, this is Mr. Zhou." We Chinese do not call people in our presence 'him' or 'her' like they are not there, we do not use our parent's first name and we certainly do not reveal familiar names to strangers.

I turn to Mrs. Sample and say, how do you do Mrs. Sample? I am pleased to meet you.

Her green eyes sparkle as if a light shines out of them from the inside. I am fine. Thank you, she says. I am pleased to make your acquaintance as well Mr. Zhou.

Thank you for keeping her company, Ellen says, before returning to her seat.

I want to say, 'what a polite daughter you have. You must be very proud,' but I am from the north and cannot bring myself to say something that is so far from the truth.

Instead I try to move the conversation past this awkward moment. Mrs. Sample, I say. Will you do anything special during your visit?

Not that I know of, Mr. Zhou.

I am sure your daughter has big plans. Maybe that too is a surprise.

How about you Mr. Zhou? What might your plans be?

I will see my grandchildren. They were born in America and speak to me in good American English. I am a proud grandfather.

In truth, my grandchildren no longer know their mother tongue, and because of that, my son and daughter-in-law do not speak to me in Chinese when the children are present. They are like the lizards I once saw on television. The ones that surrender a limb to escape their attackers. They must lose something to gain something else, a limb for their freedom.

Mrs. Sample asks me if I would watch her purse. I say, yes, of course. I notice she says 'restroom' instead of 'toilet.'

She grips the headrests with her right hand to steady herself as she moves up the aisle. On the way back, she pauses to speak with her daughter who is seated in the center aisle five rows ahead of us. Mrs. Sample's face does not glow like a mother's should when speaking with her daughter. As Mrs. Sample departs, her eyes narrow, her lips tighten and a worry line appears, like a dry river bed, down the center of her white forehead. It is the face of an old person suppressing the kind of tears only a child can cause. After a few steps, Mrs. Sample stops, turns and makes her way back to the restroom one headrest at a time.

When she returns, the rims of her eyes and nostrils glow bright red. The added color has awakened her bland face. I want to tell her that red suits her, but I know this is not a polite thing to say on this occasion. Instead, I ask Mrs. Sample if she will be staying long, forgetting for a moment that she does not know where she is going or who she is visiting.

No. Mr. Zhou. I never know how long I will be staying. I guess you could say it is part of the surprise.

But this cannot be part of any surprise. Mrs. Sample is queen of her chess board, regal, but moved without consultation like a pawn. Perhaps I might distract this kind lady from her troubles. Perhaps I might provide some comfort from her sadness.

Mrs. Sample, I say. I hope you won't think it too forward of me, but I must confess a fondness for the dignified way you carry yourself. So rare today. You must come from a cultured family?

Why Mr. Zhou, I am flattered by your kind words. Quite the opposite I am afraid. My parents lost our ranch during the Depression. My father worked the rest of his life as a hired hand on the very place his grandfather had homesteaded in his youth.

And your good mother. What of her?

She raised eight children, five boys and three girls, with only a grade school education. But she made sure we all had choices. Mine was to teach school. I suppose if there is any dignity in me, it came from facing a room full of unruly farm children for forty-two years.

Yes. That explains it. Teaching is the most noble of professions. Those who teach earn the respect of all those who enter their classroom. I am sure you are a fine teacher, Mrs. Sample. And I am equally sure you have enriched the lives of many students.

Well. Some of my former students do contact me from time to time. It is heartwarming to know they still remember me.

I have finally diverted Mrs. Sample's attention from her unwanted surprises. Old people do not like surprises. Maybe this is why my two prior visits to Houston were not as joyful as they should have been. Too many surprises. Surprised by the way my grandchildren speak to their parents, surprised by the way my son speaks to his wife and she to him. Surprised by the food and the confinement. Surprised by feeling like a guest in the home of my own son.

The pilot interrupts to tell us that we have begun our descent. The line to the restroom extends deep into the middle of the plane. Mrs. Sample was wise to have gone when she did. I decide to wait. A few minutes later, a flight attendant directs the passengers back to their seats.

We exit the plane together. I tell Mrs. Sample to go ahead, judging that Ellen is impatient and that I can overtake them after a brief stop. I reach the restroom just in time to save myself from embarrassment.

I leave the restroom without drying my hands. I hurry to reach Mrs. Sample. Ellen lumbers like a water buffalo five steps ahead of us. She glances back to see if we are keeping pace. Mrs. Sample walks in her dignified manner, purse swaying from the bend in her left arm, Audrey Hepburn hat resting elegantly on her head. I am pleased to accompany such a poised woman.

Ellen turns again and says, hurry mother, we have another flight to catch.

So Houston is not their destination after all. This sounds like more of a surprise than Mrs. Sample can bear. Ellen stops in front of a departure kiosk and searches for their gate. She points in the direction opposite the sign to the baggage claim. Even though we Chinese do not interfere in other people's business, I do so now.

Ellen, if I may be so bold. What is your final destination so that I may offer Mrs. Sample and you a proper farewell?

Why it's El Paso, she says.

Thank you. And who will your good selves be visiting in El Paso?

My brother, Alvin.

And if I may, how long will you be staying with brother Alvin?

Really, Mr. Zhou. Is this necessary? We have a plane to catch.

I'm sorry to be such a bother. But yes. It is necessary. For the farewell you see.

If you must know, I will be returning next week, but she will stay for two or three months until other arrangements can be made.

I see. Then on to my farewell. I wish you a pleasant stay with your brother Alvin in El Paso and that you understand that I mean no offense when I say we Chinese . . .

I'm afraid we have no more time for nonsense, Ellen says as she grips Mrs. Sample by her bent arm and turns her in the direction of their gate, leaving me to swallow my half-finished sentence.

By the time I reach the baggage claim, some passengers are dragging their luggage off the conveyor while others hold their ground with anxious faces. I do not see my son among the people standing just beyond a low wall separating the baggage claim from the arrival area. Then I remember that he always waits for me curbside so he doesn't have to park.

I find a less crowded spot where the unclaimed bags disappear into the wall. After a few minutes pass, I see my brown plaid suitcase moving towards me. I grab it with both hands, jerk it from the conveyor and bring it to rest on its four wheels. I remove a strap from the pocket, attach it and pull the suitcase towards the gap in the low wall. A middle-aged Caucasian man in a green and white uniform checks my claim ticket. He waves me towards the automatic doors that flutter open and closed as passengers spill onto the sidewalk.

I sit on an empty bench and remember my first visit to Houston. One afternoon, I went for a long walk in my son's neighborhood. The houses all looked the same, and the streets curved and ended abruptly in circles. My son found me after dark sitting on the curb under a sign that said 'Not a Through Street.' I was not afraid. I am too old for that. But my son was. That was why he did not speak to me on the ride home and why he raised his voice and told me in front of his family never to wander off like that again. And so when the subject of where I would stay came up, we all thought it best that I return to Beijing where the streets are not curved and they do not end abruptly in circles.

Don Schofield

SHEPHERD

Above the canyon road I saw a shepherd
descending toward me, crook behind his neck,
wrists dangling, whistling softly. *Ti kaneis?*
he asked and looked me in the eyes as I
continued on, not wanting then to stop
or talk or lose the pain of loss, the knowledge
that parting's now inevitable. *How are you?*
he asked again, this time insisting, so
I stopped. I saw his tanned and wrinkled face,
his pitted, curving nose, eyes deep-set
and kind. He asked me where I'm going,
adding that he's seen me walking here
before, and then, *Do you have children?* "No."
Married? "Yes, for now." *So why no kids?*
with a look of grave concern. Then where I'm from
and where I work and what I pay for rent.

I asked in turn where he was from (*Albania*),
how long in Greece (*For years*), how old (*Fifty*),
and where he lived. He pointed to the depths
of Thermi Canyon. "Children?" *Yes, a boy,
sixteen, back home in Korçë, still in school.*
Then where he takes his herd and who he sells
them to and at what price and isn't herding
dangerous since trucks come barreling down

the slope. "And when your son is done with school

will he come work with you?" He scratched his head

at that, said, *Let's go have an ouzo* one day.

His flock came leaping down the cliff just then.

I saw them spread across the asphalt, rams

with heavy curled horns and faces lined

as if with grief, ewes skittering off, their young

not keeping up. Surrounded by a hundred

tinkling bells, the clop of hooves, the stench

and coarseness of their hides, their heavy breath

against my wrists, those penetrating eyes. . .

I know I heard him say, *We'll walk these roads,*

you and me. At dawn we'll wake the goats

and press them up what ridge we choose. At dusk

my wife will take your coat and set you close

to the fire, pour a glass of tsipouro.

"Relax," she'll say, "Take off your shoes and stay

right here. You've nothing left to lose."

By then his goats had bounded down a narrow

path. I looked at him and he at me. We knew

we'd never have that ouzo, never could be

friends. I thanked him for his company,

went up the road as he went down. Now nothing

left to do but shepherd what I've lost

and make our way back home.

Iris Jamahl Dunkle

How to Cope in a New Landscape

First, learn the promise of water. Listen
to the wind, believe what it will carry.

Get a shovel, dig. Under every
town there is a secret room no-one talks about.

Sometimes, this room is spotless. But sometimes,
it contains a small, forgotten child.

Work tirelessly to retrieve the child
even if no one says that she exists.

Second, learn to forget the press of fog,
the sharp taste of salt in the air. Forget

the landscape you've stitched into your skin. Wash
yourself in the new air—no matter how cold.

Third, step off of the crumbling asphalt
onto the spongy earth. Find acceptance

in what rebuilds each Spring. No matter where
you end up there will be birds, some unknown.

Identify them. Follow their jagged
ascent. Identify trees and common

plants and animals. Don't infer meaning

from names alone. Look deep into the woods

until you see what was unseen. Soon a

song will rise in your throat.

Melissa Roberts-Fishman

RESURGAM: PORTLAND, MAINE

"The task of history as a cliché / about forgetting." —Susan Stewart

Palimpsest

of cobblestone, asphalt, and packed, potholed dirt wedged

      between low buildings—

            scaly, edge-

eaten, salt-scrubbed skins

of board, aluminum, plywood, rust, bird shit, and moss—

      that lean together,

          hunched,

as if to hold themselves up

under the wharf's insane rooflines where clutches

      of miserable pigeons

          cling to buckling eaves

and exposed tarps fray

and flap, like flags of a gentler, fallen country, over the easy

      down-shifting of weight-

          bearing walls.

Four times

this city burned to the ground, torched first in 1676

      after some English fishermen taunted

         a native girl

upended her birch bark canoe and tossed her baby in the icy river

       to see if a papoose

              would swim

on its own accord.

The young mother pulled the infant out alive,

       but her baby died

             of exposure.

The briny air

on the wharf today is thick and damp; the gulls master it,

       soar over dumpsters,

             complain, perch

like kings.

Inside the fish market, buckets of lobsters just off the boat

       clack their red-black,
             banded claws.

The second time, 1689,
native warriors razed the city *until nothing remained*
       save burnt foundation pilings....
        the brittle skulls

and empty ribcages

of the slaughtered settlers left in scattered heaps

       along the shore

           as warning....

Everywhere, beds

of ice hold clean rows of freshly dead

       fish, filets of turbot

and sole glowing

as youth glows;

and whole bodies shimmer in the artificial light,

haddock, striped bass,

branzini—

silver skin

under sheer scales,

the functional pageantry

of fins,

grace

not yet undone by the mouths curved

in varied degrees of gaping

and the big, dead,

milky eyes.

Nearby oysters and clams lie still as stones,

cold, calcified around viscera-

soft insides.

The city slowly rose

again from ruin, its new settlers survived

trading muskets and rum

for fish and pelts,

supplying ship masts

to the Royal Navy, receiving payment in pounds

sterling from the crown

that sailed

its wooden ships

back, mid-October, 1775,

to the stony coast to punish

the rebel militias;

they rained bombs,

mortar, musketry down on the abandoned town

all day until nothing

remained

of the buildings that stood

along the muddy lanes of Lime Alley, King Street,

Love Lane, or Fish Lane

that sloped dorsally

down this way,

to the bay's burnt wharf pilings,

the smoking hulls

of ships.

But up out of the rubble

came another brave century, a newly-won identity,

the muddy lanes turned

to real streets:

Congress, Market,

Exchange, Silver, Free. The new century

sped by steamship

and railroad

through the veins

of citizens drunk on rum

and abundance, and the bright flag

waved

that day a boy

tossed a firecracker into a barrel of wood shavings

on the fourth of July 1866

setting the city

ablaze.

The beams of the Sugar House burned, history says,

like napalm. The fire blasted

through the city

like a blowtorch

until eighteen hundred buildings and three hundred twenty

acres of city were *reduced*

to black ash.

Rebuilt with now-

predictable grit, branded with motto—*I shall rise again*—

and symbol, phoenix, fiery, false, so we know

today's accidents

of patriotism, too,

will become the ash that softens our footfalls, we

who glory in the blind erasures

of transformation.

Quotations from A Concise History of Portland, Maine by John B. Robinson

Jaydn DeWald

EPITHALAMIUM (OR, LANDSCAPE WITH SOLDIER)

My husband stands, among our green tomatoes,

    In the Kabul square. More and more, I fail him:

        I remain on the patio, slathering chicken wings

With barbecue sauce,

        and do not enter our past—

    Wandering Vienna before sunrise, for example,

        With the shopkeepers hosing down their walks—

        And thus forget him, my husband, my husband,

Before the war messed with his head.

        He is not

    In the Kabul square, in other words. He is here,

        In our gated sideyard, facing the lavender light—

The way all soldiers, at one time, looked to me:

    Watching the recruits, through my car window,

        Upon the purple hills, nose pressed to the glass.

        More and more,

            I find this distance pleasurable:

I, in the patio's dappled shadework, watch him—

    Setting the two halves of an apricot on the grill—

Jaydn DeWald

And feel, again, that pent-up, long-ago longing,

With which he might be restored.

My husband

Whose face is fixed upon our wilted cornfields;

Whose arms hang at his sides, massive, useless,

On such a meditative evening; whose red mind

Sees red alone—no, no:

you must not believe it.

You must walk up to him, over windbent grass,

Over wisteria petals, and caress his lower back,

His hulking shoulders, his little sunburned ears,

Even when he moves forward, then looks back—

Like you: remembering him, in the Prater Park,

Under the chestnut trees,

thronged with leaves.

Brent van Staalduinen

BUDDY'S MIRROR

*YOU WAKE UP AND FEEL LIKE YOU'LL
never be able to tell the difference between the grey clouds and the
smoke. Your head aches so bad you dream about puking. The stench is
so thick you swear you could roll it between your fingers like Plasticine.
You're sweating hard and you worry about heat stroke as you pee
yellow, so yellow, like syrup. Tiny needles of itching threaten to rip
your crotch to bits. Your socks are more thread than fabric, and no
matter what you try you can't wash the salt stains from your armpits.*

 You think about dying.

 *Not enough to kill yourself, but enough to know that
sometimes suicide's not as crazy as everyone thinks it is. You know
for a fact you're not crazy. The chaplain says that everyone deals
with mortality in different ways. Everyone. As though you weren't
alone. As though Buddy sitting next to you is scratching himself and
thinking the same thing.*

And that's what gets your ass out of the sack every morning, ready to face the same windowless walls that ache to kill you.

    I didn't believe Buddy when he told me. Sat me down and laid it all out, like a guru who'd seen it all. As though I'd climbed the highest peak to see him rather than just up the elevator and past the nursing station. The amazing thing is that he was younger than I am. I don't want to sound cliché but, man, they were right when they said you could read it in their eyes—you couldn't stuff anything more mechanical into his skull. When he talked it was as though his emotions had been replaced with cement. He just talked and stared and scratched. The antibiotics had killed the infection. The memories still made him claw at himself.

    My decision was purely financial, I said. It was hard to shock Mom and Dad. But what about school, they'd asked. I told them that the registrar had intervened and promised to re-register me when I returned: "Good for you. They need you over there," the grey man behind the desk had said and then returned to his paperwork.

    Dad was more careful. "I know you volunteered," he said, "you don't have to go." I told him it was a part of being a soldier. I told him that they needed medics and that I wanted to go. I told him that it wasn't combat it was peacekeeping. I told him I wouldn't be part of it. I told him about the money: basic rate plus isolation pay plus danger pay plus displacement allowance, and it was tax free. My dad hated taxes, as though the danger and isolation were secondary. So that's the argument I adopted. "It's good money," I'd say to anyone who asked, "and it looks good on my resume."

    But my professional prospects were as far from my decision as the registrar was. I had never forgotten Grandad's face the day he died: grey, dry, lined. For the first time since adolescence he'd had a shave in the afternoon, and folded hands, the irony of the peaceable atheist. The way his skin was cool to touch, not cold like people said, cool. Before, I had always enjoyed those wrinkling valleys and the sandpaper stubble of his face when he spoke; its new stillness was as unfamiliar to me as the surface of the moon. I pulled a chair up and sat with him for an hour.

    I wanted to see what real death was like. The way it really is, not like CNN's jumpy images of grainy explosions and after-the-fact cleanups: so distant, so sanitized, so clean. I would love to explain it, but no one asks. People wouldn't have understood my real reasons, like there's no way to see it without participating in it.

    But it's impossible not to be a part of it, really. Six months of training then off you go. Great promises of worthiness, as though the world should stand and applaud our nobility on the six o'clock news.

    We'd arrived in late afternoon. The bunker was new. No ventilation yet. Hot. It smelled of canvas and rubber as we trundled in with cots, foot powder, sleeping bags, barracks boxes, rifles, pillows, rucksacks, radios, ammunition, web gear, soap, toothpaste, gas masks, flip flops, pictures, and detcord. We had new desert boots, new helmets, new blue berets, new satellite phones, new pistols, new underwear, new all-weather matches, and new field caps. I had new combats, new body armor, new socks, a new blue ball cap, new rain gear, new pens, new medical bag, and new Red Cross stickers to put on everything. They promised to send stencils and spray paint for the final, permanent red crosses. I put one on my first letter home, reassuring, as though it was bulletproof.

"Get squared away," McNicoll had said, like he'd been there longer than we had. We just sat there and sweated, draped over our piles of gear like khaki tarpaulins.

"It's Eastern Europe, for God's sake, why's it so hot?" asked Buddy in the far corner. I felt dizzy and sick from unloading the truck; my first casualty, I thought, and I hadn't even unpacked my sleeping bag. I drained my canteen, grabbed my web gear, and went out to grab an extra water jerry.

It took me almost an hour. The bunker was cooler when I got back. Some engineer had rigged a meat locker fan between the sandbags and the roof. Sacrifice: one window. Somehow everyone had sacked out despite the constant whining from the overtaxed fan motor. Loud as hell, but it cooled us off. I unpacked my gear alone.

That night, McNicoll said that the CO hadn't known we'd arrived. Strange baptism, it seemed, to be forgotten. So we went to bed early; it was cool enough to sleep. A bunch of snoring cocoons, lying in the dusty corners of a bunker, a million miles from anyone we knew. The fan noise drowned out the snoring. I dreamt of red crosses and high school and meat locker fans whining, whining, whining.

I lay awake as the bunker grew stuffy and smelled of sleeping men. Buddy ran through the door yelling, "Stand to! Stand to!" He was very concerned. His flashlight flitted from face to face, and he fidgeted while we dressed in the danc-ing flash-lit darkness, groggy and bleary. Pants. Shirt. Boots. Helmet. Pistol. Buddy looked at Buddy then Buddy for instructions. Confusion. No one moved. McNicoll, in charge, swore, grabbed his web gear and stormed out, half dragging the offending soldier, leaving me in charge. The fan whined on. I turned on my flashlight; its red filter dimly illuminated a half-dozen expectant faces looking for guidance. I heard myself tell them to hold tight, then walked out.

We hadn't heard the shot that killed Buddy. Caught him on the way back from the latrine, buttoning up his combats. McNicoll and an anonymous lieutenant shone their flashlights on Buddy all sprawled in the dirt as cold as a museum exhibit. Some medic administered CPR. He stopped, shook his head and sat back. The bullet had caught Buddy under the rim of his helmet, which lay in the dirt a few feet away. No one returned the sniper's fire. The rules said that we weren't allowed to, unless he shot at someone who wasn't already dead. We just stood around waiting for the sniper to decapitate someone else. He didn't. Buddy just lay there, obscenely splashed with white light as his brains soaked into the ground.

I stayed and watched while Buddy was zippered into a body bag then went back to bed, my introduction to violent death fading like a bad movie.

You can't imagine the anticlimax. Months of anticipation, intense training, and all you do is walk the same patrol route day in, day out, hoping that someone doesn't feel like blue helmet target practice. Sometimes, you get to ride the white iron horses bristling with virgin weapons. They shoot over you at each other. You crawl over the landscape, fat, white maggots peaceably cradling your rifles and hoping never to use them or even imagine the reality of where you are.

I'm looking at my third case of heat exhaustion. Buddy complains about the treated water: "Hate that shit. Smells like a fucking swimming pool," he says. I forgo yet another medic's I-know-best-so-listen-to-me speech and give him my best don't-fuck-with-the-heat look.

"I forgot to drink," he says. "Landmines, you know."

A cow had triggered a bounding mine the day before, cutting its owner clean in half. The old man had lay down beside the crossing, dead and bloody, while nearby his cow stood against a fence, its side torn open by shrapnel, trying to graze but too weak to do so. The old farmer had been a lost cause so I did what I could for the cow. Sacrifice: two 9mm rounds between the eyes and a chunk of my psyche for watching a cow live through the first bullet. The quartermaster had looked surprised when I handed him my magazine short two rounds.

He laughed when I told him. I hadn't thought it was funny.

"I know," I tell Buddy, who's not interested in my memories and whines about the water and his growing dizziness.

The road's melted, and our section walks on the shoulder. The guys are edgy. Gravel's the best for hiding landmines, so the engineers sweep the shoulder first. Slow. Irony spills into our labors: this is what we call "quick-time country," open and dangerous.

Every now and again a forgotten landmine vaporizes some unlucky soul, and your patrol stops. The reporters stand off a ways as though they're at a barbeque, away from the smell of charred flesh and shit. You act as though you could ever get used to that smell, and give your candy to dirty, bloodied children and hope it helps.

So death grabs you slowly, gradually. You feel it pulling gently, the way you crave cigarettes. An extra look here, a longer pause there. You don't even realize it.

I'm thinking about how thankful I am that I'm not infantry: months of patrols, stopping, starting, waiting for your tax-free million-dollar round. Long hours spent pacing between two armies who don't care if you're in the way. Almost never shooting back, never really knowing the satisfaction of real combat.

I am glad that I'm as restricted as I am; I'm almost not allowed to think about combat. So I fix people. Medical thinking helps pass the time: save some, lose others.

I move the salt tablets to the top of the bag and wonder if I'll lose anyone from heat stroke. No matter how many times I lecture them, they're always forgetting to drink enough water. "Heat stroke'll kill you just as dead as bullets," I say. They nod and smile and forget about it two days later. Buddy from Bravo Company had cried just before he went into a coma. His body had shut down hours before we sent him to the field hospital. There's nothing harder to watch than a man cry without tears. He made it back to Canada. Probably.

McNicoll calls a halt and stands in front of me, sweating. I notice the large salt stains on his body armor and pull out a salt tablet.

"I can't believe this heat," he says, swallowing the tablet dry. "How many guys are down?"

I tell him.

He grunts then looks at the overcast. "It's not supposed to be this hot. Indian summer, we'd call it. Wonder what it's called here?"

I say I don't know. A white helicopter chatters by towards the buildings on the horizon. McNicoll seems to be waiting for something as we shift uncomfortably. I imagine we must look strange, a small army of green with bright blue helmets waiting beneath the umbrella of someone else's war. I notice for the first time that I can't hear gunfire.

"It's quiet today," I tell McNicoll.

I almost expect him to say that it's too quiet, like in the movies. It feels like a movie, what we're doing, moving frame by frame and hoping the film stays on its guides. McNicoll says nothing. He's edgy too, unhappy about the necessity of waiting in the open. I keep moving, restless, to stave off boredom. Salt tablet here, foot powder further down the line for jock itch, ibuprofen for the strained knee that I think is bad enough to send Buddy home. We wait for the engineers to finish their sweep and pray that the screen writers don't pencil in a mortar round.

The artillery rounds screaming overhead sound like freight trains. We never hear the guns in the valleys, just the wailing, an eerie reminder of our fragile steps under this deadly sky. Buddy looks up at the sound and shudders; unease, contagious, ripples through the section.

"Like waiting for the sky to fall and not wearing a fucking raincoat," someone yells.

McNicoll gives Buddy in front a shove. "Move," he says.

The buildings grow. Our spirits fade. We weave through twisted concrete, craters, and pockmarks, the staples of village life. Hunched figures move through the wreckage, spirits that drift through the constant haze. These are the few brave souls. Others seek privacy in the corners and holes, away from our unfamiliar eyes and safe from random bullets. We feel the same way. A bond. A growing mental reprieve from the destruction and the graffiti. Growing. Like cancer.

The section tenses as we pass the first ruins. Speed is a new enemy; it blinds a person here, where nooks and holes are both refuge and danger. "Never look where your weapon's not pointed," I remember from Basic. I finger my holstered pistol and stroke the red cross on my bag.

The echoed shooting reaches every ear simultaneously. Sounds bounce off the walls and shattered buildings, piercing and surrounding us, as though we've been thrown blindfolded into a concert hall. McNicoll fingers his rifle, clicking his safety on and off. Once. Twice.

You know they're not shooting at you. Doesn't matter. You get to cover and try to be invisible. You almost wish they would so you could do something. It's like porn – you only watch.

We're bathed in gunfire that drives noise into our bellies—it's not like the movies at all, polite machine gun chattering in your ears. No, you feel it in your gut the way you feel boxing gloves. Cordite stings our nostrils as we feel bullets smack into the walls inches from where we've pressed ourselves. I'm caught between studying the pattern of pockmarks in the wall and trying to melt into it when McNicoll collapses next to me.

"Jesus," he yells.

"What the hell is happening?" I shout in his ear. I wonder if he can hear my voice crack.

"Somebody's making a push," he says. Red tracers streak like lasers between the buildings and over our heads. So fucking close. Never been this close before—are they shooting at us? One in five's a tracer; I'd never see the other four. The antenna from Buddy's radio dances as McNicoll yells at the crackling voice in the handset. He yells something in my ear about spacing. I can barely hear him. My head feels as if it'll split my helmet and I'm caught between screaming and puking. My eardrums must be bleeding—I hope McNicoll can hear me.

He shakes his head. "We have to wait it out."

"But they're shooting at us," yells Buddy with the radio. McNicoll doesn't answer. I know what he'd say, though: we'd be in a lot more trouble if they were.

McNicoll points at Buddy behind the concrete flowerpot and shouts. Buddy starts as though his parents had just caught him with his hand up some girl's shirt.

I see where McNicoll wants him ("Damn flowerpot wouldn't stop a snowball," he adds). Buddy gets up and runs across the street, hands over his crotch like he's facing a penalty kick. The shot stops him. I watch his hands—they're still stuck in his groin—as he folds face-first into the pavement. Someone broke the rules, I tell myself, as Buddy lies in the middle of the street like a pothole.

McNicoll drags Buddy under cover; I hear a snap as a bullet catches him in the shoulder. He's a stone, not a noise even though the pain must be unimaginable. So silently he drips blood all over Buddy.

Buddy doesn't care. I see the others looking. They know Buddy's dead and that they're statistically safe, but they'd gladly crawl through McNicoll's exit wound to get away. I'm mentally writing out forms in triplicate as McNicoll slumps, faint, against our wall. Somehow he finds voice enough to yell about conserving ammunition. I try not to tell him about the fist I could stick through the hole in his shoulder.

Buddy down the line points and yells, jumps up—McNicoll wants to scream at him but can't—and empties his magazine into a dark, crumbling window. We're not here for this, I know. We're here to watch, not shoot at blind buildings. I should say something. I'm second in command but there's no way they'd listen to me now. I catch blurred movement out of the corner of my eye as the section storms the building. Fuck.

I hope the shooter is dead before they get there. Building assaults. Bloody and fatal. I hate them more than syphilis.

My hands are gloved, yet I can still feel the warmth of McNicoll's blood as I rip open a field dressing. I'm alone with McNicoll and dead Buddy whose eyes are wide open as though he expects me to say something. I know that it's not quiet, but I can't hear the violence—I've sucked myself into a soundproof tube. My headache seems out of place, a holdout, hung over. I feel as if I've had my ears boxed; my field of vision jumps and dances as though I'm watching through a Handycam. Through the ringing, I sense an explosion of light and noise as I tighten McNicoll's field dressing. I have to do this right, I say to myself, I'll be damned if I lose McNicoll from a shoulder wound. A puff of air, a first-kiss breath, brushes against my cheek as I stuff McNicoll's shoulder with dressings. God, that stings, I think as I see drops of blood—my blood?—on McNicoll's sleeve. McNicoll points suddenly behind me—he's trying to bring his rifle around but can't, because of his wound.

I don't even think. My virgin pistol is suddenly in my hand and roaring, pounding, kicking. I'm willing the bullets through the barrel at somebody—anybody—and I'm yelling as if I'd been insulted in a bar fight. I point and point and point and pull until I'm clicking at nothing but empty street. I turn back to McNicoll and add another bandage, swearing to myself that I'm not ready for this shit.

McNicoll places his good hand on my wrist and stares at something behind me. I look, and for a moment think that Buddy has moved. But the eyes are closed. There are no lines on the grey, peaceful face. His camouflaged green hat is askew, and covers his long, dark hair and the smear of blood on his jaw. His AK-47 leans against

Buddy and its bayonet digs into the asphalt. It's not Buddy, but he's just as dead all right, his uniform mottled with wet, black spots. McNicoll looks at the pistol in my hand and at the body. He's trying to speak, I know, but I'm distracted by my pistol's unfamiliar warmth. I'm saying things to him now, about being okay and help is on the way and I'm looking at his identity disks and looking for the radio operator I'm looking everywhere at once but I can't look further down the street at the man I've killed.

I wonder about what I've done and I don't really feel anything other than the blistering adrenaline in my veins. I'm amazed at my indifference and lack of philosophical reflection. Calmly, yet with my hands distantly shaking, I pop out the magazine, notice that it's empty, drop it, rustle through my web gear, and slide in a new one. The reporters are still cowering behind us, retreating into their scratch pads and clicking cameras. I turn back to McNicoll's wound, noting absently that I'll have to answer for what I've done. Maybe a medal, maybe something more serious.

But above all, I count the missing rounds in my head and I wonder what I'll say to the quartermaster because God knows I can't stand to have him laugh at me again.

You feel like you should be excited, or jittery, or ashamed. You get home a few months later and people saw it on the news and everyone wants to know what it's like. Only you can't tell them, because you weren't really there. It was someone else that drew his weapon without thinking and took a life. It was someone else who, after, struggled to keep McNicoll alive long enough to get to the hospital, forgetting about the violence of death and the smell of blood on his uniform. You can't explain this, because there's no way to make it sound real, no way to explain how survival is a kind of escape. And yet they want it all, as though you can eject the video and run it for them in their family-room. Rewind. And again.

The right thing, the wrong thing. Doesn't matter now, even though months and years have filled the gap, and reflection is only as clear as the day itself, blurry and blotchy. There's no line, no boundary. And all you keep thinking as you stare and fade away that the only difference between then and now is that by now the pistol barrel's cooled down and you could put it back into your holster if you wanted to.

Robin Michel

THE BOY AND THE MOON

—for Giovanni

How many months of your tender life
have you and the moon been in deep conversation
as I have held your growing body next to mine,
eavesdropping with delight?
Little Poet, will words be your salvation, too?

At home, the stuffed lions in your crib
roar their ferocious roars
and the storybook roosters
crow their cock-a-doodle-do
and in this wide open
world outside
the moon walks with you.
Is he a cool and remote father,
all too often absent and asleep?
Or is she a mercurial mother who weeps
a galaxy of broken stars when each night falls?

"*Hello,*" you whisper. "*Hello.*" I hug you tight.
What lies before you as you walk this uneven path
lit by a careless moon?
Will you remember to open wide your arms
and scoop up joy when beauty falls from the sky?

Will you find the words to keep you safe and whole?

Please. Thank you. Goodbye.

"*Hello,*" I whisper. "*Hello.*"

Heather Altfeld

ANNALS OF THE ORPHELINES

I. The Boxcar

Pretend our parents are dead.

And we had to go to the funeral

but we got to wear new dresses.

Here is a handful of Johnny jump-ups

and two little stones you can see from the window

with their names engraved in crayon.

And we can visit them sometimes,

if we want to. Pretend that we live

beneath the dining table

which is really a train-car full of cookies

whistling on to that place in the mountains

where we can pitch our new tent

with the windowed ceiling

and look out at the lake of stars.

II. The Swim

Or pretend that we are going to drown in the lake.

I mean, pretend that we are pretending

to drown in the lake. Make your glasses

float in the water so everyone thinks we are dead.

Then let's swim down into the little hole at the bottom

and out the other side and have our picnic

in the mossy shade with chopped-up eggs

and apricots from the tree.

And pretend we brought our blankets with us

in the tunnel we swam through

in case we are cold at night. And we can sing

the alligator king song

and the lantern song

if you are afraid.

III. The Drawing

I am already invisible. Pretend I am not here

and that you can't see me

because I am already gone.

and you can't hear what I am singing

because my song is invisible.

I have gone deep into the trash can

and out through the underground tunnel of light.

I am off traveling to the houses

of other disappeared children.

We are very busy

having snow-cones and grape ices.

I know how yesterday I was your heart contracted with joy

and today I am not even going to be

the warmth in your kitchen.

Don't worry. I have a satchel

of blank photograph paper and tin plates

that I can use to see you

and a looking-glass to see myself

if I get lonely.

IV. The List

In the grain elevator north of town

I composed some important lists.

Things to take with me

when I really leave. Games

that can be played alone.

Photos I have taken

recklessly in poor light. Core samples

from my certainties. Things I will need

when I am gone. Who I will miss.

Who will miss me. The last list

is scrunched onto a tiny square of graph paper

and is composed mostly of elderly spinsters

who thistle up in houses

and still read newsprint with their tea.

Not even the town parakeets

will notice the missing morsels of bread

I traded for their cheeps.

V. What we saw in the snow

Sleds are for gliding,

bicycles for riding. Ropes are for jumping

if you want to stay in place.

At the bundle of fog at the bank of the river

some other children were gilded

to the ditch. Moat-children

with popguns in their pockets,

faces cracked and smeary

with oil tar. Someone had said

let's pretend to be lily pads

and sleep above the tadpoles,

with our ears plugged deaf like god.

What a dumb game. Like freeze-tag

in the middle of the road, or statues

in the boulevard. And now they are

being pulled from the sloughs

like wishing-well buckets

with rope and some dogs.

Sleds are for gliding, hay carts for riding.

This is the hour that you are still real.

Away down the hill, past the clay village

and into the powdery light.

VI. Pewter

Fifty pewter digging spoons ago,

everything was a hatch to elsewhere.

inside the sea-shell was a lighthouse

inside the sugared egg, a tulip-house

in the mouse-cove at the baseboard

there is a thimble-vase

full of butter-and-egg flowers

and a tiny pub and a plate of cheese and crackers.

Inside the little cave in the mountain

there is a room tiled with jewels

and in the glimmery room there is a tomb

with someone expecting you.

And so I kept digging.

But when every doorway

was just a pillar of dirt

and I was a stone in the quarry

I had to invent my own country.

I said goodbye and thank you. I said goodnight.

I exited through the hole in my body

filled with light

and willed all my spoons

to the wind.

VII. The Voyage

And now I am going to pretend

to be dead. Like one of those

frozen children skating in the blue blue

icing pond on a birthday cake.

I will marry myself off to the hole of light

as my scarf slaps at my cold cheek.

So now the towns get smaller and smaller.

From the mirror it is only blinking lights behind

and the familiar trees catching my tailwinds.

And then it is only a road

with the memories scooped out of the window

into the passing scenery. And even being able

to remember was fleeing my heart

through the buttonholes. My breast pocket

forgetting the shape of hankies.

The radio off so I could pretend

music had never been invented. I did not want

to be reminded of anything.

I had to imagine every wind

touching my skin through the window

was a brand-new wind,

that the mountains I was seeing

were a new country, that the small lump

of cash in my pocket was a foreign currency.

I could be empty, swallowed

by the sky, instead of being the one

trying to swallow it.

Matthew Keuter

VERISIMILITUDE AND OTHER UNTRUTHS

1

The table says
> She's waiting for a letter

The letter says
> When the pain starts like a motorcycle in the morning

The painkiller says
> Take with beer

The sunny girl said
> Wait for the night

After dark she said
> Can't you see what you're doing?

First she said
> Buy me a drink, and we'll see

The last day of our marriage
> Asked for the key

2

The wind says
> Walk with the cold Easterly in your nose
> Back to your Western hovel

The day-moon says
> Tonight will be no different

The moon in the raindrop says
> Go to touch the earth

The ants in the garden say
> Funny moon, that's what we were thinking

The full moon says
> I like children running in circles
> Laughing their heads off

The tide
  Swallowed the great lung-shaped rock
  Where you stood in June, singing hymns, and casting ashes

   3

The feather in the cap says
  I should have been a painter

The poem says
  Just write what comes up

The poet says
  It's hardly enough

The poem says
  Cross that, try this

The poet
  Vanity!

The poem
  Humility

The painter to the poet
  What makes you think I have money to lend?

   4

Letter to John Berryman
  Bless your soul

Letter to Anne Sexton
  Bless your soul

Letter to Virginia Woolf
  Bless your soul

Letter to Sylvia Plath
  Bless your soul

Letter to Spalding Gray
  Bless your soul

The clairvoyant
>*A great sadness awaits you*

5

The river says
>Have you come alone?

The black-slate rock asks
>For your clothes before walking into the river

The river mirrors
>The clouds

The clouds mirror
>The river

The snake enters the river
>It's shedding becoming another cloud of the river

6

The woman at the bar says
>C'mere

The man at the table says
>I'd leap the table if it weren't for my beer

The kiss says
>This is love, so here is my tongue

The jukebox
>Is my retirement plan

The bartender says
>I ought to be sorry, but I'm not

The trumpet says
>Turn the tables! Break their legs! Dance!

The tables
>Yes do it, we're exhausted

The man at the bar says
>That's my ex-wife at the jukebox
>Wanna know the next 5 tunes?

7

The folktale says
>   Shh. Don't tell them in the brighthouse
>   That we're talking about them

The brighthouse
>   Come on in, if your hands are clean

The window at night
>   Go out.
>   Get your hands dirty

Dirty hand-prints
>   At the bedroom window

The ghost story around the fire
>   The lady of the house carried the lantern to the barn

The barn fire says
>   It was the lady of the house, I tickled her chin

Gossip in the kitchen
>   Shh. Don't let the lady of the house hear

8

The nail
>   I'll be singing when my sisters fix your coffin lid

The scalpel
>   I'm unconcerned with your dreams

The librarian says
>   In the dream I enter a cavernous library through my closest.
>   There are no books.
>   Bookcases bow under the weight of mason jars.
>   What look like silenced hours drowned in amber

The shrink
>   Stop wailing. It's not as though I've kicked you

The couch
>
> You should hear the Doc when he's alone

After the pain pills
>
> The humming starts

>
> To loosen my tongue
> To your name.

Lynn Tudor Deming

In Gipsies' Cant

—Argot spoken by beggars, hustlers and vagabonds in Great Britain,
starting in the 16th century, often to disguise criminal activity.

You dimber wapping dell, my pretty, winsome girl,
if you flaunt gipsies' cant, a roguish speech, I care not
and will take howsoe'er it comes, just so it come,
will not recant whether thieves' or Pedlar's French,
flowing so plash as we roll it on the tongue, [1]
fine as the King's English, better than, I say.

Marvelous funnel that opens at dusk, whiddling words [2]
to spangle like rain on the roofs, let me patters flash with you; [3]
let me steal your rings, your thimble of ridge; [4]
when my panter is weeping, my quarrons heavy, heal me; [5]
I won't couch a hogshead 'til you simmer wild syrup [6]
to smooth my stutter, brewing delight in the darkey. [7]

Come fresh as a blowen in your horse-drawn rattle, [8]
decked in your downy kicksies, bobbish with knowing rigs, [9]
sly wink of your peeper; only your soothe will do [10]
for me now, else I am lost in mumps and mulligrubs, [11]
lushing blue ruin and heavy wet, fullied to nether sorrows. [12]
When dusks lay heavy, where shall I stalk you, down

in the gin shops, swigging bene bowse, or high [13]

in Andean blooms, traipsing the greenmans in meadow glim? [14]

I squeek as a maunder, snabbled by longing and begging for rhymes, [15]

neither canter nor filcher, nor ready yet for the morning drop, [16]

lilly slats or the winding-sheet. It's your bub and grub [17]

I'm after, by lightmans or darkmans, your swag and rum fambles. [18]

Lass of the moon men, scampsman's trollop, do not bing awast, [19]

but stay; I'm muzzy without you. Lend me your double-tongued squib [20]

and blue plumbs, don't drop me like brimstone. Pour in my ear [21]

your wondrous potion, irresistible diddle, and pass me no flimsies [22]

or flam. Wench of the lyric, straggling on clouds and striding [23]

the wind, quit your sallies and rambles, be my pretty tonight!

[1: fine] [2: speaking] [3: talk slang] [4: gold watch]

[5: heart; body] [6: lie down and sleep] [7: night] [8: girl; coach]

[9: flashy cut trousers; light-hearted; smart tricks] [10: eye] [11: "the blues"]

[12: drinking; gin and port; remanded] [13: strong ale] [14: fields; light]

[15: speak; beggar; imprisoned] [16: gallows] [17: white sheets; drink and food]

[18: day or night; booty; fine rings] [19: gipsies; highwayman; go away]

[20: muddled; double-barreled gun] [21: bullets; an abandoned person]

[22: gin; false notes] [23: nonsense]

Gwendoline Riley

A. Born etc

I MOVED HOUSE TWICE LAST YEAR, FIRST JUST across town and then further away, up to Glasgow. Each time my Mum was the first to offer to help.

I moved into my friend Maxine's flat in April. That was a small room; there was a single bed, a clothes rail, no floor space for anything else. Her last flat mate, Nico, had been there for eight years, since she and Maxine started college together. But she'd moved 'round the corner now, into a place she'd bought outright with an inheritance.

"God," she said, having come by to pick up some last bits, "coming from the new place back to this, it seems tiny. I don't know how I managed all that time. Can't wait to spread out now. Mind you, it is very, very cheap here. It's a great deal. You'll want to get a mattress topper for that bed, though," she said, "That mattress is horrendous."

Mum didn't look at the room. I only remember her sitting, hunch-shouldered, on the edge of one of my boxes in the living room. I'd brought two boxes with me and two suitcases; the rest of my things—my books—were going to the spare room in Mark's house. Mark was Mum's husband, back in Liverpool.

Mum had said: "Well, don't pay for movers Ash, we can use our friend Gerry. Yes, he's a 'man with a van,' he does all sorts of odd jobs. No, don't pay anyone. Don't pay anyone, Ash."

Well, I had no money—I mean, obviously I didn't—so that sounded fine to me.

They showed up one Saturday morning. First there was Mum's chin, her mouth, in the grainy intercom screen, saying Ash? Ash? And then she was following this Gerry out of the lift. He was a grim- looking old man, in jeans, boots, a fisherman's jumper; he barely nodded hello, by which I understood that he was one of Mark's friends, actually, as opposed to anyone Mum knew or got along with. As he lifted the first box, his breathing was heavy; and as we followed him out with our own heaved-up boxes, Mum gave me a worried look over the top of her box. I gave her a similar look back, and as we all waited for the lift, I gave her a very sharp look, and maintained it, until she said: "Gerry, why don't you wait downstairs and load in. Yes, we'll bring everything down. Yes, save us all getting in each other's way won't it? Yes. Okay. Yes, downstairs."

All this in her go-to anxious, strident voice, which she used on everyone these days, I'd noticed, which you normally only heard certain English horrors using abroad, with waiters. Still, I was glad she said it. I hadn't liked having a non-professional stranger in my flat—my late flat—which really wasn't anywhere to be proud of— just one of those pasteboard nesting holes they used to build in city centres. I'd rented there for three years.

So we lifted out the boxes, and then wheeled out the suitcases, relaying them to the landing and then into the lift, and from there shuffling them through two sets of heavy fire doors and out to Gerry's van, which wasn't much of a van either, as it turned out. It was an old, mossy-windowed camper van.

Mum and I sat squashed together in the high front seat. The drive took ten minutes. As we rounded the last corner she said, "Oh! Princess Street. That's your old place isn't it, Ash? Up there. Is that it, Ash?"

I didn't answer that at first. And then—I couldn't help it—I said, "Yeah, thanks for reminding me of that."

After Gerry had gone, I paced about searching in my phone for my new building's door code. Mum still looked unsure, frightened even.

"Well, I gave him thirty quid for that," she said. "That's enough, isn't it? For a morning's work?"

It didn't seem much, as useless as he'd been, but then—it wasn't me who was paying, was it? Or —oh, I got it, that was why he'd been useless, wasn't it? How horrible.

"I don't know Mum," I said.

With Maxine at work, Mum and I were alone in the flat. Only when I'd pulled in the second box did she finally sit down, perching on the edge of it, as I say; and with her narrow shoulders hunched, and not looking around at all: she kept her eyes on the floor. She'd asked for a glass of water and I was getting her one, running the tap, when I found myself saying, "I've got too many books, haven't I? Maybe I should throw them all out, get a Kindle. Make life easier, wouldn't it?"

"Yes, well why don't you, then?" She said, still not looking up, "Yes, get rid of them. Do that."

When I was growing up she wouldn't throw anything away. If I tried to take a bin bag out before she'd 'checked' it I'd get clawed at. "You can't throw out other people's things," she'd say, on her knees on the floor, snatching all that she'd rescued to her chest. Rotten food, for instance.

She behaved differently towards my brother. And if she didn't? I have one memory of him forcing her into a corner of the hallway, using the smallest of a nest of occasional tables, thrusting the legs at her like a lion tamer with his stool. He must have liked that—been pleased with the innovation, I mean—because he did the same to Grandma one afternoon, again thrusting the table legs at her chest. As Mum had done, Grandma held her arms up in front of her face, turned her face away and made a rising moaning sound. A Punch and Judy noise. That house seemed to elicit them: various don't-want-to wails and can't-make-me wails; braying distress.

Grandma knew not to throw anything out. Instead, she put things in piles. If I got in from school, and there were piles of old newspapers and clothes on the stairs, I'd know she was there. She came over if Mum was working late, or if she was going out after work. (This happened precisely once a year, for her office Christmas do.)

Mum hated her job. 'Well, everyone hates their job,' she used to crow. Still, I remember the strange urgency, the pinching excitement—I felt it, anyway—the day she called in sick so she could go to this 'career change clinic' she'd found. I also remember how having filled out a comprehensive questionnaire there, taken personality tests, aptitude tests, been interviewed 'one-on-one,' the results that came back had her temperamentally suited only to doing exactly what she was already doing. I knew that because she kept those results, along with the clinic's leaflet and the brochure she'd sent for, in a box-file: labelled JOB. A few years after that—hard to credit this, but it's true, perhaps it's even magnificent, in a way—she decided she wanted to be an 'interior designer.' So—more leaflets, more brochures, and then she started a correspondence course, and took out a subscription to LivingEtc. magazine. Her assignments arrived in white A4 envelopes and these she'd snatch up and take upstairs. She didn't finish the course, but again kept all the material, again shoved and stuffed into a series of box-files.

The one advantage to Mum's midden-ry was a box-file, labelled DIVORCE DOCS. I found—oh, all sorts in there. This creased page of lined A4, for instance: notes made after a meeting with her solicitor, I supposed:

<u>Can't</u> reasonably be expected to live with>

violence
threats
constant nagging
the longer going on
forced to leave home

List 1st , most recent, worst

Violence: started within few weeks of marriage—friends party—disagree—in taxi, forced out, slapped, strangled etc. pushed across road

continued on very frequent basis—sudden unpredictable rages

culminating in slaps, punches, kicks, twisting thumbs, throwing things—dishes, shoes, biscuit tin

Threats: throw tea if didn't go out for the day mark for life

throw out of front door

2 slaps when declaring his absolute forbidding me to take child to grandparent for hold

Hit about head when suffering migraine

" " " while breastfeeding baby

paint on face

hot scrambled egg thrown over me, children hysterical

hot casserole thrown across table—plate not hot enough
Breakfast + plate smashed—bacon too crispy

suffered severe bruising, kick on base of spine caused pain when sitting for several weeks

Pile of washed clothes dumped in dirty washing up water—not hung properly

walked off in supermarket—didn't pay

If dishes not neat—smashed into sink

Pulled out of bed—made to stay in kids' bunk three months

parking

Constant nagging: fault-finding +criticism of me +everything I do

Comes at night + looks around for anything out of place

corrects cooking, driving, shouts, grabs wheel (he can't drive! failed test x3!) in front of people

not allowed to wear trousers

Totally domineering—completely uncompromising—
>wrong if not done 'his way'

last autumn—3 mnths in children's room

Fear mental illness—violent mood changes

—extremes of opinion—frightens guests

—irrational behavior

—obsessions—tidy, wash up, parents, A. born etc., trousers

—delusions—things done before met

—denies what he's said—adamant

—I can go anytime—never have children +kill us etc.

None of this came as a surprise, I should say. I had to spend every Saturday with the man, after all. Still, it was a useful find; useful to bear in mind whilst in his company, and in hers too in a different way. I found the page again while I was packing to move into Maxine's; read it through again. 'A. born etc.' Now what had that related to? I phoned Mum to ask.

"Where've you got that?" she said, "Have you been going through my things?"

"Mm…it's something I took years ago. You know I'm a terrible nosy parker. Come on, tell me. What was he obsessed with when I was born? It sounds sinister. It might hold the key."

"Ooh, might it? Well, let's see. 'A. born.' I don't know. I mean, the thing with my Mum and Dad was, there was this terrible row. They came to visit, you see, to see their new granddaughter, and on their first morning I was getting some nappies out of the machine and your Dad said something like, 'Don't do that now,' so then my Dad said, 'Don't speak to my daughter like that' or something like that, and so they had this huge row then, this sort of prodding-each-other-in-the-chest type row, and then my Mum and Dad announced they were leaving; after that, you see, having planned to stay a week, so…"

"That was good of them."

"Yes, and we didn't speak for ages after that."

"You and your parents."

"Mm…"

So—no revelations, there. It was the same old Twister game. Still—I did find myself thinking about that scene. I thought about the near-painful acuity of my father's satisfaction, for instance, seeing Mum on her knees like that—because I could certainly guess at that, knowing him. And proceeding from that, I thought about his thinking, musing rather; that Hmm… Actually he wanted her up now, now that her position had been demonstrated. (Her position was: Negligible Drudge.) Yes, his mercurial munificence (in the galley kitchen) would extend to that, wouldn't it? To a barked: Don't do that now.

I thought about it and found myself shaking with rage, actually, and feeling suffocated, sick, and as bewildered as ever, too, that Mum seemed to have no feelings at all about what she'd been through with him. When pressed, she said brightly: "Oh yes, it was dreadful, yes."

Reading that list when I was younger, it was that 'made to' that always struck me in that way. That plaint. 'Made to stay in kids' bunk.' Because—could she really take a plaintive tone? A pious telltale wounded tone, against a regime like that? Seven years she was submitting to this, and worse. And then—here she was submitting to making a list about it, with precisely the same placid obedience. That was a hollow

I couldn't seem to sound out. I kept on trying to. I couldn't seem to stop that. Like this for instance: May 1997—I was seventeen—I stood in the living room doorway one afternoon, and asked her how she'd voted.

"My vote is private," she said, "I don't have to tell you."

"But you vote Tory don't you? Because that's what your Dad voted."
At that she only smiled, sort of, or at least she bared her teeth, looking past me, as always, as if looking for help.

"How could you vote Tory?" I said.

"Well," she said, "I could never vote Labour, could I?"

"Couldn't you?"

"Well, my Dad always said that what Labour want is to make everyone the same, bring everyone down to their level, down to the lowest common denominator…"

"Okay. That's intelligent. But you're not six are you, so who cares what he said. What about equality of opportunity? Social justice? What do they mean to you? Anything?"

She held her arms up in front of her face then, started making that noise again. "Oh stop harassing me," she said, "Stop bullying me. Oh you're a terrible bully, Ash."

Another memory, from around the same time: coming back from town one Saturday, for the sake of something to say, I decided to pretend I'd caught the wrong bus home, and deliver a shaggy dog story about where I'd ended up. Now, why did I do that? What kind of what-are-you-like was I expecting from those people? I can hardly say. All I know is that instead, standing in the filthy, curtains-drawn living room, I saw Mum and my brother look up from their TV watching—he was stretched out, she was perched on the edge of the settee—as if dumbly lifting their heads from the drear imperative consumption of an obscene feast. Hearing what I was saying, their lips curled in unison, and they started to bark out together their absolute incomprehension and disgust; finding, I think, a sort of lack of hygiene in my straying…

"What?" Mum said.

And he said, "Ugh, you fucking retard."

And she said, "Are you thick? What do you mean you got the wrong bus? Can't you read?"

But she was happy, I remember thinking, quite happily mollified, to be joining in with him like that. This seemed an efficient way to live to her, clearly. And I could see the logic, sort of. Within all of that clamour there must have been a very peaceful space, mustn't there? Where she could abide, finally. Unmolested, I mean. By people like me, I mean. Because that's what I was realising: that whatever my Dad had done to her was pretty incidental, all told, compared to what I'd done, and wanted, since

I'd appeared on the scene.

Funny way to live though, isn't it? As if always with your fingers crossed behind your back, and with everything in your life a front: a marriage, a marriage left, and now the hoarding, the squalor; all a front, a flight, a handful of grit thrown with terrible desperation into the eyes of—people like me, as I say. People with my particular agenda.

Anyway, the pair of them finally turned back to whatever show my brother had on, and I went upstairs, and they went on sitting there—oh, for the next six years or so. And then, after my brother left home, Mum got married again very quickly, to this Mark character.

The mattress in Maxine's spare room really was bad: lumpy and dusty. I couldn't sleep on it. I could only lie there, curl up there, and if I tried that without the radio on, I was in tears very quickly, or in a cold sweat very quickly and having to sit up and latch my head forward to try and breathe. After six months I could afford to give notice, and I had to get out of that city, too; I was done with it. Where to go, though? Where I wanted to be: there was no way to get there. Or at least: it was an occult proposition, and it was going to take time. I wanted to live alone again, so I needed somewhere I could do that. When I mentioned Glasgow Mum said, "Ooh Glasgow! Yes move to Glasgow. Shall I come and help you look? I love Glasgow. Oh yes, any excuse to go up there!"

Or as I saw it, again—anything to save me money.

We took separate trains up, arranging to meet at the hotel Mum had booked. She gasped in from the rain an hour after me, laden with bags and with her glasses steamed up.

For tea we went to a Turkish café back near the station. Mum brought two of her tote bags with her, each full of useless old maps and guidebooks, and printouts of flats she'd found on the Internet.

"Look," she said, handing these pages over to me after we'd ordered, "Just look, Ash. It doesn't hurt to look."

"It does though," I said, "If it's all out of date. Thank you, but there's no point, is there?"

"Mm…" she said. "Okay." She looked deeply unsure, though.

In fact she'd seemed agitated all afternoon, but I'd held off on asking her what the matter was, which meant that we were drinking our coffees before she said, "Well, I've had a horrible week."

"Have you?" I said.

And then she told me very a nasty story about Mark. I felt my stomach lurch.

"Jesus," I said, "It's the same old thing isn't it? Could you not tell he was a prick, Mum? I mean, it's not like you were blinded by love, is it?"

She winced at that.

"Sorry," I said.

But she went on wincing, drew her shoulders up. "Mm…I don't know…" she said. "He seemed fun. But now I think he's…weird, really. Yes, just unpleasant. Just a horrible old man."

"I agree," I said," "I think he's a cowardly piece of shit."

"Mm…I mean, I was fifty-two when I married him, and I thought: okay, that's that then, winding down. But, I don't know. Fifty-two seems young now, now that I'm sixty-two. It didn't then."

"No. Best do something about it then."

"Well, yes, I did, sort of. I mean that's what started him off. I made a list of things he does that I don't like, and—it ran to six pages in the end! So I showed him that…"

"What? Mum!"

"Yes, and I said I wanted to move out. I said—Aislinn's moving and it's so exciting and it's made me think I'd like to move now, try somewhere new, and he went mad. He said—Out. Get out. So I went straight upstairs and I was looking at flats on Rightmove. But he's lifted that sentence now, so—I can go in my own time."

"And will you?"

"I was looking at places online, but I don't know. I mean, all my activities are in Liverpool, but he says that's over now. None of his friends would want to stay my friend apparently, so I'm to be ostracised you see, he said, my name's going to be mud, so—Persona non grata."

"What a prince that man is."

"Mm…well, that's what he says," Mum said, nodding.

Back at the hotel, she turned on the TV, got changed into her nightdress and then took her sponge bag into the bathroom. Her hair was longer than I'd seen it in a while, it lay in a blue-grey flap on her shoulders. She'd even bought hair straighteners.

"Like yours," she'd said, lifting them out of her little suitcase earlier, "But oh, you'll have to show me how to use them!"

The first estate agent on my list was on Byres Road. The young man on the other side of the desk there didn't know which one of us to address so he was trying to talk to both of us, equally, which was quite funny, I thought. Next to me, Mum's teeth were bared: she was concentrating, and panicking. She kept saying, "Yes, yes…" before the man had finished speaking. When he swivelled the computer screen to me so I could look at a flat, she leaned further forward, into my sightline.

"Do I need to be here?" I said.

"Ooh, sorry. Sorry," she said, sitting back, and then she lowered her eyes and made a pantomime of zipping her lips. There were her steamed-up glasses, that flap of frizzy hair. She hugged her bag and kept her eyes down. She pointedly didn't sit, only hovered in a corner. I wish she hadn't done that.

At four o' clock, we gave up. It was dark by then, and freezing; the morning's rain long since a vicious, grapeshot hail. Back in the room I curled up on my bed. I felt coshed, for some reason. Maybe for this reason: I hadn't found anywhere to live and I didn't know what was going to happen to me. Mum sat watching TV and eating the sandwich she'd bought on the way back. I watched her chewing and swallowing, and soon enough I started crying. I watched her realise that, and then I watched her pantomime her sudden yen for a post-prandial stroll (through a hailstorm); she stretched her arms out, then nodded to herself, before standing and putting her wet shoes back on and then her wet coat.

"Shall I leave the TV on, Ash? Ash, I'm just going out. Do you want me to leave the TV on?"

I sat up and wiped my eyes. "It's horrible out there," I said.

Adjusting her hat in the mirror now, she grinned at herself, checking for lipstick on her teeth.

"Why are you going out?"

"Yes, won't be long. I'm just going for a wander," she said.

She wouldn't look at me. She must have heard me though, mustn't she? I mean, I made sure she heard me, is what I'm saying, as she hurried away down the corridor.

On the train back we had our row. It was snowing by then; a thick, whirling blizzard. I was looking out at it, and through it, to the lead-veined hills.
"Are you interested in anything?" Mum was saying. "You're not interested in anything, are you?" She said, "Here, at the hotel, you're just—nothing."

"That's me," I said, sitting back now, and looking at her. She was looking straight ahead. "I'm sorry, I've not got much to say about the snow. I acknowledged that it was terrible. What do you want from me?"

"It's called small talk, Aislinn. It's called being polite and pleasant."

"I was polite. Where do you want me to go with that? It's the fucking weather."

"Oh I'm sorry. I'm sorry we can't all sit 'round talking about…T.S. Eliot all day long."

"What are you talking about?"

"Well—"

"Look Mum, please, I wish you did want to talk. You don't. I don't know what you want. Coloured hankies. I'm not going to take part in that."

"What d'you mean? What's that—coloured hankies? I want you to be polite and pleasant to your mother, who—"

"I can't talk about nothing with you, okay. I'm sorry. I've got my own shit going on, in case you hadn't noticed."

"Ash! So rude. My God. No manners." She hugged herself tighter then and looked around the carriage, teeth bared in anguish. "And anyway, you're only waiting to, you know, report that Mark's had a go at you again or locked you in a caravan or whatever so that I can get angry instead of you. It's bullshit. It's mendacious, actually." Her voice had a real grim force now. "Small talk is what makes life bearable. Yes it is. Yes it is, Ash!"

"No it's not. Look at the evidence. You're walled in."

"It is. It makes life bearable. Are we all supposed to march about in silence, like you, are we, with a face like thunder?"

"Oh, back to my face, is it?"

"Well...it is. Face like thunder. Face like bloody thunder. You look terribly off-putting, you know. Terribly off-putting."

And—this being our usual terminus, I didn't say anything else.

I said, "Bye then," when I had to get off at Wigan.

"Yes, goodbye," she said, standing up so I could get past.

I was on the next train for an hour, sitting with my bag on the seat next to me. I was very tired by then, which felt luxurious in a way. I didn't seem to give a damn about anything, Mum was right. It all seemed pretty funny and not much else, after all. And I had this to contemplate, too: another bit of paper I'd taken from her. From her handbag this time, while she'd been in the loo. It too seemed pretty funny now.

MARK

CONS>

Antisocial: burping scratching farting—in public

Always takes 'news' section of paper

Extreme opinions—loud—in public

Constant name-calling—arsehole, dimwit, s
tupid cow, 'mad,' 'pathetic,' 'no-one's interested'
'no-one gives a fuck what you say'

Made to sit in caravan on my own

Birthday—'tricked him,' no present.

Always in front room> I'm alone

Silent treatment

Out with friends, am I invited: 'No'

Supermarket—'old bitch'

Reads on trains—might as well be alone

'Thrown out'—if I 'mention Thatcher again'

PROS>
Allotment

Funny, and then not so funny. I went back and forth with that.

I did move to Glasgow in the end, taking a six-month lease on a flat in Partick. It had two rooms, dusty cane furniture throughout. The windows rattled behind thin curtains and the place had the feel of an out of season B&B, I thought, especially in the mornings, with the seagulls screeching in the courtyard. I wasn't happy, but I liked being alone again.

After three weeks I saw Mum's handwriting in my mailbox. The card she'd sent featured a photo of an old lady: a cheery old dear with watery eyes and a gurner's grin. The caption read: Get in Touch or I'm Coming to Visit! and this Mum had appended with a yellow Post-it note, on which she'd written: *Only joking*!!!

I was going to reply. Before I got 'round to it she texted me: "Cut all my hair off. Do you want brush straighteners etc.? MUM"

I wrote back: "No, thanks." And then, because I couldn't help myself, "That's instead of getting a divorce, is it?"

No reply to that. A few days later, though, walking to the shop one morning, I found I had to ring
her. "Hello," I said, "How's your hair. Has anyone noticed it yet?"

"No," she said, "no-one. I think—no-one's looked at me for years, so no-one's noticed!"

"And are you still looking at flats?" I said, "Please say yes."

"Oh—well, no. No, it's too embarrassing. I can't stay here if he's still here. Anyway he thinks it's all hunky-dory now, so...he thinks I'm some mad old cow now, you see, who was having an episode, so…"

"Right. But God forbid you leave him, hey? Anyway, listen Mum, you can't come and visit me, you know. I've been having panic attacks, thinking about it. I can't sleep, so could you not ask again please?"

"Ooh. Can't sleep. What d'you mean, can't sleep?"

"I mean the thought of you coming to visit is making me ill. The thought of you making comments about my appearance or my things, or telling me stories about Mark when you won't leave him. I don't want you to have no-one to talk to but you can't keep—"

"Ooh—anything else I can't say? I'll keep my eyes on the floor shall I? Making you ill, oh, aren't I a monster. Aren't I terrible."

"Do you enjoy being on your belly?" I said. Actually, I was shouting now. I was standing on Dumbarton Road and shouting, "Why is that your default? For Christ's sake. Yeah, keep your eyes on the floor. I'm only trying to save us both some grief here after last time."

"What about last time? What are you talking about? My own daughter phones with this tirade of what I'm not allowed to say or look at."

"That's not what I did. I don't want you to come, it's pretty simple. I'm trying to save my life here. I'm trying to get away from you. If you come up here I will end up slitting my own throat, do you understand? I will slit my own throat if you try and come near me. I'm trying to save my own life. You are not a tolerable presence. I won't be able to stand it and I'll have to cut my own throat do you understand?"

"Ooh…sorry… What do you mean? What do you mean, Ash? Goodness me. My own daughter. Pardon me for breathing. Not a tolerable presence. *You're* not a tolerable presence."

"No, I know…" I said.

But she'd already hung up.

Desmond Kon Zhicheng-Mingdé

MARLENE DIETRICH MEETS DIETRICH BONHOEFFER

> *"I have now finished Dostoevsky's Memoirs from the House of the Dead. It contains a great deal that is wise and good…. And if even illusion has so much power in people's lives—that it can keep life moving, how great a power there is in a hope that is based on certainty, and how invincible a life with such a hope is."*
> —Dietrich Bonhoeffer*

I.

Between the weatherboards of two heavens is a waiting room.

Bonhoeffer's corner was simple.

Calming, awash in a cornsilk light.

Just beside it, a humid room.

Its infill panels were infested.

Maggots.

A pet muskrat nibbling at salted pork rolled in a baking tray of breadcrumbs.

The room's occupant was on the floor behind the futon, and you couldn't see him.

II.

Marlene, on the other hand, kept herself busy.

She had thrown out five big boxes.

She hadn't bothered taping down the tops, as if to say closure wasn't the point.

There was nothing to seal of the first twenty years of her life.

There was only the forgetting and the discarding.

III.

"What will you take with you when the carriers come?" Marlene said.

Someone desired a beef casserole and a Chardonnay.

And both suddenly appeared on the gateleg table.

Along with a soft cheese and satsumas.

IV.

"These two books," Bonhoeffer said.

He raised his favourites, Goethe and Plutarch, with a big smile.

He surprised Marlene with his candor.

Today, he told her she had beautiful eyes.

That she drew them perfectly, the way his fiancé did.

V.

"It's easy. You leave your lids at half-mast and draw the arch."

Marlene said this with a thick accent.

"The way you'd pencil your brows.

And everything becomes shaped like almonds."

In the casualness of her voice—a tint, a gaze.

A proposition is on its way. And sadness and comedy.

And hope gets mixed in, mixed up into one big emotion.

VI.

No grilles or cell doors here, Bonhoeffer existed for his daily walks.

He still wore his simple shirt, grey slacks.

These were perfect days, of a cool wind.

The same languor as that April Friday when he looked out the truck.

Its uncovered windows.

How he saw the monastery at Metten.

VII.

"What will you remember most of everything?"

Marlene said softly, hoping for something she wanted to hear.

"The Tuesday of that last Easter," Bonhoeffer replied quickly.

"We played chess, and shared a tobacco ration.

The next day, we were allowed off the truck.

The farmhouse, its small yard.

The rye bread we were given.

And honeyed goat's milk too, into which we dipped the bread."

VIII.

Marlene straightened the front of her blouse and smiled.
It was a look that said the next journey was a long time coming.
That it was time to inhabit the light.
Bonhoeffer knew his decision, biting into his satsuma.
It was seedless, and easy to peel.

IX.

The waiting room still seemed homely enough.
Walls like thick curtains.
Stirring with each occupant's immediate sentiment and passing feeling.
Colors shifted like seasons.
Changing scenes, waves of frescoes.
Memories sputtering on a screen.
Like a vintage Merkur projector.

X.

"I think my heart is blurring. I've given up on fuzzy logic."
Marlene confessed this in the low country of her voice.
She gave Bonhoeffer a nod, hooking her left arm under his elbow.
"No more theatre or illusions."
"No more curtains for me."
"No more April winters."

Epigraph excerpted from one of Bonhoeffer's many letters, dated July 25, 1944.

Michael Caleb Tasker

THE VISIT

THE WINTER COLD KEPT THE HUMIDITY AT bay. Spanish moss hung still in the live oaks that lined the street, and looked twisted and haunted, and tortured into the shapes that gave them their name. The air was warm and soothing and carried with it the smell of salt water from the Gulf and the smell of the Mississippi that ran a few blocks away, deep and brown and dangerous. The sky was a soft gold and edged with the purple of the coming night and it was the time of day when the streets emptied and were quiet but for the locusts, whose call would grow and steady into a hum. Far out over the Gulf an electrical storm cracked in the sky.

Abel came to his door and stood behind the screen and looked out at the street. His faced was tanned chestnut and lines like carvings ran from his eyes and along his cheeks and though his nose was no longer swollen he had the gin blossoms and burst blood vessels of a lifelong drinker. His eyes were tired and sad with age and knowing and he breathed in deep and the air was cool and damp and dusty to his lungs and warm and soft on his face. His feet hurt and his bones hurt and he opened the screen door and went to sit in the wicker chair on the side of his veranda. He set a glass of iced mint tea down on the table beside him. A highball glass filled with ice and crushed mint leaves. Sweat beaded the outside of the glass and Abel looked at it and wished it were a real drink, wished it had the sting and fire of bourbon, wished for the hollow warm feeling as it hit his gut, wished for the release of when it hit his mind. But he sipped the tea and crushed the ice in the back of his mouth and watched the street and watched the gold of the sky become stained with a dark orange and always the fringe of purple growing, slowly following the sun across the sky and down. The moss swung lightly in the trees and the seagulls flew violently, telling of a coming storm and Abel remembered hearing of a supposed windstorm in the news. Abel thought it would rain too as he could feel the atmosphere dropping and his feet felt swollen inside his loafers. He shuffled them off and stretched his bare feet out in front of him and listened to the locusts growing louder and the cries of the gulls. The sky was the color of burnt gold and the purple had become black. It would be dark soon.

Abel heard the soft steady steps on the pavement and the whine of his wrought iron gate swing open. A tall skinny man walked slowly to the steps and stopped at the bottom of the veranda. He held himself straight and tall but his steps were carefully chosen. The house behind Abel was dark, causing the visitor to be a black silhouette with the dusk behind him and Abel wondered if it were death finally come to take him. The visitor walked up the step and behind him wind blew and darkness came and Abel looked away from the man and at the jasmine flowers along his gate and he wished he could smell them but the wind wasn't right. A man in a worn suit and as old as Abel but with deeper lines came to a stop at the top of the steps. His face was tired and old and ready for the end, not scared of it and not hungry for it, simply accepting. He took off his hat and nodded at Abel.

"Hello."

"Abel," the man said.

Abel nodded to the chair opposite him and the man sat down slowly, resting his hat on a knee. He looked at Abel's glass.

Abel watched him and again he felt that need and that wish for a drink. That need and that wish for the bitter and sweet taste and the calm dullness of mind and the release and again he remembered that alcohol was the most giving of lovers. But it took the most in return. His stomach turned and his face felt flushed but he stayed quiet and seated. Thoughts he didn't like came to him and he wondered what his visitor was thinking. Something similar, he imagined. Abel remembered what the girl had been like and he remembered what he had been like. He had been too old and she had been too young, much too young, and he remembered his face in her hair and smelling that wet copper smell. He looked at the visitor and he knew they were both thinking of her.

"Haven't seen you in some time," Abel said.

"Yes." The visitor looked away from Abel and to the dusk, the sun was gone but stains of purple turning to blue mixed with the white light of the moon. The wind blew, catching the moss in the trees and making them swing and with the wind the locusts called louder.

Abel hadn't seen her in some time. Years, really. It had happened because he drank, he knew, and afterward he drank more. At first to ease his mind, to help think of other things, and then he drank because he didn't want to forget, because he could not let himself forget. When he was drunk he thought of her, he saw her and felt her and smelled her and for those moments he was with her again and all was well. And one day he stopped. He supposed he had drunk his fill. He knew he had hidden more than a man can. And he knew it would happen again. He wanted her to be the only one. So he stopped drinking. Though he never stopped wanting a drink.

Abel looked to his visitor.

"Are you drinking again?" the visitor asked.

"Tea. Only tea now."

The man nodded. When the man first started visiting, so many years ago, that was when Abel drank the most. He had to. And he would be drunk when the visitor came and he would feel embarrassed and he would feel weak but he drank more.

The first time the man came to see Abel he came to kill him. They were both younger, the visitor full of hate and Abel full of gin. When he saw how weak Abel was the man was sickened and he left nauseous and disgusted. Anger and hatred and ugliness had kept him alive and kept him full of tension and purpose but Abel's impotence drained him.

The second time the man came to see Abel he came to understand him. He came to listen to Abel explain, to understand how Abel could do such a thing to someone so young, someone still nearly a child. He came to listen but Abel did not say a word.

The third time the man came to see Abel he came to forgive him.

And then he came to punish him. He came many times to punish Abel for what he had done, to remind Abel, and to make sure Abel would never forget how he had hurt her and how that hurt and that damage could never be reversed. He would come every week and they would sit on the veranda together. They didn't talk. They didn't need to and there was nothing to say. And slowly he visited Abel less; every month and then every year.

"Do you still see her?" Abel asked.

"Yes," the visitor said. "Once a year. Do you visit her?"

"No."

Abel looked out at the sky and saw the electrical storm over the Gulf and saw the lightning breaking through the sky and he could see the shadows of the gulls still flying overhead and though it was winter and the air should have been fresh and light and clean Abel could feel the heavy air he felt in summer and he could feel sweat building on his forehead and feel sweat running down his back. He had a swallow of the mint tea and wished it were a mint julep, and he remembered a bar he went to years ago where a beautiful Creole girl named Gilda made him the best juleps in town and he would let himself believe that her smiles were not solely for the tip he would leave. But now there were no more juleps and no more bars and he knew better than to delude himself into believing he could have the affections of beautiful young women. He no longer deserved and he no longer wanted the affections of any young woman. He only wanted her back.

"Have you forgotten her?" the visitor asked. "Have you forgotten what you did to her?"

Abel shook his head. No, he would never forget. He saw her when he closed his eyes, when he slept she was with him. He remembered her wide blue eyes and her confused smile. He remembered the heat and the air on his face as he drove and the streetlights' glow on the road. Fog was coming off the Mississippi and rolling onto the streets and though the dawn was a couple hours away the sky was streaking with grey and as he drove he thought the fog looked like steam rising from the earth. Abel remembered the way the car felt when it hit her and the bump of driving over her leg before he braked.

When he stopped the car he sat still and waited for something to happen. His first thoughts were selfish and he looked at his knuckles tight on the wheel and he knew he had to get out of the car and see what happened. He stepped out and saw her on the side of the road and ran to her, swallowing the vomit in his mouth and trying not to look at her leg where the bone had come out of the skin. She was alive when he reached her side. She was crying and smiling and had a confused look on her face that made Abel think of a young dog that didn't understand why it was being punished. Blood came from her leg and from her head where it had cracked itself on the pavement and the metallic smell of her blood mixed with the smells of the night; the dew in the earth and the rotted fish smell from the river and the clean air smell of a night without people and without cars. Her body was warm to the touch and her skin was soft and wet. Abel held her close to him and buried his face in her neck and apologized while she softly died.

Abel had not forgotten her.

"I dream about killing you," the visitor said. "I still dream about it and still think about it."

"I know."

"I guess I don't have it in me."

"I guess not."

"You did once."

The moon was high and bright in the sky and Abel looked at the man's face and saw the pain and saw the anger that had been there years ago. But now the pain and the anger were worn and tired and Abel knew they were only there to fight the sadness. The night was quiet now. The locusts had stopped calling and the gulls had flown away and though the storm over the Gulf could be seen it was still too far away to make any sound but the wind was blowing stronger and moving the trees a little and Abel remembered the wind storm. Though it was too dark to see, Abel could hear leaves and piles of dirt and dust being gathered up and blown down the street.

"You know why I always came by?" the man asked.

"So I wouldn't forget."

"Yes," he said. The visitor looked out at the night and nodded. "But it was more than that. To keep it fresh with you. Do you think of it often?"

"I think of her often."

"Good."

Abel's throat was dry and his tongue felt like ash but his glass was empty. He felt the visitor's eyes on him and when he met his look he felt a chill run down his spine and a hollowness in his stomach, a cold hollowness and it spread like urine. Abel did not feel the want or the need for a drink; he felt death and shame and hatred. The man's eyes were hurt and sad and the creases on his face deepened as he laid a small and ugly revolver down on the table. Abel looked at it.

"I don't miss her," the visitor said. "I think about her but I don't miss her and I don't like that."

Abel felt the air and wished it were cool but it was warm and soft and blanketed and he felt claustrophobic and he smelled the storm over the Gulf and knew it was coming closer. Sweat came to his forehead and he knew it was from tension and not the heat and his shirt started to cling to his skin. The air blew strong and warm along the street and up to the veranda. Abel looked at his visitor, at his sunken eyes and pitted cheeks. He knew those lines had once been the dimples of a laughing man. Wind blew what little hair the visitor had, white and thin and delicate.

The visitor stood. Abel noticed how straight the back of his neck was and watched as he put on his hat and walked off the veranda. He could see the white shadow of his back as he walked the pathway to the gate, and the change in the sound of his steps on the pavement. Abel listened as his visitor walked down the streets his steps going softer until the sound of the night drowned them out.

Abel sat alone and looked at the night and at the sky and there were no stars but only the moon and some clouds glowing soft and gray. He breathed in the smell of the storm and of the sea and he wondered when they would come. He looked at his empty glass and it shined with light and he remembered how gin would shine and sparkle in a glass and how a bar's neon lights would reflect in the glass and he remembered how her eyes shone with water when she looked at him. He looked at the revolver that had been left on the table and thought it was ugly and dull.

He sat for some time and listened to the night and to the wind and he watched the lightning break over the Gulf and he felt old and tired and thirsty.

Terese Svoboda

CAR PROBLEM

I drive fast. Mom in the other car coasts.
She swerves, but only for robins.
The tacks she left in my gas tank make their music.
Don't all moms do this? Teams of friends
replace parts while I climb back in.

She's 24 years ahead, and lots of her big black
curled rubber awaits my own kids
strapped into their vehicles,
puzzled still about the finish line, but game.
The dark alleys on their screens make them adept

and alert at the console, inept elsewhere.
Mom? I radio ahead, her line dead.
I want to know if the deer I keep hitting
she's trained to my headlights.
But Mom's counting dinner parties

to keep herself awake, stocks and bonds
she should have bought, Pietas she didn't need.
Scotch is what she needs, to improve her performance.
She's left a great ape standing in the highway,
its fur so motherly I remember which coat.

I'm forced to stop. My offspring sense a show,

they break their laps to watch. The ape

lifts me over the hood. I'm ornament!

My kids wave their maps, googled so recently

the streets aren't named, the turns lead to parkways

yet to be built. The ape, distracted, drops me.

The overhead copter, my husband,

yells Left, go left but my steering wheel

runs out of fluid, the kids pile up,

they need bandaids and coffee.

Mom's totally cruise control now,

mascara-wand flying. She waves.

I gun what motor's left in my car

so she can hear me, so she knows where I am.

Her engine coughs back.

The road ahead is dark, trees capsize on either side,

the thrump of the overhead spouse dies out.

I calculate the hypoteneuse between her and the end.

She's doing 80, top down, driving wild, though hospice has the keys.

The kids say they're safe in underground parking.

They're tunneling to the end point

just to show me they can. I turn my head away.

That's when Mom's tires squeal,

she's peering over the dash, foot heavy,

the sun blinding at that angle, her eyes slits.

Her engine switches to another source of power,

unknown. The hours, days, lives that she burns

fill the air with smoke until her sleek low fast car

becomes the dark all around.

No one dares turn off.

Kathleen Spivack

THE GREAT RAILROAD TRAIN OF ART

"Farewell, little Katya,"
My Russian Lit. Professor
at Oberlin College called.
He was running alongside
the train in Cleveland, Ohio.
His little legs churned,
his belly pumped in and out.
"Farewell, my little Katya
on the Railroad Train of Art..."

And the great Lackawanna
locomotive pulled
out of the station
and I graduated from college
and the years
started to pass by the train
at first distinctly
like trees, then faster,
merging into a green smear
of landscape
always moving ahead of me,
converging into a great "V"
somewhere beyond, sucking
the silver train forward.

Is this what was meant
by "Perspective:" college
Art History class, yawning
in darkness, slides
of "Old Masters," and occasionally
too much light, a shocked
glare at the end of the show?
There were other travelers, too,
on the train, clutching chickens
and boyfriends, sleeping
through boring parts of Rome,

Florence, and Renaissance Man.
and even children, peeping,
wide-eyed out of baskets,
and amazed young girls
and grandmothers no one could
startle, lit by white
streetlights by which the train
passed quickly, before entering
tunnels where, if one opened an eye
one could still see Leonardo
up there on full screen,
straining and clawing,
trying something new.

We had taken our notebooks
and bundles, smoothing them down,
scribbling, in a clandestine way;
we were special with secrets,
and anesthesia was invented
and mid-wives supplanted
by surgeons taking off legs
and Michelangelo
hacked at his marble
while the train rushed
on through violet evenings.
And in Holland a woman
set a table and light shone
on the draperies and fruit: we
could see, looking into the
quiet room with longing.

"Peasants," my Prof.
scoffed, as we pleaded
for make-up exams.
I was hopeful, my college
diploma, virginity lost
to that Russian professor
and now, perhaps, a job.
Yes, a job, typing
to the clack of the wheels
as the relentless locomotive

thundered on through the
Industrial Revolution, the
horrors of Hogarth
the Song of the Shirt.
I typed faster and faster,
tapping, teaching American
children, although
at some point the Greeks
invented beauty: Keats
called it something else,
and the train
puffed through stations
steaming like the filthy
ones of Monet. Had we reached
French Impressionism so fast?
Had the Curies
already discovered radium?
There is no time for
a quiz. "...Truth; 'tis all ye
need to know." No time.

Who could have foreseen
the villages we passed
where the station master
ran out of his cuckoo clock
office and gaped in wonder
like the bears at Berne.
Who could imagine the comfort
of cows, seen from the train
that never stopped; how peaceful
the shepherds, dozing at crossroads
of Flemish art. But we
were moving faster
than Turner's clouds.
Smallpox was cured,
Fleming found penicillin
in a cave, and the train
entered a tunnel.
A new tray of slides:
Gogol, Pasternak, and
Marx were writing madly,

all at the same time.
We passed pine forests,
snow fields, and on
the smooth white sheets of
marriage, somewhere between
the Russian revolution, I made
love to a husband whom
I promised to cherish
all my days, and birthed
children on the train.
And did not
throw myself under it.

And other passengers also
gave birth, as if in
emigration, lying together
under that great shawl
of silence, hardly crying out;
and our children grew
while the train sped
away from the Czar,
past the Irish Potato
Famine, toward that "V"
on the horizon: "0, My America,
my new found land:" the vanishing
point. We were going
to be taught to plant corn.

And there was sadness
too, of course, and bitter
words. (We entered the Depression.)
and a turning away of the
husband. Outside, the air
was lacy with new birch leaves,
everything stretching its arms
and crying "stop here!"
And a hunger for love
after the Great War:—
for all the beautiful young men,—
roared up in me like
the huge boundless cry

of the locomotive
hurtling toward summits
and Yalta, the Axis powers,
death of the Archduke,
and promises of collaboration.
They were dancing at Maxim's;
and somewhere in here
Modern Art seemed to begin
as well as Movies.
As we looked out
at the darkened towns,
passing them too quickly,
the train whistle left
its dark moaning sound
to which vacancy
was the only response.
After Pearl Harbor
and Polio, while Picasso
and Braque discovered
Cubism, we petitioned
the train to slow down.
Attendants came to us
and told us to be quiet,
and porters, too, respectful
with luggage, tipping
their caps. We offered to get
psychoanalyzed,(not on
the syllabus) for Independent
Study, to go to the Far
East, or gaze impassively
over Great Plains
from the back of a horse.
These requests were denied.

This was before Vietnam
still. This was before napalm
and hippies. This was before
Eleanor Roosevelt "became
a lesbian." One still had hope.
Crossing these decades on the great
Railroad Train of Art

becomes more difficult.
But at the terminal station
when the train does "kindly" stop
I shall find my Russian Lit.
Professor waiting; he will look
exactly as he did. I'll embrace
my parents, loves, and children,
hand in my final bluebook
on Tolstoi, whisper "The light,
the light. Turn out the light."
and get an A plus for the full course.

Cortright McMeel

PAINTERS

WHEN I GO OVER TO GRIFF'S FOR BEERS AND chess, he tells me what he thinks about The Fraze.

—He comes over here and drinks and stares at the wall and says nothing.

—Iron Man, I say.

Griff gives me a blank look. I hum the famous Black Sabbath bass chords, but it isn't Beethoven or Bach so it is lost on him.

—Rock and Roll, Griff spouts from his well of prejudice. —That is what got The Fraze into this mess. Drugs. Excess. MTV. It is nothing but vanity. You stick to your Brahms and your Beethoven, read sections of The Autobiography of Benjamin Franklin every once and a while and this kind of thing doesn't happen to you.

—A job will be good for him, I say.

—He's crazy, says Griff. —I would not be surprised at all if one of these days he came over here, drank a bottle of vodka and then murdered me in my sleep.

It's hard to take Griff's word at face value; after all, he spends his spare time painting the words to the Old German epic poem The Nibelungenlied on the ceiling of his crappy living room. Looking up at it, I can see in the tiny, detailed script, Griff's hundreds of hours of work. Griff worships the mythical heroes above him, heroes beyond human defeat. Griff lives the text, and following its dictates, scorning mercy and the here and now.

The six-foot-five, two-hundred-and-fifty-pound "The Fraze" lives above Father's First, the pub where he works as a bouncer. Father's First sits in the afternoon shadow of Fenway Park's legendary Green Monster. The pub's owner, Joey Laziano, is a relic from the Bob Cousy and Ted Williams days; Beantown's sports Renaissance. He's got framed pictures of himself with the old idols to prove it.

The Fraze's apartment smells like old books. The air is stale and dusty. He, like Griff, engages in scholarly undertakings. It is his goal to condense the entire Encyclopedia Britannica onto cassette tapes. No one asks him what he plans to do with the tapes, afraid of the answer. When I enter, he looks up at me from his book-scattered desk.

—What's going on, my friend?

—I'm fine except when my studying gets interrupted. He looks over at me and shuffles his notecards together. Then he lets out an exasperated breath.

—The constant studying helps, he continues. —I am also screwing a Chinese girl who works at the library. She's teaching me how to speak Mandarin. I've got over three hundred Chinese characters memorized right here on these note cards. Test me.

The Fraze's eyes seem to quiver. His face is heavy from the complimentary booze downstairs. Whiskers sprout off his cheeks in sporadic patches. I can tell he is thinking of China and the strange Chinese characters: some endless, useless exotic knowledge.

—She comes over and sings in Chinese, he says.

—Sounds cultured, I say.

—It is nice, he says.

His chin drops to his chest. The conversation is wearing him out. I can tell, in his strangely patrician way, he feels it's beneath him to lose his mind.

It's early morning at an old lady's house, and another worker and I are taking turns reading the newspaper, while the other works the sander. Technically, we are both supposed to be sanding, but as long as one sander is on, it sounds to our boss Patch like we are both hard at work. When the sanding is done, it's time for a mid-morning coffee break.

Later that afternoon, as I am priming the baseboard in one of the upstairs guest bedrooms, Mrs. Bigelow, the owner, corners me.

—Buzz, I'd like a word with you, she says. I stand there, a laborer, waiting for my retainer's command.

—About that job I mentioned before, if you are interested. It's my summer house in Cotuit. Mr. Pingree has agreed to paint the exterior for fifteen thousand dollars. I was wondering if it was a job you could handle, with perhaps another painter for a lesser price.

What Patch says is true, nobody loves saving money like the rich.

—I saw a picture of that house upstairs, I say. —I could do the work for around ten thousand.

—Of course, she says, nodding at my price. —I wouldn't want you to start until a month from now, when summer begins.

—Thank you, Mrs. Bigelow, I say. —I'll drive down to the Cape this weekend and check out the house to make sure my estimate holds.

—You're a fine young man, she says, preparing to make her exit. Standing there, poised in the doorframe, she wears a motherly expression on her taut cold lips, at once superior and concerned. Her eyes are grayish-colored, like dusky pearls. Then in a kind voice, icy with disdain, she says:

—I'm sure you'll do an exemplary job, Buzz.

It is a balmy spring day, opening day at Fenway. I make my way through the crowds to meet The Fraze at Father's First. The scalpers call out like circus barkers. The air reeks of the sweet, rancid smell of caramelized peanuts. Cops stand in a group at the corner of Landsdowne Street, laughing and smiling, drinking bottled water.

The inside of Father's First is cool, air-conditioned, a pleasant escape from the masses of Sox fans. The Fraze is sitting at the bar, drinking a bottle of Miller, staring at some of his Chinese character note cards. A few feet away, Dom the bartender is hunched over in thought, picking away at a scab on his bald head. He is an old man, a friendly soul who has been working behind Beantown bars for half a century. A little boy wearing a Red Sox cap is sitting at a nearby table, loudly sipping at a Coke through a straw. He looks up at me.

—It is getting harder and harder to study in this place.

—I got a proposition for you, I say. —You want to make five grand painting a house on Cape Cod this summer? I ask.

The Fraze puts down his notecards.

—I would like that, he says.

—How about a free beer for me then, I say.

—You don't want a free beer from here, he says. —We get cockroaches in the tap lines. Every once in a while a dead one shows up in somebody's pint glass.

Joey saunters over to us, red-faced from his conversation. He is breathing heavily from his twenty-foot walk, his sumo wrestler belly stretching his XXXL Celtics T-shirt to the breaking point. He makes no garrulous remarks about opening day or the Curse of the Bambino. Instead he slaps The Fraze on the shoulder.

—I was supposed to take little Louis here to the opener today, Joey says, pointing to the boy. —It's just not going to happen. You two going to the game?

—No, we mumble in unison.

—Here's two tickets, says Joey, handing them to me. —I was going to take my nephew but I got this visit to deal with. You two go. They're good seats. Right behind third base.

The boy looks confused.

—Louis, we are not going to the game today. Uncle Joey has business, says Joey to his nephew.

The little boy begins to cry. Joey goes over to his nephew and gives him a napkin to wipe away his tears.

We exit the bar and head up Landsdowne Street in the shade of Fenway's left field wall, the Green Monster. The Fraze gives the tickets away to the first scalper he sees. He doesn't even ask for any money. The sun is shining and I can hear the last line of the National Anthem being sung. It is followed by one second of silence and then the stadium erupts into cheers. The walls of the ballpark seem to vibrate from within. My associate doesn't take notice. He is staring down at his note cards as we walk.

Across the bay from Mrs. Bigelow's summer cottage stands a battered lighthouse, which scans the horizon at night like a lantern-eyed Cyclops. She tells us how the jetties on either side of the bay are supposed to be two welcoming arms, reaching out to greet the returning sailor's home to safety. She relates us the story like she herself has personally saved the lives of half a dozen lost mariners. The Fraze gives me this frown which tells me that he already has no patience for putting up with Mrs. Bigelow's shit.

We bring the equipment via The Fraze's El Camino. Right out of the gate Mrs. Bigelow tries to talk to me about something, but I pretend not to hear her, remembering Patch's rule about clients. Number one: work, don't talk. If the client tries to talk, just wave at them and keep working. That is why it is always good to have a radio on. It makes it easier to ignore the client. Otherwise, the client will have a painter do things other than work, extraneous bullshit that slows down a job, like babysitting a kid or taking out their trash or feeding goldfish. Painters paint, nothing else, and a client is always out to take advantage of you—but if you are always busy or seem busy, they can't hassle you as much.

The client gains confidence if the painters move big ladders convincingly like they are your slaves and not vice versa. We walk the thirty foot ladder across her lawn and around to the backside of her house with ease. Knowing how to talk about paint also lends credibility. I give Mrs. Bigelow my spiel about the pros and cons of latex versus oil-based paint. I stress the importance of primer and let her know that the old standby, Ben Moore oil base, is what I plan to use. It's expensive but more resistant to the corrosive salt spray you get living by the ocean. Also, since I know the Mrs. Bigelow is a neat freak, I bust out our new plastic and cloth drop cloths for her teak wood decks. At the end of the first day, Mrs. Bigelow brings us out some sugar cookies, which means she's sold on us. The good impression has been made and will last until the first, and inevitable, big fuck up.

The next day Mrs. Bigelow insists on making our lunch, a single half-dollar sized hamburger on a bun for each of us. But this isn't enough. When she leaves for her daily tennis game, we head into the house and begin to search for food. Most of the cupboards are bare. It turns out that the widow is something of a miser. There is a bar of cream cheese in her refrigerator. The Fraze cuts the bar in half and devours the white slab.

—Those hamburger buns have got to be around here somewhere.

—Honeypot, he says. He is cradling a ceramic jar in the shape of a beehive. We each take huge swigs out of the honey jar, letting the golden ooze spill into our mouths like a heavy mead. The sugar high makes our eyes shine over. We are talking about how good chugging honey is when I hear a shuffling sound behind us. That is when The Fraze commits the first fuck up. He panics, trying to put the bumblebee lid back on and drops the beehive jar. It shatters, sending honey and ceramic all over the kitchen floor. An ancient lady, stooped and withered, stands in the living room, looking somewhere vaguely near us.

The ancient lady walks about with a cane and taps it in front of her.

—Oh my! she says to herself. Then she turns about-face with her cane still in front of her, and marches up the stairs.

—Who was that? he asks.

—I have no idea.

—Did she hear us?

—I think she's blind, I say.

—She looked about a hundred years old. But who is she?

—Who cares. Go get the cat, I say.

—What?

—Get the fucking cat.

The Fraze goes into the living room and lifts the Persian off the sofa and brings him to me.

—Now rub him in the honey. He's the culprit.

—He might get nasty.

—Just dip him in it like he's a mop, I say.

The Fraze does this and the cat resists, staring at us with a questioning look. The cat takes off and we slip out the patio side door to get back to work. Mrs. Bigelow comes back from her tennis game around two o'clock. We keep sanding away at the shutters, glancing nervously at each other, waiting for Mrs. Bigelow to come out and accuse us of treachery. It isn't until an hour later when she emerges.

—How's it coming along? she asks.

—So far so good.

—Can I ask a favor of you?

—That's fine. We got to finish these shutters here, I say. —But if you don't mind us getting behind schedule.

—Oh, don't worry yourself, she says. —I don't want to slow you down.

Patch would be proud. Fuck up concealed, favor averted.

After work, The Fraze and I stop by a packey on the way to my stepfather's place in New Bedford. Its only thirty minutes commute to Cape Cod so my mom gave us run of the place. At the packey we pick up a couple forty-ounce torps of beer and then head to the beach cottage. We unpack our gear and throw it in the garage.

Then we go for a jog. We run in silence along the side of the road, making our way down to the Padanaram Bridge. Standing out in the low tide of the harbor are Portuguese fisherman in waders bent over sand sifters, digging for quahog. Halyards clang against mastheads from sailboats out in the bay. The sound rings out, ghostly and faint, carried by the wind. By the time we return to the guest cottage, the summer evening has come on, enveloping the landscaped lawns in a purple gloom.

In the cottage we sit in the wicker chairs and start drinking the cold forties.

—It is peaceful here, says The Fraze.

—It's the crickets, I say. —The chirping makes you sleepy.

—And I could get used to the jog, he says.

—No more city for two months.

I lay my head back on the chair and begin to relax. As my lids shut, he wakes me up with a sudden proclamation.

—I am going to be reading all night. I hope you don't mind.

—We're waking up early, I say.

—The book's called The Philosophy of Civilization by Albert Schweitzer. It is about how the individual spirit must triumph over institutions. It is part of my comeback. My grand plan.

I wake up once or twice during the night. The Fraze still has the light on and I can hear him turning the pages of the book, trying to stay awake and stave off darkness.

—We got an early morning, I shout. There is no response.

At ten to six we wake up and put on our uniforms, white painters pants and ragged T-shirts. We get into the El Camino and cruise down the Cape Cod highway to Cotuit, blasting his favorite tape, AC/DC's Dirty Deeds Done Dirt Cheap. By the time the tape rolls around to Big Balls, we are entering Mrs. Bigelow's driveway.

By noon I have a severe sunburn on the back of my neck and arms. I'm up on the thirty-foot ladder painting the trim and the rooftop shutters. With the sun bearing down on me and the heat coming off the tar shingles, I'm ready for a break. The Fraze, meanwhile, is down below me in the shade, working at a snail's pace, slowly inching his brush along the edge of the window panes, trying not to ding the glass.

—I'm getting bar-b-queued up here, I say.

—How about a lunch break? he says.

—We're behind schedule.

—So come down and help me paint these windows. We can talk.

It is an unusual request for my stoic counterpart. But, eager to get out of the sun, I unhook my paint can and climb down the ladder.

I start in on a window. I can see his point: in this spot the offshore breeze and the shade make the job easy, and allow for pontification.

—I've been thinking about this book by Schweitzer all morning. You should read him, he says. —He is a good guideline. He insists that each living human should engage a theory of the universe. What's more, it must be optimistic and ethical.

—Sounds simple, I say.

—It isn't, he says. —You have to build from the ground up. We deceived the old lady yesterday. We lied to her. That fact stands in the way of my grand plan.

—We're painting a house, not restructuring the universe.

—I dropped the honeypot, he says. —Until I tell her the truth about it, I cannot continue.

—You're damn right you can't continue. She'll fire our ass.

—Schweitzer says you got to have courageous faith and absolute resolve. If the old lady can't make way for my truth then she has lost her optimism about the universe.

—Are you high?

—No, I'm slightly pleased with myself.

—Jesus. Go ahead then. Just don't tell her I was involved.

—No. That's right. That is for you to do, he says, walking to the front door.

Ten minutes later, The Fraze comes out and picks up his paint brush as if nothing has happened.

—Are we fired, I ask?

—She wants to speak with you, he says.

—What'd she say?

—Nothing. She seemed fine with the truth.

—What'd you tell her about her cat?

—She didn't ask. So I said nothing about the cat.

When I go into the kitchen to speak with Mrs. Bigelow, she is sitting on a stool. She is visibly shaken.

—What possessed him? she says. —Did you know anything about this?

—He told me this morning, I say.

—And what do you think about this, Buzz?

I do what Patch always says to do when the first fuck up has been committed, offer money immediately.

—I would like to reimburse you for the damaged goods, Mrs. Bigelow.

Her response is textbook for a wealthy client.

—I won't hear of it, she says. —But I don't want that man to ever step foot in my house again. If he wants to use the bathroom, he can go behind the shed.

—Very well, Mrs. Bigelow. Is that all for now?

She nods her head and glares, her lips drawn tight in an accusing line.

On the drive home, I tell him about the old lady's request. At first he says nothing. Then he pushes the play button on the car tape deck. AC/DC blares once again. When the song Problem Child sparks up, he says:

—She lost her optimism. She is out in trash heap with the mercenaries. She's done. He wears this grin, leering and supercilious, the kind a hangman must have underneath his executioner's hood.

—So, Buzz, how do you like your first taste of courageous faith in the truth?

—We lost her respect, I say. —We have to be perfect from here on out.

—I am working towards perfection, he says. —It is my number one priority. Schweitzer, like The Fraze, is laconic in his revolt. Schweitzer often speaks of the "homeless, drunken mercenaries" of the world. He goes on about the people of the modern world, wandering hither and thither in the gathering dusk of thoughtlessness without any concrete theory of the universe, enlisting in the service of one thing or another, not being able to discern between that which is great and that which is common. He is referring to me, of course, Buzz McBain, the common mercenary. And to The Fraze, too.

Once again we pick up forty ouncers at the packey. When we arrive home, we go on another long run. After the run we fix up some frozen dinners and relax with our beers in the back cottage. The Fraze brings up the idea of reading The Philosophy of Civilization out loud while we drink.

The reading of Schweitzer becomes central to our routine. In the weeks that follow it evolves into ritual. We wake up and let AC/DC batter our minds on the drive to work. We paint. We eat the old lady's small hamburgers. We resume painting until dusk. We go on long runs farther and farther out past the Padanaram Bridge. The Portuguese quahoggers are always there, a fixture of the landscape bent over their sand sifters in earnest toil. We consume beer and take turns, reading Schweitzer aloud.

Schweitzer was also a doctor and a missionary who went to Africa to heal the sick. He was a good man, and being in his presence like this and working hard each day has a cleansing effect.

Schweitzer might be the patron saint of painters. When you paint a house, your mind is unoccupied, and to combat the tedium you must find thoughts within the rhythm of the moving brush. Schweitzer's a friend to the moving brush.

—Spirit is everything. Institutions count for little, he says.

Swoosh. Swoosh.

—The materialism of our age has reversed the relation between the spiritual and the actual.

Swish. Swish. Swoosh. Swoosh. Swish. Swish.

With about four weeks left to finish the house, The Fraze and I get our first taste of Painter's ESP. Patch once mentioned the story of Painter's ESP, a phenomenon that he said mostly occurs on interior painting gigs where two guys are locked up in a room with heavy fumes for a couple of days. According to Patch it has to do with the ammonia fumes in the paint and if two guys are friends or not.

—I've had jobs, said Patch. —Where guys are finishing each other's sentences and thinking the same damn things.

I am up on the ladder, staring out at the lighthouse across the bay. The sun has baked my arms and neck, welting the skin, making it feel tight. The pungent ammonia smell of the paint has made me dizzy. There is no fear at being up so high on a windy day. Just me in a dreamy stupor looking at the lighthouse, wanting to swim out to it. The lighthouse is a mile offshore with strong currents that could sweep a person out into the Atlantic in a matter of minutes. Still, the urge to swim out to the lighthouse remains.

The Fraze hails me from beneath the ladder.

—Mrs. Bigelow's not around today, he says.

—That's right.

—Let's take a long swim. Out to the lighthouse and back. You up for it?

—That's fucked, I say. —I was thinking the same thing.

We stroll down the boardwalk steps and make our way onto the pebbly beach.

—It's what, I say. —About a mile.

—About, he says.

—There are currents.

—Maybe. I'll see you out there or I won't, he says stepping into the surf.

I step in after him and the cold, dark Atlantic water sends a chill throughout my sunburned frame. Soon I am striking through the waves, trying to catch up to The Fraze. One stroke after another, I try to cut a straight path to the lighthouse. The sea is flat and calm except for some white-capped waves in the distance, whipped up by winds that don't make it into the bay. The act of swimming is not unlike painting, focusing on a motion and repetition. It's a tiring chore. When I start to feel the deep cold water, freezing my underbelly and numbing the tendons in my legs and back, I look up to see the lighthouse. It still lies a good distance away, although now I can appreciate its imperious height. The current has drawn us a hundred yards or so to the eastern side of the bay.

—We're getting dragged, I say.

He stops swimming and looks up.

—Only a quarter of a mile or so.

—We're far out, I say. —It's been a good swim.

—Are you tired? he asks.

—Tired and cold, I say.

He spits salt water out of his mouth. His teeth are chattering.

—I can make it, says The Fraze.

—I'm going back.

—Like I said. I'll see you out there or I won't.

Then The Fraze turns his head to the lighthouse and plunges back into the brine. I tread water for a few moments, biting at my bloodless lip. Frigid water from the current below lifts and moves about me, feeling like aquatic fingers. My body is slowing down. Something tugs at my calf muscle and I realize it's a cramp. Drowning seems like it might be a gradual process.

Angry and cold, I aim my eyes back to the shore and begin to crawl back through the waves. No longer fighting the push of the surf, I glide with the tides towards the beach, not thinking at all of the lighthouse or of The Fraze, just the warmth of the sand.

When I reach the shore, I limp out of the water and sit down on a mat of seaweed. I begin kneading the cramp out of my calf. It was a good thing I turned back. I look out across the bay to the lighthouse. He is nowhere in sight.

I make my way across the lawn, and once again, up the ladder. Two hours later, The Fraze strides up the pebbly beach. Once or twice he stops on his way to the house and begins a strange sort of shadowboxing, throwing punches in a downward motion like he's punching some invisible dwarf in the head.

On the ride home, he blasts the Dirty Deeds tape. The tape has been overplayed at high volumes for far too long. The warped sound is grating. It has a garbled, nightmare quality to it; less Aussie heavy metal, more acid rock played inside a fish tank. He taps his knuckles on the dashboard to the distorted beat.

The night after the swim, we head out for our routine jog. As we turn out of the driveway, two young women on bicycles ride toward us. One is a freckled brunette and the other is long-legged blonde. As they pass by they smile at us, and the brunette says "hello" in a British accent. Immediately, we stop, our heads looking back to see what driveway they will turn into. We watch as they continue biking, nearing the end of the street and almost out of our sight. Then abruptly they guide their bikes into the last driveway on the left.

—The pale blue house at the end of the drive, I say. —The big house.

—That was close, says The Fraze. —We almost lost them.

—Did you hear that accent? They're nannies.

—Perfect, he says, in a daze. He is silent for a moment and then he says— The blonde is mine.

I shake my head. We can enjoy the luxury of becoming mortal enemies.

—She was that good, wasn't she? I ask.

—She is part of my grand plan, he murmurs.

After the jog, I hit the shower and try to get the paint spots scrubbed off my face and arms. It doesn't take long before The Fraze and I decide to go visit the girls. We walk down the dimly lit street, kicking at the gravel as we go. Everything has changed since seeing the girls on bikes. Sitting back in the cottage drinking beer and reading Schweitzer would be a thing of defeat.

—Who talks first? I say.

—If the blonde answers, I talk, he says.

We make our way down the center of the street like we're in some wayward ghost town about to enter some saloon and get our faces shot off.

—I have this weird feeling, I say. —Like being in an old western.

—Let me talk, then. No matter who answers.

When he rings the doorbell to the pale blue house, it is the blonde who answers. She is tall, as tall as me, but only about shoulder level with The Fraze. Her face has sculpted cheekbones, a velvet curve of lips and blue eyes that are so crystalline they don't seem to belong to the rest of her face. I hear him exhale.

—Hello again, says the girl in a strong Scandinavian accent.

—We came over to invite you and your friend for cocktails tomorrow night. We live down the way at 111 Narragansett. My name is Frazier. And this is Buzz.

—I am Gnelia, she says slowly.

—Will you accept the invitation? asks The Fraze.

—Maybe. I don't know if Julia is working tomorrow.

—Well, we hope to see the both of you, he says, bowing his head and stepping back.

The girl thanks us, nods her head and closes the door. The whole interlude, with The Fraze's formal speech pattern, had a Transylvanian vampire feel to it. I tell him so as we walk back down the street.

—I wasn't expecting a goddess, he says.

—You were creepy. I could've done better.

—She doesn't speak good English. She wouldn't be able to sense my fucked up inflections. Besides she'll tell the British girl what happened and the British girl will make her go.

—What makes you think that? I ask.

—Because the British girl turned her head and looked back at us when she passed by on her bike.

—So.

—So. Chances are she is a slut. And sluts are curious by nature.

On Saturday evening, The Fraze and I are in the garage playing ping pong, waiting for the bell to ring. Even though it's only ping pong, the game has gotten intense, because we are pissed. We don't say anything about the fact that the young ladies have bailed, we just smash the little plastic ball around, dreading the idea of a night without women.

—The nearest bar is how far away? he asks.

—Far, I say.

The Fraze smashes his paddle against the table. It breaks in two. Then the doorbell rings.

—Ah, they're here, he says, throwing his half a paddle gently onto the floor.

We walk through the kitchen and open the front door and there stands Julia, the British nanny, followed by Gnelia, who looks at us with a detached stare. After Julia introduces herself, we make our way into the living room where The Fraze and I have set up some wine and cheese, as well as some choice liquor. Julia tells us how impressed she is with the house and asks if we own it. I tell her it is my family's summer home.

—It's a brilliant little house, Buzz, she says, and from there on out, Julia sets her focus on me and the pair-offs are set. Julia and me. The Fraze and Gnelia.

Julia likes to talk. She tells me how she would rather drink Boddingtons beer than wine. She doesn't like wine primarily because of the taste, but also because French people drink wine.

—And everyone knows, she says, —that the French are turds.

Once she drinks some gin, Julia begins to talk about the family she sits for and how the husband is a horny bastard and sad lush case who has on two separate occasions begged her to get it on. Then she goes on to talk about how she has a serious boyfriend back in England who is in the Royal Navy and how she doesn't get it on with anyone but him. Her breath hits my face. She touches my leg with her long-fingered hand.

Julia has dark hair and knowing eyes that shine with a filth-loving glee. She wears too much make up for her pale complexion. When I touch her leg with my hand she starts telling me stories of how her brother is a skinhead back home and how he loves to beat up foreigners and immigrants. I don't know what to think of this. She goes on telling me weird details. Within the space of three drinks, she mentions her boyfriend at least two more times before we are on the couch in the living room, taking off our shirts.

—I like to go to motels, says Julia.

—There is a bedroom upstairs if you like, I say.

—I like American motels. There is something rotten about them. Let's go to one.

—Now?

She starts to put her shirt back on.

—I've got a boyfriend, she says. —But in a motel one can let oneself get carried away with the moment.

Then looking straight into my eyes, Julia slowly reaches her hands around my back. Then she rips her nails down either side of my spine.

—Did you like that? she asks.

Before I can answer she slaps me across the face with an open palm. My ears ring. Then her nails tear down my back again.

—Jesus Christ, I say.

—Do you like it?

Even though her body is skinny, her face in the cheeks and around the chin has a soft, roundness to it. A gluttonous face, I think.

—You do like it, she says, now taking my nipple between her thumb and forefinger. She squeezes until it hurts. Then she digs into my back with her nails again. There is a ping pong paddle near my elbow and I think about smacking her across the face with it. But I let her continue her game, which moves on to more pinching and then to biting. I am not necessarily enjoying it. I am being patient. Maybe curious. And hoping it leads to better things. I play the game back, being careful not to get too rough.

Her agile body moves from one side of me to the other, inflicting small wounds. Her bites leave teeth marks, and one bite in particular leaves a small purple contusion. She inspects the bite, probing it with her finger.

—This is a nice one here, she says, pleased. —I came close to breaking the skin but didn't.

Her manner is definitely more clinical than passionate.

—That one hurt, I say.

—Almost done, she says with a sigh. Then she unzips my pants and takes my penis in her hand. She strokes up and down. I watch her. The feeling in my groin is isolated pleasure, surrounded by a sea of stinging scratches and aching bite wounds. Exhausted from the extended session, and then made alive from her expert, gliding touch, I come in a matter of minutes. Julia, like some surgeon, zips me back up and with a grim, little smile, gives me a pat on the shoulder. Then she lies down by my side.

—Did you like that? she asks.

I nod and lean over to kiss her.

—No, she says, pushing me down on the bed. —I'll kiss you before. But not after. Only Roger can kiss me after.

—Where's Roger now?

—He is in the Falklands.

She goes into her purse and pulls out two cigarettes. We lay on our backs, smoking.

—This is a nice house. You must be well off to own two houses, she says.

—It's not mine. It's my stepfather's.

The cigarette has a bitter taste. The air around us is hazy with smoke. The scratches on my back sting with sweat.

—Just don't be one of those people who gets attached, says Julia. —That sort of thing makes me sick.

The next day, The Fraze has little to say about his night, and I'm not jumping at the chance to tell him about mine. Around lunch he takes off in his El Camino and when I see him later that afternoon, he is in the backyard, reclining in a lawn chair. I walk up and see that he is absorbed in a thick textbook.

—Five hundred and one Swedish verbs, I say, repeating the title of the book aloud.

—Go away, he says.

—Are you in love? I say jokingly, knowing full well that he is not capable of the emotion.

—I am learning Swedish.

—Obsession is unhealthy. It will take fifty pounds off your bench press.

—I am going to Provincetown with Gnelia on Tuesday night. I should know two hundred and fifty words by Tuesday.

—That's good. You can tell her you love her in Swedish.

—I dreamt about her last night, he says. —It was one of the first good dreams I've had in some time.

—Shit. Sounds to me like you're done. Already bought and paid for.

—You're pissed, he says. —You got the painted whore.

That night we eat our frozen dinners in separate rooms. I retire to the hammock on the porch, drinking wine from a bottle, thinking of motels with paper-thin walls. No mention is made of Schweitzer and a day of work looms over us.

The way I find out about how bad The Fraze has it for Gnelia is from Julia. Most nights we meet at The Sandpiper Motel in Dartmouth. It's thirty-five bucks a night or twenty-four for three hours. The rooms have faux wood cardboard walls, and petrified bubblegum stuck underneath rickety night tables. Orange lampshades emit a sickly, jaundiced light and the air is rank with cigarette smoke, which has settled in, a hidden toxin in the bed and pillows. Julia thinks The Sandpiper is perfect.

Mostly, Julia likes to listen to couples screwing in the adjacent rooms. Through her general mild flirtation, she's gotten buddy-buddy with the check-in guy and we get the kind of rooms she likes. Sometimes we sit back in bed and watch professional wrestling on TV. She finds it very moronic and very American, and watches it whenever possible. She goes for the vicious bad guys like Rowdy Roddy Piper and Captain Lou Albano with rubber bands pierced in his cheeks, and his monster cohorts, the Wild Samoans.

—I love Captain Lou, she says. —He's brilliant.

She says Captain Lou typifies the complex nature of a man and the stupidity of Americans: he is grotesque, pathetic, hilarious, and loveable all at once. The truth is, she likes him because she enjoys those who engage in cartoon-like behavior: ship captains, pervert fathers who hit on babysitters; and sun-tanned, drunken painters.

Once she sees Captain Lou get put in a sleeper hold by Superfly Snuka. Captain Lou struggles for air and then passes out in his opponent's grasp.

—That's fake, says Julia. —You can't knock someone out by just doing that.

This makes me smile.

—Want me to show you? I ask. She lets me go to work. I slowly apply the pressure to her neck and then jugular veins, squeezing my forearm, boa constrictor-style around her throat. Eventually her eyelids flutter and she passes out. I lie her down on the bed, arms outstretched. The room seems lonely. Some part of me feels like a seedy private eye, investigating a homicide in a cheap, seaside motel. If I had a cigarette, I would smoke it and stub it out on the carpet with the heel of my shoe. Case closed.

A few seconds later when Julia comes to, I put my arms around her. She gives me a cynical sneer. She knows what I know. We are staving off boredom. We light cigarettes.

Julia then tells me about The Lovesick Fraze. Expensive gifts. A valiant attempt to learn the Swedish tongue. Romantic trips to clean, quaint, artsy villages by the ocean.

—She is practically engaged to her boyfriend back in Stockholm. Doesn't he know that? asks Julia, accusing.

—I know nothing about it, I say.

—Gnelia's going home in a week. You should tell him that he's wasting his time.

—You don't like Frazier, do you? I ask.

—He is a lout. All Americans are louts. You're a cheeky lout, she says, blowing smoke in my face.

An hour or so later as I am putting on my pants, getting ready to leave, Julia surprises me with a kind tone in her voice.

—I only have a week or so left before I go back home, she says.

—Life in a motel passes quickly.

—It has, she says, and the coy, worried, sentimental look on her face makes her seem like a young girl, or a little sister, even.

—Next time we'll do something special, I say. —Something nice.

I close the door on the way out. It makes a hollow sound when I shut it.

Back at the cottage, The Fraze is walking out the door with Gnelia. He smiles when he sees me. It is apparent from his glow that he is escorting his own Valkyrie Queen, his final step in The Grand Plan.

—We are going to a café in Westport tonight, he says.

—You're big on cafés these days, I say.

—Just like I hear you are big on motels, he says.

Then The Fraze descends the porch steps alongside Gnelia, holding her hand in the protective way a groom holds the hand of his bride when leaving the chapel; people throwing rice and cheering. I look at Gnelia as they walk by me. Her beauty has an ethereal, vaporous quality to it. A person whose voice you can never really remember.

The next day at lunch, we're eating quietly under some shady elms when Mrs. Bigelow calls me over. She is upset. There are long trails of white paint all over her teak wood deck. I tell her I can't understand how it happened, since we covered it with plastic tarp. Then I spot the culprit writhing in the grass: a thick-bodied, slug-like, four-inch-long tomato worm. Instead of being neon green, the worm is completely white, having been dunked in a bucket of paint. I do not bring the worm to Mrs. Bigelow's attention, because the worm has very bad implications. I have seen The Fraze, before today, dunking tomato worms in the paint when he thought I wasn't looking.

—I'll clean this up right away, before it dries, Mrs. Bigelow.

—You've done a good job. I hate to see it all spoiled, she says.

—I'll get the paint off. Every drop.

When she's out of sight, I pick up the worm and take it back to our lunch spot. I throw the thing down in front of The Fraze. It twists about by his foot.

—A tomato worm, he says. —I hate those things. They have a little spike on their end.

—This one crawled all over the god-damned deck.

—Wow. He's still alive, says The Fraze. —I dunked him hours ago.

—You're going to help me clean the deck if it takes all day. Go get the turp.

The Fraze looks at me, his expression serious, filled with finality. Before it even happens, before he says a word, I am reminded of a scene from The Good, the Bad and the Ugly. That classic moment of betrayal, when Clint lets his partner in crime, Eli Wallach (the Ugly), know that he is going to leave him to die in the desert.

—You are going have to find a ride back home, he says. —I will be taking the El Camino.

—You're going to clean the deck, I say.

—No. I am leaving for the airport after lunch, he says. —My flight for Stockholm leaves at four o'clock.

—Sweden can't wait a week?

—I am afraid not.

—This is not good. You don't fuck your friends like this.

—I must go, he says. —She left yesterday. She has some guy back at home waiting for her.

—Does she know about this? Gnelia.

—In essence she does. She knows my grand plan.

—She is going to ruin you. The woman is made of air! You remember that, when you commit murder in Sweden.

—It isn't like that. She is the most pure specimen of absolute woman that I have ever seen.

—You can keep my last paycheck, he says. And then The Fraze walks off in search of icy beauty, Sweden and beyond.

I look over and notice that the tomato worm has surrendered. His fight for life over, he lies in the grass encrusted in white paint, looking like a small broken bone.

After work I take a taxi to The Sandpiper Motel. I have the special surprise for Julia in a paper bag. I go to the check-in guy and he tells me that Julia is already waiting for me in #14. I ask him what the smile is fucking about. His beefy chin quivers and apologizes, saying:

—Nothing, man. Nothing.

—Well, okay then, I say. —I have had a shitty day.

—Welcome to my life, he says, as I move past him.

Julia is lying on the bed in #14 in a red bra and panties. She's wearing dominatrix dark brown lipstick. Her black fingernails shine like bugs against her pale flesh. She is smoking a cigarette and watching TV.

—There is a show about the giant rats of Borneo on the telly, she says.

—Name one thing that isn't on TV these days?

—True love, she says. —True evil.

—They try, I say. Julia says nothing. She doesn't like being contradicted.

—I brought something, I say, hoisting my bag.

—I brought a surprise too. It's in my purse.

I open up her purse. Inside is a vibrator.

—You know what to do, she says, reclining. It's all part of her mechanized fidelity to her Navy boyfriend, Roger. I hold the plastic device in my hand and feel the weight of the batteries inside it.

—You have to flip the switch, she says.

Later on, when Julia tells me I have soft skin for a man. —Roger has very rough skin, and a hairy back, she says. —You make for a good contrast, I think.

—You like me better, don't you, I say.

—You know the boy at the front desk? she says in a voice between playful and cruel. I made him show me his willy.

After one more session and more cigarettes and bad TV, I produce two shot glasses and my promised surprise, a bottle of my stepfather's purebred Russian vodka, Russky Standart, conduit to oblivion, and proven antidote to misery.

What happens next after multiple vodka shots makes me understand how Ozzy Osborne ended up a mile from his hotel, wearing his wife's green dress, urinating on the Alamo, explaining to Texas Rangers "All I wanted to do was take a piss."

With me the episode involves a woman in the bathtub and Klingons. Julia is the woman in the tub. The vodka has filtered into my pituitary glands. Comments are made. Insults are exchanged. Julia brings out the Wild Samoan in me. I warn her that it might be time for the Cobra Clutch or, better yet, a revisit with the sleeper hold. Julia tells me her Navy boyfriend, Roger, will kill me. I throw her hairbrush at her. It splashes in the filmy water. A moment later it is floating beside Julia's leg. She screams bloody something. That is her favorite hairbrush.

On the TV Spock and Captain James T. Kirk are fighting Klingons in gladiatorial combat. I'm marching around the room, singing the American National Anthem. It's getting dark out. In the motel parking lot the driver of a minivan begins honking the horn as if he is my getaway driver, signaling me to leave the scene of the crime.

Next thing Julia is passed out on the bed, face down. I go over to the counter and take The Sandpiper Motel "Do Not Disturb" sign and place it on her ass. It sums up our time together. I have no one to talk to or yell at. The white trash symphony needs a crescendo finish. I begin breaking things. First I punch the cardboard wall. My fist goes through it. Then I go into the bathroom and smash the mirror.

—That is highly illogical, Spock says in the other room.

—Mr. Spock, responds James T. Kirk. —I don't care. Mr. Chekov, prepare to fire photon torpedoes.

Then a brutal Klingon voice is screaming at the door. Only it is a real voice, the fatboy from the front desk.

—Open the door, he says.

—You Klingon! I shout.

—I am going to call the police.

—She gave you a hand job, you bastard! I scream.

This calms us both down a bit.

—Is everyone okay in there?

—We're okay.

—I won't call the police, he says. —But if you broke anything. You're going to have to pay for it.

—Fair is fair, I say, before passing out on the bed next to Julia.

It is harder without The Fraze, but inside a week I finish painting Mrs. Bigelow's house. For a couple of days after the job, I do nothing but eat macaroni and cheese, and laze about in the hammock. Each night, Julia visits for a few hours. After she leaves, I sit out on the porch and watch the fireflies blink, small summertime Christmas lights in the darkness.

The morning of her departure back to London, Julia comes over and we drink lemonade in tall glasses at the picnic table. She shows me the gift that her kids got her, an imitation whale tooth scrimshaw carving of Cotuit Bay. I grab her by the hand and start to guide her toward the house. She pulls away. Not enough time. Once she is gone, I notice the brown smudge of her lipstick pasted to the rim of the glass. I close my eyes. The growling hum of a lawnmower next door begins to put me asleep. I sway in the hammock, suspended, smelling the freshly cut grass. Dirty Deeds, Done Dirt Cheap. Albert Schweitzer.

That fall I'm back in Boston, standing atop a forty-foot ladder, swinging a paintbrush across a rooftop gutter. The man I replaced died painting the same stretch of trim. He fell the distance and landed face-first onto the red bricks below. The ladder slid out from under him.

Real painters don't need someone to hold the ladder, is what I am told by Conley. He stands below me, recounting stories while I paint. Conley goes on about how another friend of his died in a motorcycle accident back home in Ireland. His motorcycle hit a wet patch of road and flew off the Connemara cliffs. He lets out a long whistle at this, testifying to the length of the fall. Conley's mood brightens with the telling of each tale.

—The deceased had been a real painter, Conley says, serious. —No one had to stand guard over his ladder.

When I finish with the trim, Conley tells me to go inside; the foreman wants to see me. For the rest of the afternoon, I am caulking and painting the six living room windows. The foreman has a rangy build and a fighter's face, with a crushed nose, sunken eyes. He stops working from time to time, and watches me. The only sound besides the radio is the swishing of moving paintbrushes, whispering throughout the sunlit room. The soft sound is constant. A mantra, breeding inner thought. Dull philosophies.

When I ask the foreman about the guy who fell off the ladder, he says:
—Are you kidding me?

I go over to the aluminum jug of turpentine and begin cleaning out my brush. The foreman stares at me for a moment and then finishes his harangue.

—You got to use your brain, kid. I had to fire that head case Conley was lying to you about. You want to know what he did? The dipshit painted a swastika on a wall. Even after two coats you could still make it out. We got rules around here. No artistic license with the paint. None whatsoever.

Theodore Deppe

A CHOREOGRAPHER IN CORDES

"In Cordes, everything is beautiful, even regret." —*Albert Camus*

Perfect, the sunlit pigeons. From these heights

he watches them sweep around the hill town

then fly in together to the red tiled roof below him

wings outstretched and riding gold light.

From his table on the terrace, the grieving choreographer

waits for the moment the flock will rise

and circle Cordes-sur-Ciel, a movement perhaps

for his next dance which he tentatively names Regret,

though at once he knows that's too mild

a word for the dance he imagines, something to do

with the genocide of the Cathars who once thrived here.

Breath held, he waits for the birds to ascend,

but they now seem settled for the night, so—

when his bill is paid and the late sun is just right—

he checks to be sure he isn't seen, then flings

his fork across the alley, where it bounces

on the roof below him. The pigeons startle

but stubbornly hold their place, and it's his old problem,

how to set things in motion. He studies the silverware

on the tables around him— twenty dancers—

pictures them prone on the dance floor,

glowering at the audience. He makes them refuse

to dance. And what did he think,

after the extermination of a people, he could make art?

Then sees, at that moment of negation, the body

of his former lover, or what seems

to be his carved and handsome image,

as on a sarcophagus, at peace.

He picks up his spoon and wants to hurl it too,

then stops, closes his eyes, begins to draw.

ONE WAY SHE APPEARED TO HIM

She didn't, of course, start the fire, though he thought
she'd set the whole Music School ablaze,
the orange sky puckered and creased above it

and he couldn't pedal fast enough to get there.
Earlier that week he'd stepped into a practice hall
and seen her at the dress rehearsal of Ravel's

Piano Concerto for the Left Hand. He was lucky,
he'd been kicked out of high school English
and creative writing, so he took classes at the university,

and arriving early he'd watched as her fingers
bi-located on the keyboard and the whole orchestra
rose above her like a storm cloud.

No sign of her at the scene of the crime
and it turned out to be just a single practice hall,
a disappointment maybe, though he reveled

at the thought of all those scales and finger positions
roaring into the night—who needs analysis and rote?
Then he realized how many instruments

were in there, every piece of the orchestra

igniting, and maybe he just imagined this,

or maybe he could hear heat pluck the cello strings,

hear flames sear a tightened drum skin,

hear the chords a piano makes as the floor opens

and it falls and strings, brass, and winds follow.

He rode back through a maze of glowing streets,

but once home, where none of the windows

reflected fire, he suddenly felt lost:

this boy, who couldn't read music, wanted

to play Ravel, wanted to perform on the piano he'd heard

crashing through the burning floor, wanted

a cadenza of flame, the pulse and flare of the impossible:

the piano resounded through the trap door of embers,

and everything else followed.

ANOTHER LIFE

How has this happened?
I've stepped outside
on a summer morning, alive,

dressed in a hospital johnny,
and no one tries to stop me.
I must have been ill

but now bare feet
try out cobbled streets,
cool breezes caress

my calves, and everyone
in the bird market
seems so happy.

Still, what good is this joy
when I come to the caged
sparrows? What good

is a hospital johnny
and this life without pockets?
Which is when I meet the nurse—

she may have followed me,

she offers me a smoke,

asks what my plans are,

and when I have no plans asks

would I like to go home now?

She is the angel of resurrection

who appears each morning

with coffee. I know this

but thank her and keep walking,

and how to explain that? They let

me keep walking!

I am alive on a summer morning,

I've reached the old bridge,

I've started composing

a little anthem for the road,

and no one yet makes me turn back—

Twenty Questions

TESS GERRITSEN

1) How has Maine informed your writing life? And how does place affect your work in general?

Maine has given me the peaceful setting and long winters that help me focus on the writing. There's also a sense of creativity that seems to be part of the Maine landscape, which may explain why we have so many artists and writers in this state.

2) How did you come to be a writer?

I knew I was a writer when I was seven years old, which is when I wrote my first "book," about the death of my beloved cat. All through childhood, I wrote stories and even bound the pages with needle and thread. But writing is an uncertain career, as my father impressed upon me, and he urged me toward a more secure job—as a physician. It wasn't until after I started work as a doctor that I returned to writing stories.

3) What are your biggest roadblocks as a writer?

Life! So many things intrude upon one's concentration, whether it's family emergencies or illnesses or those dozen thank-you notes I forgot to write. And, of course, the internet is a huge distraction. As for blocks in the writing itself, I'll admit that every single book I've ever written has hit a point somewhere in the middle where I just stop, because I don't know what happens next. I have to let the story stew for a bit before I know where it's going. That's "plot block," and I consider it just part of my own creative process.

4) Who are your writing heroes? What are you reading?

My writing heroes include every author who's written a book that made me stop and think: "Wow! If only I could write so magnificently!" That would include Barbara Kingsolver and Larry McMurtry and JRR Tolkien and a whole host of writers who pushed me, by example, to want to improve my craft. At the moment, I'm reading a galley of a really fun thriller called *Dark Magic* by James Swain.

5) What are you working on now, and how did you get there?

I'm now working on the tenth book in my series, featuring homicide detective Jane Rizzoli and [medical examiner] Maura Isles. When I wrote *The Surgeon* (published in 2001), I had no idea it would be the first book in a long-running series. Now here I am, a decade later, and Jane and Maura continue to grow and change. In this tenth novel, Maura heads to Maine to visit an isolated boarding school attended by the boy whom she's unofficially adopted. After she arrives, of course, bad things begin to happen.

6) How do you work—please let us know something of your writing life and discipline.

I start off with a premise, figure out a way to intimately connect it to the personal lives of my two characters, and then just start writing and see where it takes me. I can't seem to plot out the stories in advance; instead, I let the first draft tell me where the story's going. It means I write myself into a lot of blind corners and I'm forced to do a lot of revising, but I love this process of discovery. While in the first-draft stage, I try to write about four pages a day, and I write with pen and unlined typing paper. I go all the way till the end, then I'll type it, print it, and again work on paper for the second draft. I seem to like the security of real paper.

7) How do your characters speak to you? Or not? Is it a process of engagement with yourself or with extraneous voices?

Oh, they definitely speak to me. If I can't hear their voices, I can't really develop their characters. Sometimes I'll just write in a "placeholder" in the story, a faceless character who says the things I need him/her to say to advance the mystery. But as the chapters go by, that character will start to take shape. And eventually he'll seem real to me, and I can go back in later drafts and really make him come alive.

8) How much do politics and/or personal/cultural identity weigh for you in terms of your writing? Do you aim to create a greater message in the body of your work? And, do you think your separate works create their own overall narrative arc?

Not every book has a message. Sometimes, I'm just out to tell a good story. But every so often, there'll be an over-arching theme or moral that works its way into the tale. Most of my books share the same theme that other mysteries do: good triumphs over evil. But I've also explored medical ethics (should the young be sacrificed to prolong the life of the old?), sex trafficking (*Vanish*), and the Asia-American experience (*The Silent Girl*).

9) How much impact does your childhood, or personal life, have on your writing?

Generally speaking, does your work live in the present, past or future?

My personal life occasionally directs the story. *Bloodstream* was launched because of the difficulties I had with a teenage son. *The Silent Girl* explores my own experience growing up Asian American. But some books are just about topics that I don't know much about, but want to explore.

10) Writers are often encouraged to "kill their darlings," as the saying goes. Does this come easily? Do you enjoy it?

It's always hard to kill that paragraph you feel is so exquisitely written—but I've learned to do it if it doesn't serve the story. And a great little bit of writing that gets excised from one manuscript just might make it into the next.

11) Are you jealous of other writers/how do you feel when you read a bad review/ why do you think what you do matters/who do you think you are?

I'm not jealous of other writers' successes, but I do envy their superior skills! When I finish reading a really, really good book I'll sigh and think: "If only I could have written that!" It's more a sense of wistful admiration than jealousy. Because truly good writing is something to aspire to, not envy. As for getting bad reviews, it feels rotten. There's no denying that. Does what I do matter? In the larger scheme of things, hardly. I'm not saving lives. I'm not changing the world. I'm simply telling stories to entertain, and it's a lovely way to make a living, but I'm under no illusions that I'm worthy of any humanitarian prizes.

12) How does humor play in, in terms of your writing? What would your alter-ego writer's name be? Or: tell us a joke!

Humor? I only wish I knew how to write it! But that's for writers whose IQs are about twenty points higher than mine.

13) If you could snap your fingers and everything would suddenly be absolutely perfect (buy the ticket and take the ride here…just imagine this is possible) what would be perfection for you?

Truly, it would be the life I'm living now. I cannot complain about anything.

14) Which metaphor do you most often use to talk about writing craft (as in food-making, music, etc.) and why? And, how important is metaphor in your work? Symbolism?

I find I often use botanical metaphors, comparing things to vines or blossoms or trees. Music is another metaphor I'll often use ("crescendo," "tattoo," "drumbeat"). It may have to do with the fact I'm both a gardener and a musician. Metaphor is useful because it uses symbols that are universally understood. If you say that something smells like lemons, everyone understands what that means.

15) It's commonly said that writing is re-writing. How do you edit? How many readers of your own work do you have—and If you feel like telling us, who are they?

I edit like a madwoman, because my first drafts are so rough. I'll often go six, seven, eight drafts before I feel a manuscript is ready to be sent in. I have no other readers before that point. Only when I think it's ready for publication do I let my editor and agent see the work.

16) E. M. Forster famously said, "How do I know what I think until I see what I say?" When you aren't able to write for some reason, what happens to you? And, are there other art forms in which you work?

If I can't write for long periods of time, I get anxious. But only because I sense deadlines looming over my head. If there were no deadlines, I'd probably feel perfectly relaxed not writing for a while. In fact, I really wish writers were allowed to go fallow for long periods of time, just to re-fill the creative well.

17) Do you enjoy writing or is it simply something you must do? Is there some other occupation you'd rather have besides being a writer?

It's a little of both. Because writing is a business, and contracts require delivery at certain dates, sometimes writing feels like a job that must be done, whether I'm in the mood or not. Other times, I can't wait to get back to writing the story. If I weren't a writer, I think I'd devote myself to botany or archaeology or culinary pursuits. There's a whole world of other interests that you can't do justice to in just one lifetime.

18) Do you have anyone you'd like to thank in particular for a writing success? And is there anything you'd like to say to your readers?

My public school teachers in middle school and high school were great inspirations. They recognized I was a writer, they encouraged me, and they gave me the confidence to tell stories. I also have to thank my husband who, after finally understanding how much writing meant to me, became as supportive as any spouse could be. And to my readers, I just want to say thank you! Every reader is a writer's best friend.

19) What advice you have to give to fellow writers?

Don't give up on a story until you've written "the end." You never know how it's going to turn out until you've finished it.

20) What question have you always wanted to be asked in an interview? The answer?

I don't think there's a single question I've never been asked!

Twenty Questions

ELIZABETH HAND

1) How has Maine informed your writing life? And how does place affect your work in general?

Much of the time my work starts out as place; the characters come next, and plot last. I've written about Maine in various novels & stories—it's beautiful and eerie, the people are more interesting than in other parts of the world, and I never get tired of the landscape. Even in winter, with the power out and sleet coming down and several feet of snow to shovel and ... well, sometimes I DO get tired of it. But not much.

2) How did you come to be a writer?

I'm one of those people who always wanted to be a writer, since I was about five years old—before I could read and write. I didn't get published till I was about thirty, so I had a long apprenticeship. Actually, I still feel as though I'm in the midst of a long apprenticeship, which is probably good. Stay hungry, stay foolish, etc.

3) What are your biggest roadblocks as a writer?

Budgeting my time. I wish I could get up at four a.m. every day and get right down to work, but I don't. I did do that briefly in my twenties, when I was working full-time in D.C.; I'd watch the sun rise and write for an hour or two before heading off to work. It was great, but there was no way I was going to keep at it for more than a month!

4) Who are your writing heroes? What are you reading?

Probably too many heroes and heroines to mention. Arthur Rimbaud, Angela Carter, John Crowley, M. John Harrison, Shakespeare... I could go on and on. I do a lot of book reviews, so I don't get to simply read for pleasure much; when I do, it's most likely to be nonfiction, as research for whatever I'm working on. But at the moment I'm reading Le Carre's *Tinker, Tailor, Soldier, Spy* which is great fun and so well-written.

5) What are you working on now, and how did you get there?

I'm working on a YA novel called *Wylding Hall*, a contemporary riff on Daphne du Maurier's Rebecca set at a summer arts camp/colony for actors in upstate NY. I went on a little du Maurier jag this summer and read *Jamaica Inn* and *My Cousin Rachel*—MCR is fantastic. Somehow the idea for a new novel came into my head. I'm also brooding on the third Cass Neary novel, *Flash Burn*, which will be set in London.

6) How do you work—please let us know something of your writing life and discipline.

In theory I am up and at my desk every day at 9 AM. The reality is less impressive. I have a magical little lakefront cottage about a four minute drive from my house, and that's my office. I usually go there every day after I pick up the mail, and write 1,000 words, and then knock off. If I can finish 1,000 words in an hour (this almost happens sometimes) I'm done! But usually I'm there till mid-afternoon. When I'm really burning on a project, I'll stay down at the cottage and just work for as long as I can, sleep, then wake up and get down to it again. I sometimes come up with a soundtrack for a novel, and I'll listen to that music to evoke a Pavlovian response. In the last few years I have more often worked in silence. When I'm on deadline for a review or article all bets are off, and I just work till it's done.

7) How do your characters speak to you? Or not? Is it a process of engagement with yourself or with extraneous voices?

If I'm very fortunate, a character's voice will just start filling my head. That's what happened with Cass Neary, and some others. More often, as with *Radiant Days*, it takes a while for me to lock in on a particular voice—with RD it literally took years and several revisions. It's like tuning into a distant radio station. When it locks in, it's fabulous. Often I feel like I'm just operating on autopilot; the character is doing all the work.

8) How much do politics and/or personal/cultural identity weigh for you in terms of your writing? Do you aim to create a greater message in the body of your work? And, do you think your separate works create their own overall narrative arc?

My work is personal insofar as it often draws on experience and autobiography; it's political mostly if/when I write about environmental issues, which often color my work, though not always overtly. My Maine story, *Winter's Wife*, is ostensibly about a Mainer who takes one of the Icelandic huldufólk, or hidden people, as a wife. But really it's about developers destroying Maine.

9) How much impact does your childhood, or personal life, have on your writing? Generally speaking, does your work live in the present, past or future?

That's a good question, about the past, present, or future. I feel like I've cannibalized my own history so much in my work that I make a deliberate effort these days not to draw on my own life as much as I have in the past. Having said that, my life is the well I draw from, so I try to keep it interesting enough that I can keep going back and finding new things there to write about, or write from.

10) Writers are often encouraged to "kill their darlings," as the saying goes. Does this come easily? Do you enjoy it?

It comes more easily now than it used to. So much of my early work was overwritten, I cringe to look at it now. I kill many more of my darlings at birth these days—I've learned over the years to write in a more stripped-down fashion, and to harness my creative energy so it's not just bleeding all over the page.

11) Are you jealous of other writers/how do you feel when you read a bad review/ why do you think what you do matters/who do you think you are?

When I was younger, I might feel a stab of envy, but for the last few decades I can honestly say no. Writing is far too difficult a career or vocation to feel much envy for another practitioner—it'd be like one coalminer being jealous of another coalminer. As for bad reviews, I try to follow Martin Amis' attitude: "A bad review might ruin my breakfast, but not my dinner."

12) How does humor play in, in terms of your writing? What would your alter-ego writer's name be? Or: tell us a joke!

Some of my characters are funny, like Cass Neary, who's a wiseass. But I'm not a good joke-teller. I'm a pretty good mimic, which is the most thankless comedic gift one can have, alas.

13) If you could snap your fingers and everything would suddenly be absolutely perfect (buy the ticket and take the ride here…just imagine this is possible) what would be perfection for you?

Believe it or not, being able to work at Tooley Cottage is pretty much all the perfection I need. I love London, where I also spend a lot of time, so the ability to travel instantaneously between Maine and here (I'm in London as I write this) would be nice.

14) Which metaphor do you most often use to talk about writing craft (as in food-making, music, etc.) and why? And, how important is metaphor in your work? Symbolism?

Hmm. Another interesting question. Maybe the metaphor of building a house, which I used in my novella, Illyria, as a metaphor for putting on a play. I like metaphor as a descriptive technique, but I shy away from it as overarching symbolism within a novel, which seems too close to allegory and preaching.

15) It's commonly said that writing is re-writing. How do you edit? How many readers of your own work do you have—and If you feel like telling us, who are they?

I rewrite constantly. I think it's the single most important part of the writing process. My partner, John Clute, is nearly always my first reader. I don't show my work to too many people. John; my friend Ellen Datlow, who's a brilliant NYC editor; and my friend Bill Sheehan, another writer. That's probably about it. When I'm working on something that relies on a field of expertise, I will show it to someone more knowledgeable than myself, as I did with *Available Dark*, which I gave to a friend who's a professor of Icelandic and knows the language, culture, and people.

16) E. M. Forster famously said, "How do I know what I think until I see what I say?" When you aren't able to write for some reason, what happens to you? And, are there other art forms in which you work?

Not writing makes me crazy: I am not a happy camper when I can't work. I always feel like one of the people in that Vonnegut story, *Who Are We This Time*? I don't have other abilities, alas, so it's writing or nothing for me.

17) Do you enjoy writing or is it simply something you must do? Is there some other occupation you'd rather have besides being a writer?

I love writing. I can't think of something I'd rather do, though if I had another life, I'd like to be an interior decorator (really).

18) Do you have anyone you'd like to thank in particular for a writing success? And is there anything you'd like to say to your readers?

My parents, who put up with me and gave me a lifelong love of reading. And my children, who grew up in a family of writers and never complained. Not about the writing part, anyway.

19) What advice you have to give to fellow writers?

To read widely.

20) What question have you always wanted to be asked in an interview? The answer?

I've always wanted to be asked what question I have always wanted to be asked in an interview. The answer, of course, is 42.

Twenty Questions

BARON WORMSER

1) How has Maine informed your writing life?

I hope my memoir *The Road Washes Out in Spring* demonstrates that living and working in Maine informed my writing profoundly. I wouldn't be who I am as a writer and human being if I hadn't lived in Maine and particularly in Somerset County. It was an education in many ways. I grew up in an urban environment very different from the world I'd inhabited for twenty-five years or so. I was hungry for rural authenticity. Maine certainly satisfied that need.

And how does place affect your work in general?

Living on a particular place on earth matters enormously to me. I couldn't be someone who takes a job in this city or that state. Whether it's been directly to the land or to the old house we worked on when we lived in Hallowell (after we left our house in the woods), the connection to a place on earth has been crucial. Northern New England for me is a hospitable place, one that has allowed me to do the work I have wanted to do with a modicum of distraction. I love the seasons of northern New England.

2) How did you come to be a writer?

I started writing when I was an adolescent and never really stopped. I wrote two prose books in my twenties that never got published—a rather wooden novel and a book on the limitations of modern architecture. I started writing poetry in earnest when I was around thirty.

3) What are your biggest roadblocks as a writer?

I haven't had any to speak of. Writing chose me as much as I chose writing, probably more.

4) Who are your writing heroes?

I'm keen on Shakespeare. Otherwise there are hundreds of good writers I've read over the decades. As far as American poetry is concerned, Dickinson, Frost and Plath resonate particularly for me.

What are you reading?

At the moment I'm reading Barry Hannah's stories, Mark Twain's *Roughing It* and a poet from Nevada named Joanne de Longchamps. I just finished reading *A Time to Keep Silence.*

5) What are you working on now, and how did you get there?

I "finished" a semi-autobiographical novel set in 1962-63 around the end of May, 2011. I keep picking at that. It's hard to get that many words (112K) exactly the way you want them. It's a book I didn't think I would make it to but I did, so I'm pleased about that. I keep writing poems and literary essays. I've written a few of what I call odes lately. The most recent is about the photographer Diane Arbus—one of my artist heroes. I just finished an essay about Quentin Anderson's book *The Imperial Self.* I have a nonfiction book about 1965 floating around in my head and a book of short stories set in 1968.

6) How do you work—please let us know something of your writing life and discipline.

I can't say I've ever had a schedule. I'm episodic—even writing the novel was that way. When you're with it, you're with it. As to poetry, it's random. Something strikes you and you go with it. If it doesn't strike you, then it doesn't. Worrying about it is not going to help.

7) How do your characters speak to you? Or not? Is it a process of engagement with yourself or with extraneous voices?

I've written a fair number of persona poems, poems in which others speak. It's more of an engagement with that which is not me. The world is much bigger and more interesting than my ego. I've always been haunted by this massive coming and going on the face of the earth, the sheer drama of it, the oblivion of the particular. As to fiction, what everyone says about the characters speaking on their own is true. I experienced some of those remarkable moments in writing the novel.

8) How much do politics and/or personal/cultural identity weigh for you in terms of your writing?

My historical sense informs my work. I'm interested in how the weight of historical time intersects with moments. That sense includes politics, though not in the sense of protesting this or that event. Without a doubt, that sense includes my being Jewish. I've never particularly pursued any agenda. As to identity, I'm a practicing Buddhist so I've been working on giving up identity rather than taking more on. Identity can be empowering; it also can be a shackle.

Do you aim to create a greater message in the body of your work?

No. As the remark goes, if you want to send a message, use Western Union.

And, do you think your separate works create their own overall narrative arc?

I may have learned a bit more about life and writing as I've aged. That's about it for a narrative arc. I called my new and selected poems *Scattered Chapters* for a reason. Some people have complained about how all over the place I am. I can understand that but I'm a fairly various character.

9) How much impact does your childhood, or personal life, have on your writing? Is there a writer whose childhood and personal life haven't impacted his or her writing?

They are the soil writers grow from. They may directly address it or they may not but it's crucial as to who they become. As for the personal life, though I don't write much about mine, the loss of my mother when I was twenty-one, my marriage, having children, have had enormous effects on my writing, much more than I could articulate.

Generally speaking, does your work live in the present, past or future?

The past is a pretty long tail we carry around.

10) Writers are often encouraged to "kill their darlings," as the saying goes. Does this come easily? Do you enjoy it?

I'm not very attached to this or that line or phrase or sentence so I can't say I have "darlings." I'm trying to write well and I go from there. I like revising because it's a wonderful illusion—I'm going to perfect something. I don't seem to tire of that illusion. I think it was Zagajewski who defined poetry as "an impossible art." Not that prose is a piece of cake.

11) Are you jealous of other writers/how do you feel when you read a bad review/ why do you think what you do matters/who do you think you are?

Jealousy seems stupid. You are who you are. As to reviewers, they are entitled to their opinions. There's no reason for them to like me or understand me. Often they have agendas and the work before them is grist for that particular mill. That's how it goes. I've had to be a writer. How that matters to the world at large is way beyond me. As Ford Madox Ford put it, some enter by the portals and some do not. I think I'm someone who's loved words.

12) How does humor play in, in terms of your writing? What would your alter-ego writer's name be? Or: tell us a joke!

I tend to think of life as a tragic-comic affair. Both adjectives are operative for me. We don't know what we're doing here so humor comes easily to me. I know I can make people laugh but that's hardly all I want to do. Both adjectives matter. It's the balance that consumes me. My name is strange enough already without having an alter-ego name.

13) If you could snap your fingers and everything would suddenly be absolutely perfect (buy the ticket and take the ride here…just imagine this is possible) what would be perfection for you?

That's not a Baron question. I honestly feel lucky to have done what I've done in this world. To misquote one of my characters in my book of short stories, "Everything is pretty great the way it is. I mean there are spring and rain and love and dogs and Chinese food." That's how I feel.

14) Which metaphor do you most often use to talk about writing craft (as in food-making, music, etc.) and why?

Sometimes I talk about poetry in terms of recipes—some of this and some of that go into the poem. As an art, the number of ingredients that make up a poem aren't that numerous but the variations are infinite. Cooking seems like that. And cooking is a primal art the way poetry is.

And, how important is metaphor in your work? Symbolism?

Poetry is metaphor making. It's poetry's basic instinct. I wouldn't know a symbol if it bit me.

15) It's commonly said that writing is re-writing. How do you edit? How many readers of your own work do you have— and If you feel like telling us, who are they?

I write a draft of a poem and then put it down and then pick it up and put it down and pick it up and that goes on for months and years usually. Beyond that there's no rhyme or reason that I can see about how I proceed on a given poem. Prose is more a matter of sticking with it, probing the spaces between the sentences, cutting out baggage, fiddling with syntax.

My wife has been a steady and acute reader of my work. I've had miscellaneous readers of the poems over the years but mostly I've kept to myself. I like the self-critical aspect of revising. As to the novel, I've had a number of readers reading drafts. That's helped me enormously.

16) E. M. Forster famously said, "How do I know what I think until I see what I say?" When you aren't able to write for some reason, what happens to you? And, are there other art forms in which you work?

I've been a steady writer. As I noted earlier, I don't believe in worrying about the whole thing. It's about quality not quantity in any case.

I've been amazed by people like Donald Justice who painted, played the piano and composed music, but I'm not one of those people.

17) Do you enjoy writing or is it simply something you must do? Is there some other occupation you'd rather have besides being a writer?

Writing chooses you. As far as other occupations are concerned, I like cooking a lot but I don't know if that would have been a vocation. Nowadays there's a lot of energy in the world of food. It's the dominant art form in many ways. It's hard work day-in, day-out. That appeals to me. I have to say though that the vocation I did practice for many years—librarianship—was fine with me. It made for a good day job.

18) Do you have anyone you'd like to thank in particular for a writing success? And is there anything you'd like to say to your readers?

I owe a great deal to Tom Hart at Houghton Mifflin who sought me out when I was starting to publish and did my first two books. And I owe a great debt to Nina Ryan, the agent who handled my memoir.

One of my readers once described the experience of reading my work as "getting hit by a velvet baseball bat." I appreciate readers who keep coming back for more.

19) What advice you have to give to fellow writers?

I only give advice if someone specifically asks me for it.

20) What question have you always wanted to be asked in an interview?

What's your favorite beer?

The answer?

Switchback.

John Callahan

Preface to **A Storm of Blizzard Proportions** *Ralph Ellison*

Ralph Ellison began *A Storm of Blizzard Proportions* while steaming across the North Atlantic toward home after a Merchant Marine mission to the Welsh port of Swansea in 1944. He wrote first and second drafts of the story by late summer of that year. Soon afterwards, apparently setting the story aside, he clipped both manuscripts to a friend's long letter of praise and criticism dated October 10, 1944.

A Storm of Blizzard Proportions is built on reveries, influenced in technique by Hemingway and Joyce, in perspective by Jack Johnson and the protagonist's autobiographical association of the Welsh countryside with southwestern Ohio, the same landscape Ellison came to love after his mother's death in October 1937. Aficionados of Ellison's prose will compare the narrator's fictional memory of hunting quail the snowy morning his mother dies with his own autobiographical lyrical piece, February. (See pp. 1-4 of the Modern Library *Collected Essays*.) For the narrator of *A Storm of Blizzard Proportions*, that time was "the winter of Teruel." Notably he associates the snow and loss in Ohio with the Republican victory, a victory in a snowstorm that many considered a turning point in the Spanish Civil War before the brutal, fatal fascist counterattack in January of '38.

On the bottom of the second draft's last page, a note scribbled in Ellison's hand fills out some of what his narrator leaves unexplained when he tells the Welsh woman he loves he will be back, although he knows inside that he will not because in the American world they are not man and woman, but simply black and white:

> Contrast life of mother (hanging out clothes, the
> wind slapping her dress, her coat pinned at the
> throat, her hat pulled low over her ears, in the
> bitter wind, the clothes hanging stiff and icy even
> as she pinned [them] to the line) with that of girl.
> Girl used to toil, to woman's fate, but not to being
> a Negro's wife in U. S. He cannot ask her. Not because of [illegible word]
> but because she is not conditioned to the thing.

Ellison's note is provisional. So is the story. For this reason I did not include it in *Flying Home and Other Stories* (1996, 1998). But over the years the story has continued to exert a gravitational pull on my imagination. I welcome its publication in *The New Guard* because I believe discerning readers will relish the chance to read it and consider its merits.

Is the story apprentice work? Yes. Are there distinct echoes of Hemingway and Joyce, especially Ellison's re-voicing of the last paragraph of *The Dead* in his story's finale? Unquestionably. But their influence is not simply derivative. Rather, young Ralph Ellison builds on his literary ancestors' sense of rhythm and theme to fashion a story only he could tell about how the universals of love and loss are at work in his time and place and situation.

John Callahan
November 23, 2011

A STORM OF BLIZZARD PROPORTIONS

All morning he had been obsessed by Jack Johnson. It was annoying,
There was no logical reason for it, He was much too young to have seen
Jack Johnson fight, and no one had mentioned the name during the entire
voyage. Besides , he should have been thinking of how he would tell
Joan that their's was all an impossible dream. But how could he tell
her, when everytime he tried to think Jack Johnson broke into his
thoughts like the distant rumble (thunder) of a storm?

He stood at the bar and gazed mournfully at the rows of colored
bottles lined upon the shelves. Mid-afternoon now, the pub was empty;
even the bartender had disappeared. Well, it would soon be time to
cross the street to the Red Cross club to meet her. looking across the
empty tables toward the clock on the wall, he saw where someone had left
a set of darts stabbing the red heart of the target. And his own foot-
prints showed wet upon the smooth-grained floor as he gazed outside into t
the rain. He was suddenly lonely and wished that the soldiers who had
left as he came in had remained.

    Back home, he mused, there'd be someone to talk with. There'd be
a juke box with colored lights inside and for a nickle you could lose
yourself in the music. Perhaps there would be a few rummies hanging
around. Or just some guys dropped in for a drink. Maybe they would be
standing right beside you, arguing , or talking polotics, or just giving
the white folks hell. And there'd be big windows facing the street, not
these little ones, and you could see the brown girls, the kind who made
quite different problems, passing with their slow , swing-hip walk,
And maybe one would look in and smile at you just for the hell of it...

He paused, his glass in mid-air, thinking he had heard the rumble
of distant thunder. It's no weather for bombers, he thought. So it can't

293

.2   *R. E.*

be the guns at Cardiff blasting. Then through the rain-streaked window he
saw a truck transport ~~rumbling~~ thundering swiftly past, their canvas tops wildly
flapping. He sipped his beer. To him the war was an old story now, and
the thought of a raid had brought no excitement. But thinking of home had
made him feel better, and he tried to recapture his mood.

<u>You meet the damnest people in bars, he thought</u>:

> <u>Prize-fighters, foot racers,</u>
> <u>Whore-mongers, chippie chasers,</u>
> <u>Tin-horn gamblers,</u>
> <u>'Fore day creepers,</u>
> <u>Mid-night ramblers.</u>

That time I went in Smalls paying no attention to anyone and ordered and
was standing beside old Jack Johnson. Big man with a gold tooth and beret
who looked like somebody even before you knew his name. Now there was a
man in~~x~~ spite of all those women . They didn't praise him as they do Joe,
but what I like is that he went where he wanted to go and did what he
wanted to do. No matter what they said. That's what a man has to do. Wonder
what he found in all those foreign countries? He must have been lonely.
Must have been lonely in Spain alone...I'll never sail again and me the
only one of us. Fellows are all right too, not like in Old Jack Johnson's
time. Sailors the most democratic bunch of wild sonofabitching Americans
in the world. Not provincial like college presidents, politicians. Salt of
the earth...Too bad best salt goes to sea. No joke. But even with them you
miss something when you're the only one. Seems like a man's not completely
himself without others along who've passed through what he's lived.
No good to push too far ahead of your own, in somethings. But you have to
go wherever you can. Only travel light. Not politely, but lightly. But the
last one stuck by old Jack, didn't she? What hell holds? Fame gone, prestige
forgot. Yet holds? Could Joan?--Old Jack Johnson had something Joe Louis
doesn't have. Have I? Dog beneath Joe's skin. All chained up inside. In the
ring Joe's a controlled explosion. From containing himself. Joe's fight is
a machine, Jack's was a dance. Those silent movies. O humble heroes!
Old Jack reached out for life. Wasn't afraid to be called a fool. Defined

.3

his won world...own world...One World! He fought them all the way, night and day. Fought them with his fists, fought them with his grin, fought them with his high-powered car. A man with, out a man. And who hasn't. Who? 'Kills the thing he loves!' Old Jack even fought a bull in Spain. Tame stuff though, to bull he was escaping, bull he taunted.'Whiteboy, this next punch is going to bounce off your chin and jar all your old folks at home.' The bull that hollored ' Kill the coon!'....They wouldn't let me fight the bull, either. Now he's strong. Torro Franco, Torro Adolph. The old Bull changeth, but bulls is bulls. Would Joan understand that?

He looked at the clock, trying (vainly) to stop the drift of the monologue within him. So what if Old Jack did? There's a time when a man makes a choice, when it all rises up on him and he can go no further. And besides, they misrepresented the whole thing. They pushed old Jack to the limit. Sure he lay in the Cuban Sun, but his heart was covered with ice. Didn't shade his eyes from the sun , but thumbed his nose at the world...In white men they've named it anguish.'Awareness of the absolutely most extreme limitation of the possible.' Defined the world in his own terms. Old Jack Johnson, his health in bitter beer, he thought , draining his glass. Old Jack Johnson, yes! A man engaged. A man enraged. A man in rage!

He stood watching the rain, heavier now, as his eyes filled up and blurred, until beyond the window panes it was as though the sky had burst to smithereens. Well, so he would have to go. It was time, she would be waiting. Going out he suprised himself by stopping suddenly to step carefully into the grit-caked prints his own feet had made coming in.

****

In the Red Cross Club he sat and gazed into the glowing coals of the fireplace. It was warm in the club. Exept for a soldier snoring over in the lounge the room was empty. Someone had turned the radio down low and he could hear the music faintly. It was a warm melody , creating a friendly, nostalgic mood. And yet as he lounged in his chair he was cold. Cold around the edges; cold, it seemed, in the very morrow of his bones.

.4 R.E.

He sighed, waiting. Then a faint tinkling of silver drifted to him from the
kitchen and when he turned, there, coming through the doorway, was Joan.

"Darling!" she said.

" Hello," he said. The musical roll of her voice rang in his ears and
he felt a pang, though he smiled.

" Have you been waiting long?" she said.

" Not long. Not long as I'll have to wait."

He saw the quick concern on her face as she came over and stood before
the fire, the starched volunteer's apron gathering smoothly at her rounded
hips, making a pleasant sight.

" Will you be going soon?" she said.

" You never know the day," he said. " You only know that when you're
told, you leave."

" Couldn't you stay with me, just once?" she said, catching the arms
of his chair and leaning over so that he caught the fresh fragrance of her
body. " Let the ship go without you? Or at least lets get married, now, today?"

Above the smooth shapes of her breast he saw how the glow of her blue
beads deepened the blue of her eyes. Now she was smiling. How could he
tell her?"

" I'd like to," he said. " Oh but wouldn't I like to. You know that."

" Then do,"she said, her voice breaking with the sound of tears.

He could not answer. For as she searched his face he knew she would
never understand. And as she became aware of the watch ticking in the
screaming silence he saw Jack Johnson as in a troubled dream, streatched
full length upon the canvas of his mind, his gloved hands guarding his eyes
from a bitter sun...

"This war, I hate this war, " she said.

" But its the reason I'm here, dear."

" No," she said fiercely " you would have come to me somehow. I hate it
I hate it and—Oh, darling, now,..now I hate you ever came!"

.5

He watched her silently. All ready it was poisoning things, making her unhappy. She was between the horns. Five years of bombing were not enough to condition her for the war their life would be...

" But I," he said uncovering his face with his hands "I didn't make the war."

" But you made the way I feel," she said. " Why did you ever speak to me?"

" Don't be a child, Joan," he said tiredly. "Go fix your face and let's have what we can together while there's still time. And lets have it, dear, without tears.

She looked at him mutely, really like a child with the tears on her face. Then he felt her head against his shoulder and the soft movements of her body as she sobbed.

" Go on , dear," he said " This is our life together."

" Always hail and farewell, it is," she said hopelessly. "But when shall we live? I want a nice house, if only for a little while. Not a very large house, but a nice one. On a hill,.Where the mist comes down in the winter. With a brass fender where children can play and learn their lessons. And where you can tell them of America--Or," she said with sudden breathlessness ,"it could even be a house in America. A little house in Ohio..."

He watched the dimples steal into her face as she dreamed aloud, watched the soft glint of her teeth in the fireglow. And in his mind he saw the long roll of Welsh hills covered with heather, the brown and greens of the countryside, like fine tweeds beneath the cloud-hidden sun. It would have been a fine life. For, he realized abruptly, he loved this land, this country, as he had come that distant year to love Ohio--Strange he should recall that year. That was the year he had lost his mother and had hunted to keep himself alive. It was a wounderful country he thought, though connected with irrevocable loss, As now this land would be should he never return.

.6

She stirred, warm against him, gazing now into the fire, beautiful with
the fireglow on golden hair. And he watched her with a deep and numbing
anguish, for inspite of himself, she was becoming fast entwined with all
the tender , aching things within him, with buried things; merged with his
most tragic image of life,locked to his most precious symbol of death.

Entwined, she had become,with how that year he had hunted the quail
and pheasants for his living, the winter of Teurel. He remembered how
the snow-covered hills had shone in the sun the morning his mother died
and the new awareness come to him with her going. At the bomm of the guns
the birds came up along the hill in pairs and fell with a circling, down
into the thicket on the other side. And he had come down into a snow-
filled valley, soft with the last faint glow of the sunset, finding the
pheasant dead upon the snow, its plumage undisturbed, and the vapor
slowly rising from the sinking blood. He had startled the cardinals into
red tracer-bullet-streaks of flight. And there had been the apples,dark
red upon black branches that showed etched stark against the sky after
the months of ice and snow, the apples still mellow and sweet to the
taste,for all of that. That was during the early part of the war, the
first episode. A tragic moment of a pathetic year, though not many had
believed it at the time. No more than they would believe that to love one
country was to love them all. Nor would they understand that to love
this land was to more deeply love the land which gave one pain. But it
was so...So here was Joan, like the things, the peaceful things one loved,
expendible. And you couldn't tell her.

"It's time for to go on duty."

" Yes, so it is," she said wearily. " One does one's duty."

" It wont be long," he said " and maybe tonight there'll be a moon."

" No moon, a storm is expected," she said " perhaps with snow, the
first for Wales this season. Besides , it would have been a bomber's moon!"

" Oh, Joan," he said "I'll..."

.7

" But when?"

"Always...Through water, through fire, through snow, through--always, always..."

" Yes, even through what's out there you'll come back," she cried, holding him desperately " Because I love you. My Yank--Oh my Yank, I'll bring you tea with extra ~~sugar!"~~

She left hurriedly, ~~And~~ as he waited he watched the dying glow of the fire and thought of the voyage westward. Tomorrow he would sail for home. Weeks of cold , rough seas, [redacted] A cold crossing he would have of it. And at home there would be the snow. He shivered, A snowstorm of blizzard proportions, the Army newspaper had said, was sweeping the ~~mid~~-western states. Already the snow was covering the hills of Ohio, already powdering his mother's grave-stone there, and flashing the brooks and frozen rivers , where quail made tracks in the ~~quick~~ falling dusk. Snow was sweeping the hills and drifting the brairs, and drily shaking the blood-red leaves ~~left hanging~~ that hung like bandages snagged on the throns in flight--an endless snowing all over the snow-white world of home. Snow sweeping, snow falling, snow drifting down. Snow in the hills and far-away-places. A snow of blizzard proportions. Covering all.

Contrast life of mother (hanging out clothes, the wind whipping her dress, her coat pinned at the throat, her hat pulled low over her ears, [illegible] in the bitter wind, the clothes hanging stiff and icy even as she pressed it to the line) with that of girl. Girl used to toil, to woman's fate, but not to being a [illegible] wife in U.S. [illegible] not because of [illegible] but because she is not conditioned to the thing.

Ralph Ellison

A Storm of Blizzard Proportions

ALL MORNING HE HAD BEEN OBSESSED by
Jack Johnson. It was annoying, there was no logical reason
for it. He was much too young to have seen Jack Johnson
fight, and no one had mentioned the name during the voyage.
Besides, he should have been thinking of how he would tell
Joan that theirs was all an impossible dream. But how could
he tell her, when every time he tried to think, Jack Johnson
broke into his thoughts like the distant thunder of a storm?

He stood at the bar and gazed mournfully at the
rows of colored bottles lined upon the shelves. Mid-afternoon now, the pub was empty; even the bartender had disappeared. Well, it would soon be time to cross the street to the
Red Cross Club to meet her. Looking across the empty tables
toward the clock on the wall, he saw where someone had left
a set of darts stabbing the red heart of the target. And his
own foot-prints showed wet upon the smooth-grained floor
as he gazed outside into the rain. He was suddenly lonely and

wished that the soldiers who had left as he came in had remained.

Back home, he mused, there'd be someone to talk with. There'd be a juke box with colored lights inside and for a nickel you could lose yourself in the music. Perhaps there would be a few rummies hanging around. Or just some guys dropped in for a drink. Maybe they would be a standing right beside you, arguing, or talking politics, or just giving the white folks hell. And there'd be big windows facing the street, not these little ones, and you could see the brown girls, the kind who made quite different problems, passing with their slow, swing-hip walk. And maybe one would look in and smile and wink at you just for the hell of it . . .

He paused, his glass in mid-air, thinking he had heard the rumble of distant thunder. It's no weather for bombers, he thought. So it can't be the guns at Cardiff blasting. Then through the rain-streaked window he saw truck transports thundering swiftly past, their canvas tops wildly flapping. He sipped his beer. To him the war was an old story now, and the thought of a raid had brought no excitement. But thinking of home had made him feel better, and he tried to recapture his mood.

You meet the damnest people in bars, he thought:

> Prize-fighters, foot racers,
> Whore-mongers, chippie chasers,
> Tin-horn gamblers,
> 'Fore day creepers,
> Mid-night ramblers.

That time I went into Smalls paying no attention to anyone and ordered and was standing beside old Jack Johnson. Big man with a gold tooth and beret who looked like somebody even before you knew his name. Now there was a man in spite of all those women. They didn't praise him as they do Joe, but what I like is that he went where he wanted to go and did what he wanted to do. No matter what they said. That's what a man has to do. Wonder what he found in all those foreign countries? He must have been lonely. Must have been lonely in Spain alone . . . I'll never sail again and me the only one of us. Fellows are all right too, not like in Old Jack Johnson's time. Sailors the most democratic bunch of wild sonofabitching Americans in the world. Not provincial like college presidents, politicians. Salt of the earth . . . Too bad best salt goes to sea. No joke. But even with them you miss something when you're the only one. Seems like a man's not completely himself without others along who've passed through what he's lived.

No good to push too far ahead of your own, in some things. But you have to go wherever you can —only travel light. Not politely, but lightly. But the last one stuck by old Jack, didn't she? What hell holds? Fame gone, prestige forgot. Yet holds? Could Joan? Old Jack Johnson had something Joe Louis doesn't have. Have I? Dog beneath Joe's skin. All chained up inside. In the ring Joe's a controlled explosion. From containing himself. Joe's fight is a machine, Jack's was a dance. Those silent movies. O humble heroes! Old Jack reached out for life. Wasn't afraid to be called a fool. Defined his won world . . . own world . . . One World! He fought them all the way, night and day. Fought them with his fists., fought them with his grin, fought them with his high-powered car. A man with, but a man. And who hasn't. Who? 'Kills the thing he loves!' Old Jack even fought a bull in Spain. Tame stuff though, to bull he was escaping, bull he taunted. 'White boy, this next punch is going to bounce off your chin and jar all your old folks at home.' The big bull that hollered 'Kill the coon!' . . . They wouldn't let me fight the bull, either. Now he's strong. Torro Franco, Torro Adolph. The old Bull changeth, the bulls is bulls. Would Joan understand that?

He looked at the clock, trying vainly to stop the drift of the monologue within him. So what if Old Jack did? There's a time when a man makes a choice, when it all rises up on him and he can go no further. And besides, they misrepresented the whole thing. They pushed Old Jack to the limit. Sure he lay in the Cuban sun, but his heart was covered with ice. Didn't shade his eyes from the sun, but thumbed his nose at the world . . . In white men they've named it anguish. 'Awareness of the absolutely most extreme limitation of the possible.' Defined the world in his own terms. Old Jack Johnson, his health in bitter beer, he thought, draining his glass. Old Jack Johnson, yes! A man engaged. A man enraged. A man in rage!

He stood watching the rain, heavier now, as his eyes filled up and blurred, until beyond the window panes it was as though the sky had burst to smithereens. Well, so he would have to go. It was time, she would be waiting. Going out he surprised himself by stopping suddenly to step carefully into the grit-caked prints his own feet had made coming in.

In the Red Cross Club he sat and gazed into the glowing coals of the fireplace. It was warm in the club. Except for a soldier snoring over in the lounge, the room was empty. Someone had turned the radio down low and he could hear the music faintly. It was a warm melody, creating a friendly, nostalgic mood. And yet as he lounged in his chair he was cold. Cold around the edges; cold, it seemed, in the very marrow of his bones. He sighed, waiting. Then a faint tinkling of silver drifted to him from the kitchen and when he turned, there, coming through the doorway, was Joan.

"Darling!" she said.

"Hello," he said. The musical roll of her voice rang in his ears and he felt a pang, though he smiled.

"Have you been waiting long?" she said.

"Not long. Not as long as I'll have to wait."

He saw the quick concern on her face as she came over and stood before the fire, the starched volunteer's apron gathering smoothly at her rounded hips, making a pleasant sight.

"Will you be going soon?" she said.

"You never know the day," he said. "You only know that when you're told, you leave."

"Couldn't you stay with me, just once?" she said, catching the arms of his chair and leaning over so that he caught the fresh fragrance of her body. "Let the ship go without you? Or at least let's get married, now, today?"

Above the smooth shapes of her breast he saw how the glow of her blue beads deepened the blue of her eyes. Now she was smiling. How could he tell her?

"I'd like to," he said. "Oh but wouldn't I like to. You know that."

"Then do it," she said, her voice breaking with the sound of tears.

He could not answer. For as she searched his face he knew she would never understand. And as he became aware of her watch ticking in the silence he saw Jack Johnson as in a troubled dream, stretched full length upon the canvas of his mind, his gloved hands guarding his eyes from a bitter sun . . .

"This war, I hate this war," she said.

"But it's the reason I'm here, dear."

"No," she said fiercely, "you would have come to me somehow. I hate it. I hate it and—Oh, darling, now . . . now I hate you ever came!"

He watched her silently. Already it was poisoning things, making her unhappy. She was between the horns. Five years of bombing were not enough to condition her for the war their life would be . . .

"But I," he said, covering his brown face with his hands, "I didn't make the war."

"But you made the way I feel," she said. "Why did you ever speak to me?"

"Don't be a child, Joan," he said tiredly. "Go fix your face and let's have what we can together while there's still time. And let's have it, dear, without tears."

She looked at him mutely, really like a child with the tears on her face. Then he felt her head against his shoulder and the soft movements of her body as she sobbed.

"Go on, dear," he said, "This is our life together."

"Always hail and farewell, it is," she said hopelessly. "But when shall we live? I want a nice house, if only for a little while. Not a very large house, but a nice one. On a hill, where the mist comes down in the winter. With a brass fender where children can play and learn their lessons. And where you can tell them of America—Or," she said with a sudden breathlessness, "it could even be a house in America. A little house in Ohio . . . "

He watched the dimples steal into her face as she dreamed aloud, watched the soft glint of her teeth in the fireglow. And in his mind he saw the long roll of Welsh hills covered with heather, the browns and greens of the countryside, like fine tweeds beneath the cloud-hidden sun. With her it would have been a fine life. For, he realized abruptly, he loved this land, this country, as he had come that distant year to love Ohio—Strange he should recall that year. That was the year he had lost his mother and had hunted to keep himself alive. It was a wonderful country, he thought, though connected with irrevocable loss, as now this land would be should he never return.

She stirred, warm against him, gazing now into the fire, beautiful with the fireglow on golden hair. And he watched her with a deep and numbing anguish. For in spite of himself, she was becoming fast entwined with all the tender, aching things within him, with buried things; merged with his most tragic image of life, locked in his most precious symbol of death.

Entwined, she had become, with how that year he had hunted the quail and pheasants for his living, the winter of Teruel. He remembered how the snow-covered hills had shone in the sun the morning his mother died and the new awareness come to him with her going. At the boom of the guns the birds came up along the hill in pairs and fell with a circling, down into the thicket on the other side. And he had come down into a snow-filled valley, soft with the last faint glow of the sunset, finding the pheasant dead upon the snow, its plumage undisturbed, the vapor rising slowly, ghostlike, from the sinking blood. There he had cried, there in the lonely white of the snow and then felt relieved. He had startled the cardinals into red, tracer-bullet-streaks of flight. And the snow seeping through his bootstraps, chilling. And there had been the apples, dark red upon black branches, that showed etched stark against the sky after months of ice and snow, the apples still mellow and sweet to the taste, for all of that . . . That was during the early part of the war, the first episode. A tragic moment in a pathetic year, though not many had believed it at the time. No more than they would believe that to love one country was to love them all. Nor would they understand that to love this land was to more deeply love the land which gave one pain. But it was so . . . So here was Joan, like the things, the peaceful things one loved, expendable. And you couldn't tell her.

Softly into her ear, he said, "It's time for you to go on duty."

"Yes, so it is," she said wearily. "One does one's duty."

"It won't be long," he said. "And maybe tonight there'll be a moon."

"No moon, a storm is expected," she said. "Perhaps with snow. The first for Wales this season. Besides, it would have been a bomber's moon. "

"Oh, Joan," he said "I'll be back . . ."

"But when?"

"Always . . . Through water, through fire, through snow, through—always, always . . ."

"Yes, even through what's out there you'll come back," she cried, holding him desperately, "Because I love you. My Yank—Oh my Yank, I'll bring you tea with extra sugar!"

She left hurriedly. And as he waited he watched the dying glow of the fire and thought of the voyage westward. Tomorrow he would sail for home. Weeks of cold, rough seas. A cold crossing he would have of it. And at home there would be the snow. He shivered, hearing the quiet crackling of the coals. A snowstorm of blizzard proportions, the Army newspaper had said, was sweeping the mid-western states. Already the snow was covering the hills of Ohio, already powdering his mother's grave-stone there, and flaking the brooks and frozen rivers, where quail made tracks in the quick-falling dusk. Snow was sweeping the hills and drifting the briars, and drily shaking the blood-red leaves that hung like bandages snagged on the thorns in flight—an endless snowing all over the snow-white world of home. Snow sweeping, snow falling, snow drifting down. Snow in the hills and far-away-places. A snow of blizzard proportions. Covering all.

Scott Wolven

TNG Interview with John Callahan

Scott Wolven: Please describe the process of moving from *Juneteenth* to *Three Days Before the Shooting*...Did this take place at your office in Oregon, and who was involved? Truly, walk us through as much of the artistic process as you can.

John Callahan: "In the beginning was the word," Ralph Ellison said of America. In 1994, after his death, the word meant typescripts of his second novel, some of them complete, still somewhat rough drafts like Book I; others polished but incomplete like Book II; still others long riffing offshoots like "Night" or short ones like "Backwacking, A Plea to the Senator." And the *word* meant boxes and boxes of computer printouts, multiple versions of certain episodes, as many as twenty or thirty, as well as fragmentary loose pages, often piled helter-skelter, some fleshed out, others merely suggestive of what was in the writer's head. The *word* also meant the notes everywhere in his study: some typed, others handwritten, loose or in spiral notebooks, and, as time went by, most scrawled on discarded envelopes, on magazine subscription cards (a favorite), on restaurant receipts (you name the scrap of paper, Ellison used it). Finally, the word lay waiting to be revealed in computer floppy discs stacked on his bookshelves.

Then *Juneteenth* came to be: a reader's edition of what I took to be the central narrative of Ellison's ever-expanding unfinished second novel: the story of jazzman turned preacher, Alonzo Hickman; and Bliss, the little boy, whom Hickman midwifes into the world; later to become estranged from the Congregation, and much later to become Adam Sunraider, a spellbinding, race-baiting senator from a New England state who, assassinated by his own unacknowledged son, and dying, calls Hickman to his deathbed.

And then...what you call "the process of moving from *Juneteenth* to *Three Days Before the Shooting*...meant returning to the Library of Congress, where the full archive described above is housed. Once again, my former student, and by now my co-editor and friend, Adam Bradley, and I worked through the whole of it; trying to figure out if we could compile the essential materials of the second novel in the Ellison Papers faithfully and effectively enough for scholars and readers to tap into the parts and totality of the work.

Yet there was an unintended continuity. As it turned out, the contents and sequence of *Three Days* amount to a streamlined version of what I had done during the summer of 1997. Then, seeking closure to the project of publishing Ellison's second novel, I laid out on a long table Xeroxes of the various narratives in the second novel in a sequence that was as close as I could come to Ellison's most recent drafts. I was uneasy because the result resembled an archive more than it did a book accessible to everyone in Ellison's reading constituency. Next I wondered if what I took to be the most central of several narratives—the story of Hickman and Bliss—could comprise a stand-alone book. I gathered Book II (leaving out the unfinished, somewhat digressive episode seemingly tacked on to the rest) along with "Bliss's Birth" and the "Prologue" to Book I. Could this central narrative of Ellison's—his story of Hickman Bliss/Sunraider?—stand alone? Mrs. Ellison and I concluded that it could, provided that a subsequent edition of all the narratives followed *Juneteenth*. With her blessing, and Random House's, I made a pledge in the Afterword to *Juneteenth* to do just that, and also to open all of the Ellison Papers at the Library of Congress to everyone wishing to see them.

After *Juneteenth*, the next several years were, as Invisible Man described his hibernation, "a covert preparation for an overt action." In other words I prepared for editing the eventual eleven hundred page volume, *Three Days Before the Shooting...* by letting the dust settle and turning my attention to other different work first. So did co-editor Adam Bradley. While I was writing my novel, *A Man You Could Love* (2007, 2008), he finished his PhD dissertation, then wrote *A Book of Rhymes: The Poetics of Hip Hop* (2009). Along the way we each worked through the materials of the second novel, chewing over what we'd found together over the phone and in occasional meetings. I worked from Lewis and Clark and, summers, on Shelter Island; Adam from Cambridge and Hanover during his post-docs, then Claremont College in California. Neither of us was a stranger to the Library of Congress. (I should add that during 1999-2000 I worked with Albert Murray editing *Trading Twelves: The Selected Letters of Ralph Ellison and Albert Murray* [2000-2001]).

If a single principle guided the process during our concerted push to get the volume done over the last half of 2008 and 2009, it was that *Three Days Before the Shooting...* should reflect the provisional nature of what Ellison had left behind. We wanted our editorial work to reflect "that aura of summing up," which in his latter years drove Ellison toward a novel always in progress about a country also self-consciously in progress. We wanted readers to see and understand the labyrinthine nature of Ellison's material and the literary choices he faced, some of which he made and others he did not.

S.W.: With the passing of Fanny Ellison (November 19, 2005), what do you see in the future for the works of Ralph Ellison? Can you tell us anything about Mrs. Ellison that we probably didn't know? What was your working relationship with her like?

J.C.: Fanny Ellison passed away shortly before her 95th birthday. To the end, she would read Ralph's work, and she loved having passages read aloud to her. One thing is sure: without her tending of Ralph's manuscripts, notes, and letters, there would not be anything remotely approaching the Ellison archive at the Library of Congress, nor would we be able to date accurately several typescripts from the unfinished novel. It's true that Ralph threw nothing away, but it was Fanny who made order out of chaos as best she could in the confined space of their apartment at 730 Riverside Drive.

Fanny loved to laugh. Her sense of humor, her sense of incongruity, her sharp tongue in response to human foibles, including her own, and her dedication to Ralph, enabled her to concentrate on what needed doing despite the continuing ache of his loss. "My best friend," he called her, "and my best reader." First and foremost, Fanny and I were friends. On that basis, I'm happy to say, that after initial reluctance, she went along with my entreaties (and those of the Library of Congress) to give her papers to the Ellison Collection. They are a rich complement to Ralph's work and a national treasure in their own right. She was a remarkable person and a woman of distinct achievements, and I'm convinced that in time her life will be the subject of a book or two.

S.W.: Let's talk about your own work for a moment. Tell us a little bit about *A Man You Could Love*.

J.C.: Ever since 1968, I dreamed of a novel, whose characters would work out their passions, lives, and destinies in the arena of politics. Twenty years later, in 1988, I wrote a story called "A Man You Could Love"—a finished first draft but not a truly finished story…For whatever reason I was not ready to finish it. In succeeding years I took out the manuscript every once in a while, but all I did was tinker, and rethink. That was that, I thought. But it wasn't. The urge to write a novel (I called it a novel but at some level it was already my novel) stayed alive and went underground…

I spent 1996-1997 at the Wilson Center in Washington, DC, working on Ellison's second novel, and I was lucky. Gene McCarthy took me to lunch in the Senate dining room, and another old friend, a Congressman from Oregon, gave me several tours of the deserted Senate and House chambers on weekend afternoons. Consciously I chalked up my growing fascination with Washington to Ellison's Senator, Adam Sunraider, and scenes from his unfinished novel set at the Capitol, the Lincoln Memorial, and other less-known nooks and crannies of the District of Columbia. But when my work on Ellison stalled, the ghost of my fiction drifted in and out of my mind. My protagonist was a congressman contemplating a run for the Senate, but, conscientiously, I waved him off and resumed tracking Ellison's mysterious, maddening Senator Sunraider. I did not know it then, but, "on the lower frequencies," *A Man You Could Love* was beginning to take shape—no longer a short story but something more ambitious. I pushed it into a corner of my mind, I thought for good, as Ellison's enormous unfinished work claimed my attention.

That seemed to be that. But it wasn't, and perhaps how *A Man You Could Love* came to the forefront of my mind and stayed there until it was done in 2006 reveals something about how novels get to and past the tipping point. After the election of 2000 I was fascinated by the Florida recount and depressed by the Supreme Court's decision to intervene and, in effect, name the next president. In a flash I saw my narrator, a former administrative assistant to Congressman, then Senator Mick Whelan, holed up at the Oregon Coast while doctors at the Oregon Health Sciences Hospital tried to figure out his dangerously out-of-balance blood count. Suddenly it hit me: vote count, blood count. That's the hook, I thought, that triggers my narrator's memory of his life in politics from the '60s to the catastrophe that marks his exit in 1991. I'd have him veer from his blood count to the vote count in Florida and back again. If you can't make a novel with that frame, you're not a novelist," I told myself. I was hooked. And I did not listen to the voice that said not to worry, if the novel did not get written, I'd given it my best shot.

S.W.: What was the best advice you ever took from Ralph Ellison and tried to put into your own work?

J.C.: Ralph was not one to give advice. I did *take* advice from Ralph, but it was completely indirect, and did not necessarily have anything to do with me. Sometime in the mid '80s while I was writing *In the African-American Grain*, I sent Ralph the chapter on Charles Chesnutt. Late one night he told me my essay had sent him back to Chesnutt. He praised *The Conjure Woman*. Then in a taut, spellbinding monologue he said that for him the *necessity to write fiction* got closer to the bone than Chesnutt's commitment to "a fiction of necessity" in response to the stereotyping of Negro characters by the Plantation School in the late 19th century. It was a liquid evening, and by the next morning the sense of his quickening presence was more vivid by half than the actual points I had sworn to jot down.

Nonetheless I knew Ralph was saying that what drove him and kept him going was the struggle inside more than his struggles with the world. "The necessity you and Chesnutt speak of I put in my essays," he'd said. "The necessity to write fiction is the salt in your blood." It was that necessity of his to write fiction that moved me as I imagined him struggling with that intractable second novel. Maybe it was his writer's fate to contend with "the mixture of the marvelous and the terrible" in his craft. Whatever it was, was as distinctly his as his brown eyes or receding hairline or the rising timbre of his voice when he was agitated.

In any case Ralph's words that night remind me of Yeats belief that "a man may show as reckless a courage entering the abyss of himself as any who fall on the battlefield." However much the words may seem to mock from the page, the struggle to put them down is necessary to reach and shape that small part of the human story that is inside only that writer. I guess what I'm trying to say is that, that night Ralph's words bore witness to living on the inside "that same pain, that same pleasure" of being human, which is the writer's fate.

S.W.: Tell us about your just-finished novel, *The Learning Room.*

J.C.: The book began in 2008 with the image of an autistic little boy. Soon I knew his name, Fergus Scales, and the person in Fergus came to me and never left. That was a very difficult time in my life, a time of loss, and Fergus was a comfort as well as a mystery…On a solitary dawn walk in late July, a scene scrolled down before my eyes as if from a DVD screen. Though I didn't have the story of Fergus yet, what I saw that morning, I imagined would be the end of the novel, and that the narrator would pass it on to readers through a DVD that came into his possession after a catastrophe witnessed by the little boy.

Little Fergus, and the woman who cared for him and loved him more than anyone else, would come into his room knowing he was desperate for comfort and consolation. She, too, was desperate, paralyzed inside, unable to approach him or touch him, unable even to cry. And Fergus reached out and put his hands on her face, touching her features one by one. When I got home from walking, I knew that somehow Fergus, the little boy everyone assumed would stay locked up in his autistic world, would be able to comfort the woman. He loved her, and so he could give her the comfort that she could not give him. And he did. He was the first one able to love.

The story took off from there. The catastrophe behind boy and the woman's desolation happened…Gradually the story filled out in my mind, and I began drafting chapters on Shelter Island in December 2008.

Need I add *The Learning Room* is very different than *A Man You Could Love?* Interwoven with Fergus's story are those of the woman Aranza, a Basque-American and her lover, a jazz piano player named Timothy, whose secrets and troubles are buried in the past. In the novel's present of 2004, they tell their stories to Gabriel Bontempo, also the narrator of *A Man You Could Love.* He returns to Shelter Island in 2001 and has his own share of loss and tragedy. If that's not enough, I'll give you one more tease. A Ponzi schemer also lurks in the pages of *The Learning Room*.

S.W.: What have you learned about the Great American Novel, both as Ralph Ellison's literary executor and as an author in your own right? What lessons can you pass along to young novelists starting out?

J.C.: That there are great American novels but no such thing as "the great American novel." Perhaps like Ellison's Territory, the Great American Novel is "an ideal place—ever to be sought, ever to be missed, but always there." And I'll add a cautionary note. The *LA Times* reviewer wrote that "*Juneteenth* threatens to come as close as any [novel] since *Huckleberry Finn* to grabbing the ring of the Great American Novel." That said, for Ellison, there is another dimension to your invocation of "the Great American Novel." Although deep down Ralph believed he had truly hit it with *Invisible Man*, he was surprised by its staying power. Because of *his first novel's* almost mythical success, the place it seized in American literature during his lifetime, it was harder and harder for Ralph to write a second novel. To write it simply as the next novel, like Bellow did *Henderson the Rain King* as the next in a succession of novels. Maybe if he had worked like hell to shape what he had by the time of the fire into something he deemed publishable, he could have gone on to write just novels instead of *novels*. I don't know, but certainly if you believe in myth, as he certainly did, the 1967 fire was a warning, which destroyed "a section of [his] work-in-progress."

And some of what Ralph told James Allan McPherson in 1969 and McPherson put in their collaborative piece, "Indivisible Man," suggests he heard the warning. He showed McPherson the black binders full of typescript—remember, this was a dozen years before he bought his first computer. He was keenly aware of the structural choices before him. "I could publish it in three volumes," he told McPherson, clearly not very taken with the idea. If I could jump into the time machine, I'd go back to 1970 and try to persuade Ellison not to take the Schweitzer Chair at NYU. At that point I wish he had never looked back from that novel, and had finished in whatever way, and by using whatever means were necessary.

But he didn't. And I think *Three Days Before the Shooting...* shows that he never got control of his material. His reference to Proteus in "Brave Words For a Startling Occasion" (1953) provides an eerie mythic reference point. If we let Proteus stand for the second novel, it is clear that Ralph did not take the advice Eidothea gave Menelaus in the *Odyssey*. Whatever else he did with that second novel, Ralph did not "hold [it] fast and press [it] all the harder." From Proteus the novel seems to have changed into Tar Baby and held Ralph so fast that he expanded rather than contracted his treatment of the material, until the beloved form he aspired to was beyond his powers.

More than once you see and hear Ralph's flinch when he responds to questions about the difficulty of finishing the novel that would follow *Invisible Man*. Difficult? Hell, it became impossible. *Invisible Man* is *sui generis* in so many ways it's as if *it, too*, became Proteus over the years and could not be held fast.

My advice to "young novelists starting out" is simple: write your own novel. Don't chase a mythical beast called "the Great American Novel." To write a novel is to create a labyrinth; with your own novel, unlike "The Great American Novel," you can fashion a way out.

S.W.: Is your view of novels much different now?

J.C.: Absolutely: night and day, like the song says.

I read and teach novels differently than I did before I wrote *A Man You Could Love*.

Now I can't escape participating in the roads taken and not taken by the novel in front of me. Now the writer is there more vividly than when she is not, as, for example, Marilynne Robinson is more deeply present for not being there in her lovely, incandescent *Gilead*, than when she is there, as she is sometimes in her third person sequel, *Home*. After writing my novel, I take marvelous things less for granted in a good novel than I did before, and I mourn the passages, which don't come off, especially those whose effect would be truer if a word, a phrase, a line of dialogue, or an image or figure of speech had not been there.

S.W.: You have been engaged in learning and teaching for your entire career. Do you think the recent increase in MFA programs (full disclosure here, I teach at an MFA program) is producing better writers or simply more writers? Do you think it's making writing in America any better?

J.C.: I'm not really qualified to talk about MFA programs. But I'll say something about undergraduate courses in fiction writing. I am currently team-teaching one with Paul Toutonghi, a Lewis and Clark colleague and the author of two distinctive novels *Red Weather* (2006/2007) and *Evel Knieval Days* (forthcoming in 2012). In the old days, at least mine, there weren't any fiction-writing courses. Undergraduates wrote fiction only from their private compulsions and maybe for the joy of breaking into print in the college literary magazine.

Much as I enjoy reading and discussing student work, especially in tandem with a gifted, rigorous and sympathetic colleague, credit-bearing creative writing courses strike me as a mixed bag. Surely the sense of fraternity is a good thing, and it's good to have a wide variety of students trying their hands at telling and making stories. Yet however hard we try to keep the game open, to emphasize the inviolable highs and lows, whiffs of the bland, the safe, the institutional creep in. There's a sense of the potentially facile (and fatal) American how-to reflex. On the other hand, the workshop method offers sudden opportunities to point out to young writers *in their own stuff* the wonderful things it's possible to achieve in prose. There's exhilaration in seeing a young writer's sudden gift of tongues move everyone in the room. And there's satisfaction being able to identify the marks of fine prose, then walk beyond what can be identified and share with students that mystery and magic, which exists in the best prose above and beyond strict technical accounting.

And there's something else. The proliferation of courses and programs in fiction writing and poetry writing, too, can stiffen the spines of committed readers, something that's more and more at risk. In this digital age, instant communication implies instant gratification rather than the slow, smoldering understanding and appreciation that accompany an individual's encounter with works of art, or even with well-crafted popular works with a brief life span.

S.W.: After the publication of *Three Days Before the Shooting*…what was the critical response? What pleased you most, and what did you feel missed the mark completely? And what was its international reception?

J.C.: The attention paid to *Three Days* was intelligent, respectful, admiring of Ralph's work, and gratifying to its editors in its appreciation of how we were trying to present his work as he left it, with little or no editing. I like to think Ralph, too, would have been pleased that the reviewers grasped the ambition and effort of what he was up to. Malcolm Jones, who wrote a keen review on *Juneteenth* in 1999, again came close to the mark when he wrote: "There's so much wonderful writing in there. I would recommend that anybody go and poke around in it." Another wonderful response appeared in the *Huffington Post*: "The novel reads like music, a baroque rendition of the blues with layers of sounds, rhythms, and meaning communicating hopes and heartbreak, the painful smack of reality and the endurance of just getting on with it." I especially like the tip of the hat to the novel's and Ralph's "endurance of just getting on with it."

Unlike *Juneteenth*, about which and every publication had something to say, often *ex cathedra*, many of recognized opinion-shaping newspapers and journals were silent. But there was enough of a buzz and stir in print and by interviewers on radio to suggest that Ellison's formidable readership is out there still primed for and receptive to his work and his words.

Scholars, however, mostly have yet to weigh in with reviews in literary and academic journals. Likewise, there has been little international notice, at least that I've received from Random House and the Modern Library.

S.W.: Where are Ralph Ellison's papers housed now?

J.C.: Since 1996 they have been in the Manuscript Division of the Library of Congress. All of the collection is now open to scholars, general readers, citizens of all stripes and persuasions, anyone who wants to take a look. In the last year all of the papers Fanny Ellison left behind at her death have also been archived as Part II of the collection. Among these are some previously overlooked papers and letters of Ralph's.

S.W.: It seems that appreciation of Ralph Ellison has grown over the years? Is that your impression?

J.C.: I want to distinguish between Ralph Ellison and his writing. There's no doubt that Ralph's writing is more and more meaningful for more and more people. *Invisible Man* continues to engage generation after generation of students, perhaps more intensely than any other American novel. Despite the Modern Library edition of the *Collected Essays*, the essays remain somewhat below the radar screen, though the blips are a reminder that *something* of an indestructible nature is there. And when people read the essays, the blinders come off about many things, especially the enduring, up and down effect of the American experiment on individual and national wave lengths: what he called in *Invisible Man* "the principle" and the "beautiful absurdity of American identity."

Now that the projections that the United States had entered (or would enter) a "post-racial age" after Senator Obama's election to the presidency have proven false, Ellison's view of American complexity seems ever more relevant. As Ralph so often said, many Americans are more open to the idea of something or someone different than they are to the reality.

In any case for the sake of sheer reading pleasure, Americans of different backgrounds continue to relish the flavors of Ellison's prose, and the ways he puts sentences together.

Yet I think Arnold Rampersad's biography somewhat blunted, distorted, and diminished readers' understanding and appreciation of Ralph Ellison the man. In its pages, too often motes became beams. The courage, the defiant mind, the generosity, the moral, intellectual, and personal curiosity, the humor, and above all the complexity of the man fade under unfriendly scrutiny by the author and certain reviewers as if both had been waiting for the chance to knock Ralph off a pedestal he was never on. Moreover, the biography seems to suggest a kind of parity between Ralph's writing and the Ellison's social calendar over the last twenty-five years of his life. Having said that, I want to make clear that the biography also has the qualities of Arnold Rampersad's best work: its vividness, command of milieu; and the detailed, convincing respect for the work of Ralph's, which he admires.

Fortunately, perhaps confused by the biography, readers have gone back to Ralph's work and his words and come away skeptical of claims made about him in the biography and those who tried to diminish him by what they told its author. Fortunately, a writer, unlike other public personalities, gets the last word if he writes well enough. In my view the letters Ralph Ellison wrote over sixty years, from 1933 to 1993, offer a full view of the centripetal and centrifugal facets of his life and personality, and the times in which he lived. In the letters, Ellison's thoughts and feelings about what he called "every damn thing" emerge in the round. I expect the volume of letters Professor Marc Connor and I are beginning to work on to offer a fuller, richer biographical perspective than is now available on Ralph Ellison's life and times.

S.W.: Did you send a copy of *Three Days Before the Shooting...*to the White House? And what do you think Ralph Ellison's view of politics would be or could be?

J.C.: Yes, though on a circuitous road and I am not sure if the circuit was closed or the volume was received by President Obama. Your question reminds me to honor the adage, "If at first you don't succeed try, try again," and send another out over the open road.

Ralph on politics is easier. In our time the media and many politicians, for God's sake, treat that perfectly good word like an obscenity. Maybe we'll have to switch to polity or citizenship. Ellison regarded none of these three words as clichés. In his life, he took citizenship seriously enough to serve on numerous commissions, especially the Carnegie Commission for public television, and on more of his share of boards.

But it's as a writer that we know him as a man for whom politics, like protest, was part of the scene, part of life, at the heart of the human condition. So it was for Invisible Man, who dreamed of being a leader...and certainly Bledsoe was a political figure, a player in the racial politics of Jim Crow America. In *Juneteenth*, as a runaway orphan full of anger and antagonism, young Bliss metamorphosed into a powerful elected leader; the "race-baiting senator from a New England state." Politics breaks into the vocabulary of Ellison's novels and leads to similar questions of different nuance posed by Invisible Man ("And could politics ever be an expression of love?") and Sunraider (the latter in capital letters): "HOW THE HELL DO YOU GET

LOVE INTO POLITICS OR COMPASSION INTO HISTORY?" To the extent these are rhetorical questions, the answers are: "It better be," and "You better figure out a way." And "on the lower frequencies," the questions boomerang back to Ellison's characters and his readers demanding answers appropriate to every time and place, every generation of Americans.

Writers are also citizens. That doesn't mean a writer's work need be explicitly political, though Ellison believed that the novel, a form "bound up with nationhood," imposed on novelists a certain "moral [and aesthetic] responsibility for democracy." There's also a matter of craft here. If you choose to create and tell a story that portrays the political arena in fiction, you've got an obligation to get it right.

S.W.: From your experience writing *A Man You Could Love* (one of the deepest, most well-rendered stories of politics I've read in a long time) what does it take to get it right, in terms of the political arena portrayed in fiction?

J.C.: I ran for office myself, for Congress way back when I was in my late twenties in 1970. It wasn't a competitive race, but the student protests and killings at Kent State and Jackson State triggered by Nixon's invasion of Cambodia released a great deal of energy into my campaign. By the end it seemed like a real campaign. And I've worked and participated in other campaigns for national office before and since then, so I knew them from the inside and the outside. Eugene McCarthy became a close friend after 1968. From him I absorbed a great deal about politics (I was his vice-presidential candidate in Oregon in 1976) that gave my imagination a basis to work from.

In the case of *A Man You Could Love* there was also one of those displacements so often at work in the making of fiction. On search committees as a college professor I've interviewed candidate after candidate who, when they'd let their hair down, confessed a secret desire to write a novel. I'd perk up, but every damn time it seemed the young PhD (sometimes not so young) would go on to say that the novel would be a murder mystery set at a liberal arts college.

I ground my teeth, but as the years went by and I served on more and more governance committees, I came to know the fighting and infighting, the maneuvers and process, above all, the personal vendettas backwards and forwards, inside and out. Sitting through interminable meetings over trivial matters, I amused myself by imagining that if I could displace all that process and blah blah to a national stage like the Congress, and make real life and death political matters the stakes, maybe I could tell a political story in ways largely missing from serious American novels. That's what I tried to do. My characters answered Invisible Man's question about politics and love in speech and actions that brought love to politics in their experience of friendship, family, romantic, sexual relationships, and ambition in the service of country...But I knew I had to get the actual practice of politics right. So when one reviewer wrote that "the effect was like the lulling but essential poetry of whaling equipment in *Moby Dick*," I was pleased beyond measure.

S.W.: These past years, working on Ralph Ellison's behalf must have taken a tremendous amount of time and effort in the service of literature. Do you feel you are re-claiming your writing self now?

J.C.: No. I feel I've finally discovered that writing self. For better or worse, I don't think I would have had the compulsion and courage to start writing novels in 2001 without my unexpected and strange apprenticeship as Ralph Ellison's literary executor and posthumous editor.

Why? Well, working on his second novel, I came slowly, inexorably, against my will, to realize it was provisional, and would likely have remained that way even if he'd lived. Remember, ours was more a father-son relationship than a literary one. And I deeply wished that he would reappear, tell me how to edit it, and nurture my wish to see what I could do with a novel of my own...

Could I imagine and create a world? Finish, revise, and truly finish a novel of my own? Publish it? Have people read it, and a few of them live in it enough to be moved by its characters and story?

I had no idea...Yet here I am, putting the finishing touches on a wholly unanticipated second novel.

S.W.: What is your recollection of Ralph and Fanny Ellison, putting you in a yellow cab, into the New York City night, in almost the same spot where I walked and caught a cab after the dedication of the Ellison sculpture just above Riverside Drive? What is your recollection of that time and are you pleased with where it has taken you today?

J.C.: I remember swaying as I put on my coat at two o'clock in the morning. Fanny looked at Ralph, and he looked at her. Over my protests they put on light coats, and Ralph a sporty fedora from the '40s; they walked me up to Broadway and put me in a cab. "Yellow Cab, John," Fanny said as I opened the door. "In New York always take a Yellow Cab."

I also remember meeting you at that dedication six or seven years ago. Odetta was there, for heaven's sake, one of her last appearances. I'll never forget climbing up on the platform to speak. People were hanging out of windows on the upper floors of the apartment buildings. Below a dog was nipping at a police barrier on 150th Street. It was Ralph's Harlem all right. Suddenly I thought of Amiri Baraka's oft-repeated claim that one night in the sixties he'd showed up unannounced to see Ralph, and Ralph had sicced the dog on him. Of course he was a liar in the sense of telling tall tales, so he made up the stuff about the dog. I warmed up by reminding the crowd, some of whom had known Tucka Tarby (the Ellisons' dog), that Ralph's rejoinder to Baraka was that folks had nothing to fear from a militant who was afraid of a dog whose hindquarters were gone.

Afterward that wild vernacular dedication scene gave me some new imagery to use when I revised the nightmare of displacement my narrator experiences, dreaming about Gene McCarthy and Robert Kennedy's assassination in *A Man You Could Love.*

Those evenings with Ralph and Fanny Ellison made me feel like a New Yorker and a cherished friend, even then almost a son. Ah, that time, those evenings: from 1978 until 1994, they were the best ticket in town.

WINNER OF THE KNIGHTVILLE POETRY CONTEST

WINNING POEM: THE GREAT RAILROAD TRAIN OF ART

KATHLEEN SPIVACK is the author of seven books of prose and poetry. With Robert Lowell and His Famous Circle: Boston: 1959-79, a memoir, is forthcoming in 2012. A History of Yearning (2010) won the Sow's Ear Poetry Chapbook Prize and also won first prize in the poetry book category at the London Book Festival. Recent poems have won first prizes including the Allen Ginsberg Memorial Poetry Award and the New England Poetry Club's Erika Mumford Prize. She has also won several Solas awards. Residencies include the Radcliffe Institute, Yaddo, The MacDowell Colony, and the American Academy in Rome. Fellowships include grants from the National Endowment for the Arts and the Fulbright Commission. She teaches in Boston and Paris.

WINNER OF THE MACHIGONNE FICTION CONTEST

WINNING STORY: RECIPES FOR DISASTER

DAN MARMOR graduated from Stanford University in 2010 with a bachelor's degree in English. He is a scrappy, young writer from the suburbs of Long Island, currently working on a novel, Recipes for Disaster. Dan is pursuing a master's degree in English and Creative Writing with hopes of one day starting a literary journal devoted to publishing new and experimental fiction.

2011 CONTEST JUDGES

CHARLES SIMIC is a poet, translator, editor and essayist. He has put out over 30 books of poetry, has translated 15 books, and has published several books of essays. He won The Pulitzer Prize for his book The World Doesn't End: Prose Poems. Other awards and fellowships include The Wallace Stevens Award, The Griffin International Poetry Prize, The Academy and Guggenheim Fellowships, and MacArthur and National Endowment for the Arts grants. Simic was named a Chancellor of The Academy of American Poets in 2000. He was also was elected to The American Academy of Arts and Letters in 1995.

DAVID PLANTE is the author of fifteen novels and four memoirs. He is a fellow of the Royal Society of Literature and a Henfield Fellow and a University of East Anglia fellow in London, where he has been writer-in-residence. He is a National Book Award nominee. Grants include the British Arts Council Grant, a Guggenheim Fellowship and an Arts and Letters Award from the American Academy of Arts and Letters. He is an Ambassador for the LGBT Committee of the New York Public Library, where his diaries are kept.

2011 EDITORS

SARAH KOWALSKI'S fiction has been published in the *South Philly Fiction* anthology, among others; and her poetry and essays have appeared in *Small Craft Warnings* and *The Philadelphia Independent*. She holds an MFA in fiction from the Stonecoast program at the University of Southern Maine. She lives in South Philadelphia, and is currently at work on a collection of linked short stories.

SHANNA MCNAIR is the founding editor and publisher of *The New Guard*. Publications include *Maine Magazine, Roger, Naugatuck River Review, Village Soup Times,* and *Fact-Simile*. She was a Summer Literary Seminar 2010 fellowship recipient for work in both fiction and poetry. She is represented by Zero Gravity Management Manhattan for her original screenplays. McNair is an award-winning journalist, works in the visual arts, and performs music. McNair lives in Knightville, Maine.

BILL ROORBACH lives in western Maine with his wife and daughter and dozens of animals, some of which are pets. His next book is *Life Among Giants*, a novel forthcoming in August, 2012.

SUZANNE STREMPEK SHEA is the author of five novels, most recently *Becoming Finola*, and three memoirs, including *Sundays in America: A Year-long Roadtrip in Search of Christian Faith*. Her honors include the 2000 New England Book award. Her freelance writing has appeared in publications such as *The Boston Globe, Yankee Magazine, Bark Magazine* and *ESPN The Magazine*; and she contributes regularly to Obit magazine. com. Suzanne teaches in the University of Southern Maine's Stonecoast MFA and is writer-in-residence at Bay Path College in Longmeadow, Mass.

SCOTT WOLVEN is the author of the short story collection, *Controlled Burn*. Wolven's stories have appeared seven years in a row in *The Best American Mystery Stories Series*, the most consecutive appearances in the history of the series. The title story from *Controlled Burn* appeared in *The Best American Noir Of The Century*. Wolven's novels, *False Hope* and *King Zero*, are forthcoming in 2012. He is currently finishing another collection of short stories. Wolven is on the faculty of the Stonecoast MFA Program at the University of Southern Maine.

CONTRIBUTORS

SARAH BRAUNSTEIN is the author of *The Sweet Relief of Missing Children* (2011) which was short-listed for the 2011 Flaherty-Dunnan First Novel Prize from the Center for Fiction. In 2010, she was named one of "5 Under 35" fiction writers by the National Book Foundation, and she was a 2007 recipient of a Rona Jaffe Foundation Writers' Award. Stories and essays have appeared in *AGNI, Ploughshares, Post Road, Nylon,* and *Maine Magazine,* among other publications. She is at work on a second novel and a nonfiction book about adolescence.

JOHN CALLAHAN was born in Meriden, Connecticut, and raised in New Haven. He attended the College of the Holy Cross and received his BA from the University of Connecticut in 1963, the PhD from the University of Illinois in 1970. Callahan is Morgan S. Odell Professor of Humanities at Lewis and Clark College. As Ralph Ellison's literary executor, he has edited five posthumous volumes of Ellison's work including the *Collected Essays* (1995, 2003); *Flying Home and Other Stories* (1996, 1998); *Juneteenth* (1999, 2000), and, with Adam Bradley, *Three Days Before the Shooting . . .* (2010, 2011). Callahan is the author of *The Illusions of a Nation* (1972); *In the African-American Grain* (1988, 1989, 2001). His first novel, *A Man You Could Love* (2007, 2008) and he has just finished the second, called *The Learning Room.* He is the father of Eve and Sasha Callahan, and grandfather of Ava Callahan Taylor.

THEODORE DEPPE is the author of four collections of poetry, *Orpheus on the Red Line* (2009), *Cape Clear: New and Selected Poems* (2002), *The Wanderer King* (1996), and *Children of the Air* (1990). His work has been recognized with two fellowships from the National Endowment for the Arts and a Pushcart Prize. He has served as writer-in-residence at the James Merrill House, the Poet's House (Donegal, Ireland), and Phillips Academy. Recent publications include *Prairie Schooner, Arsenic Lobster, The Stinging Fly,* and *New England Review.* He teaches in the Stonecoast MFA Program and coordinates Stonecoast in Ireland. Since 2000, he has lived mostly on the west coast of Ireland.

CAROLINA DE ROBERTIS' first novel, *The Invisible Mountain,* was an international bestseller translated into fifteen languages, a San Francisco Chronicle Best Book of the Year, an *O, The Oprah Magazine* 2009 Terrific Read, and the recipient of a Rhegium Julii Prize. Her translations of Latin American fiction have appeared in *Granta, Zoetrope: Allstory,* and elsewhere. Her second novel, *Perla,* about the intimate aftermath of disappearances in Argentina, is forthcoming in March 2012. She is currently at work on her third novel, which explores migration, cross-dressing, and the tango's Old Guard in early twentieth century South America.

RALPH ELLISON (1914-94) was born in Oklahoma City and trained as a musician at Tuskegee Institute from 1933 to 1936, at which time he moved to New York, and stayed. A year later, a meeting with Richard Wright led to his first attempts at fiction. Published in 1952, *Invisible Man* won the National Book Award in 1953. Appointed to the Academy of American Arts and Letters in 1964, Ellison taught at several institutions, including Bard College, the University of Chicago, and New York University, where he was Albert Schweitzer Professor of Humanities from 1970-1979.

Trained as a medical doctor, TESS GERRITSEN built a second career as a thriller writer. Her twenty-three novels include the Rizzoli and Isles crime series, on which the TV show, *Rizzoli & Isles*, is based. Among her titles are *The Surgeon*, *Ice Cold*, and *The Silent Girl*. Her books have been translated into thirty-seven languages and more than twenty million copies have been sold. She lives in Maine.

TOD GOLDBERG is the author of eleven books, including *Living Dead Girl*, which was a finalist for the Los Angeles Times Book Prize. He is the author of the popular *Burn Notice* series and has produced two collections of short stories, *Simplify*, and *Other Resort Cities*. He lives in Indio, California, where he directs the Low Residency MFA program in Creative Writing & Writing for the Performing Arts at the University of California, Riverside.

AARON HAMBURGER was awarded the Rome Fellowship in Literature by the American Academy of Arts and Letters for his short story collection, *The View From Stalin's Head* (2004), which was also nominated for a Violet Quill Award. His next book, a novel titled *Faith for Beginners* (2005), was nominated for a Lambda Literary Award. His writing has appeared in *Poets & Writers*, *Tin House*, *Details*, *The Village Voice*, *The Forward*, and *Out*. He has received fellowships from the Edward F. Albee Foundation and the Civitella Ranieri Foundation in Umbria, Italy, as well as residencies from Yaddo and Djerassi Resident Artists Program. Currently, he teaches writing at Columbia University and at the Stonecoast MFA Program.

ELIZABETH HAND is the multiple-award-winning author of numerous novels and three collections of short fiction. She has two novels coming out early in 2012: a psychological thriller called *Available Dark*, the sequel to the Shirley Jackson Award winner, *Generation Loss*; and *Radiant Days*, a YA novel about the French poet Arthur Rimbaud. She is a longtime critic for various publications, including the *Washington Post*, and is on the faculty at the Stonecoast MFA Program in Creative Writing. She divides her time between the Maine coast and North London.

MIKE HEPPNER is the author of the novels *The Egg Code* and *Pike's Folly*. He lives near Boston and teaches at Emerson College.

MICHAEL KIMBALL is a novelist, playwright, and screenwriter. He's written four novels, including the London Times' bestseller *Undone*, and several screenplays for movie and television production companies. His play, *Ghosts of Ocean House*, was nominated for the 2007 Edgar Award.

FRED MARCHANT is the author of four books of poetry, most recently *The Looking House* (2009). He is the editor of Another World Instead: The Early Poems of William Stafford, 1937-1947, in which he focuses on a selection of the early poems of William Stafford, which agree with his conscientious objection status during World War II. Marchant is also the director of the Creative Writing Program and the Poetry Center at Suffolk University, in Boston.

JEFF MCCREIGHT is a painter from Portland, Maine. He studied fine art at Skidmore College, receiving a BS in 2000. After school, he founded the On Sight Mural Company and began working on mural and sign projects in many different medias and formats. He has also done illustrations for publication and has exhibited work in the US, Brazil, Portugal, Spain, and Norway. He currently lives in Madrid with his family and continues to make paintings, murals, posters, and drawings.

CORTRIGHT MCMEEL is the author of the novel, Short (2010). He is the founder and publisher of the literary crime magazine, *Murderland*. He is also the founder and publisher of the soon-to-be-launched (Fall, 2011) *Bare Knuckles Press*. He lives in Denver, Colorado.

Born in Vancouver B.C., ALEXANDRA OLIVER has been nominated for the CBC Literary Awards and the Pushcart Prize. Her work regularly appears in journals worldwide, and her first collection, *Where the English Housewife Shines*, was published in 2007. She has performed her poems at Lollapalooza and The National Poetry Slam, and on CBC Radio One and National Public Radio. She was also a featured performer and interviewee of the 1998 documentary, *Slam Nation*. Oliver is currently completing an MFA at the University of Southern Maine and co-editing (with Annie Finch) an anthology of poetry in non-iambic meters.

dave naybor was raised in the woods by wolves, but they were polite wolves. He has been mistaken for a Canadian. He has been a comic book guy in Portland, Maine for twenty-seven years. He began his comic novel, *Walking Christendom*, in 2004.

TIM SEIBLES is the author of several books of poems including *Hurdy-Gurdy*, *Hammerlock*, and most recently, *Buffalo Head Solos*. He has been a National Endowment for the Arts fellow and a writing fellow at the Provincetown Fine Arts Work Center. He received an Open Voice Award from the 63rdStreet Y in New York City. Anthology publications include *Manthology*, *Black Nature*, *Seriously Funny*, *The Autumn*

House Anthology of American Poetry, So Much Things to Say and *Best American Poetry 2010.*
He has lead workshops at the Cave Canem Writers Retreat, the Zora Neale Hurston/
Richard Wright Foundation, and is presently visiting faculty for the Stonecoast MFA
Program. He lives in Norfolk, Virginia where he teaches at Old Dominion in both
the English Department and MFA writing program.

ED SKOOG is the author of *Mister Skylight* and the forthcoming *Rough Day.* His poems
have appeared in *The Paris Review, American Poetry Review, Ploughshares, The New Republic,
Poetry,* and elsewhere. He lives in Seattle.

JOE WENDEROTH has published several books of poetry, *Disfortune, It Is If I Speak,*
and *No Real Light.* He has also published prose: *Letters To Wendy's* and *The Holy Spirit
Of Life: Essays Written For John Ashcroft's Secret Self.* His films and songs can be accessed
on youtube.com and soundcloud.com. Wenderoth is Professor of English at the
University of California, Davis.

BARON WORMSER is the author/co-author of thirteen books, including *The Road
Washes Out in Spring: A Poet's Memoir of Living Off the Grid, Scattered Chapters: New and
Selected Poems,* and a work of fiction entitled *The Poetry Life: Ten Stories.* In March 2011
his ninth book of poetry, *Impenitent Notes,* was published. He is a former poet laureate
of Maine who teaches in the Fairfield University MFA Program and directs the Frost
Place Conference on Poetry and Teaching. Wormser has received fellowships from
the National Endowment for the Arts and the John Simon Guggenheim Memorial
Foundation.

JAMES K. ZIMMERMAN is the winner of the 2009 Daniel Varoujan Award and the 2009
and 2010 Hart Crane Memorial Poetry Award. His work appears or is forthcoming
in anderbo.com, *The Bellingham Review, Rosebud, Inkwell, Nimrod, Passager,* and *Vallum,*
among others. He is also currently a clinical psychologist in private practice, and was
a singer/songwriter in a previous life.

MACHIGONNE FINALISTS

A native of the San Francisco Bay Area, ALLISON ALSUP has lived in New Orleans
for over a decade. She teaches Creative Writing and French part-time to under-
resourced public high school students. She also works with her husband to restore
the never-ending supply of lovely, rotting cottages in New Orleans. In the last two
years, several chapters of her nearly complete (!) novel have won national writing
contests: from *New Millennium Writings* to A Room of Her Own Foundation and the
Philadelphia Stories' Marguerite McGlinn Prize for Fiction. Two other chapters have
been published as contest finalist selections in both *Salamander* and *The New Guard.*

AMINA GAUTIER is the winner of the Flannery O'Connor Award for her short story collection, *At-Risk*. Over sixty-five of Gautier's stories have been published, appearing in such journals and magazines as *Best African American Fiction*, *The Iowa Review*, *Kenyon Review*, *North American Review*, *Shenandoah* and *Southern Review*. She has received scholarships and fellowships from Breadloaf Writers' Conference, the Ucross Foundation Residency Program, and the Sewanee Writer's Conference. She has also been awarded the William Richey Short Fiction Prize, the Jack Dyer Fiction Award, the *River Styx* Schlafly Beer Micro-fiction Award, The Danahy Fiction Prize, and a grant from the Pennsylvania Council on the Arts.

CARON LEVIS' story, *Permission Slip*, won the 2010 Summer Literary Seminars prize and was listed in *Best American Nonrequired Reading* 2010; her plays have recently been selected for the Estrogenius and Samuel French OOB Festival; her first children's picture book, *Stuck with the Blooz*, is forthcoming in Fall 2012. Caron works as an arts educator in her hometown of New York City. She is lucky to have spent some amazing summers in Maine as a kid.

LISA LOCASCIO's work has appeared or is forthcoming in *American Short Fiction*, the *Northwest Review*, *Faultline*, *Reed*, and *Fifth Wednesday Journal*, among others. She is the winner of the 2011 John Steinbeck Award and is the 2012 Emerging Featured Fiction Writer as chosen by *Grist: The Journal for Writers*. Lisa lives in Los Angeles, where she teaches writing in the honors college of the University of Southern California.

GRETA SCHULER's work has appeared in *Creative Nonfiction* as the winner of the magazine's 2009 MFA Program-Off Contest and in *Crab Orchard Review* as the winner of the journal's 2010 Jack Dyer Fiction Prize. Her fiction and nonfiction has been placed as finalist in contests such as the *Fourth Genre* Michael Steinberg Essay Prize, *Narrative Magazine* Fall Story Contest, the *New Letter* Alexander Patterson Cappon Prize for Fiction, and the *Hunger Mountain* Frank Mosher Short Fiction Prize. She recently received fellowships at Yaddo and The MacDowell Colony, where she worked on her first novel.

BRENT VAN STAALDUINEN's work has appeared in *The Storyteller Magazine*, *Bazaar Magazine*, and *Fringe Magazine*; his poetry in *Cadenza* and *Minstrel*. He has published essays and creative nonfiction in *The Christian Courier*, *The Banner*, *The Kuwait Times*, and the *Al-Watan Daily*. He lives in Hamilton, Ontario with his wife Rosalee, and is working on his second novel.

MICHAEL CALEB TASKER was born in Montreal, Canada and raised in New Orleans, Louisiana. His stories have appeared in numerous literary journals including *Wet Ink*, *The Long Story* and *Storyteller Magazine*. He was recently shortlisted for the 2011 and 2009 William Faulkner-Wisdom Creative Writing Competition, and was a finalist in the 2010 Walker Percy Prize in short fiction. He has worked as an actor, house painter, ranch hand and journalist. He has a BA in Music Studies and Literature and recently completed an MA in Professional Writing. He lives in Sydney, Australia.

KIRK WILSON'S true crime novel, *Unsolved*, has been published in six editions in the US and UK. Kirk was selected for the anthology *The Wordstock 10: Finalists from the 2011 Wordstock Short Fiction Competition*, and more new work is forthcoming from *Eclipse* and *Midway Journal*. Kirk lives in Austin, Texas with his wife, Donna Johnson.

SAM WILSON'S stories have appeared in *The Sun, Connecticut Review, Canteen*, and *Cold Mountain Review*. He earned his MFA from Queens University of Charlotte, and now lives in Olympia, Washington.

MACHIGONNE SEMI-FINALISTS*

JACKIE ZOLLO BROOKS has worked as a professional actress, director, and script writer. She holds a BA from Tufts, a master's degree from Antioch and a doctorate from Harvard. She taught English at the University of Massachusetts in Boston until she decided to join the Peace Corps to teach English in Madagascar. Publications include *Serving House Journal, Montreal Review, Glimpse Magazine*, and *Omby*, a literary magazine out of Madagascar. Jackie's *Selected Poems* were published in 2009, and she recently placed as a finalist in the Iowa Short Fiction Awards. Jackie now lives and works as a full-time writer in Gloucester, Massachusetts.

GWENDOLINE RILEY was born in London in 1979. She is the author of four novels, *Cold Water* (2002), *Sick Notes* (2004), *Joshua Spassky* (2007), and *Opposed Positions* (out Spring 2012). *Cold Water* won the Betty Trask Award and *Joshua Spassky* won the Somerset Maugham Award and was also shortlisted for the John Llewellyn Rhys Prize.

MITCHELL STOCKS was raised in Michigan and Montana and has lived in Asia for eighteen years. He has logged, ranched, carpentered, gardened, sorted, troubleshot, taught, drafted, negotiated, managed, mentored, and volunteered. He recently retired from the law and is a second-year MFA student at City University in Hong Kong where he writes stories that give voice to the ignored. *We Chinese* is his first published work of fiction.

Please see Knightville Finalists for Soma Mei Sheng Frazier's biography.

KNIGHTVILLE FINALISTS

IOANNA CARLSEN'S poems and stories have appeared in *Alaska Quarterly Review*, *Agni*, *Beloit Poetry Journal*, *Field*, *Poetry Magazine*, and many other literary magazines. She was a featured poet on Poetry Daily.org in 2001 and 2006 and a featured poet in 2001 at Poetry.org. She won the 2002 *Glimmer Train* Poetry Open. Her work appears in the fiction anthology *Mother Knows*, and *Pomegranate Seeds: An anthology of Greek-American Poetry*. She lives in the country, outside Santa Fe, New Mexico, with her husband.

KEVIN CAROLLO lives in Fargo, North Dakota, and teaches world literature and writing across the river at Minnesota State University Moorhead. He writes for *Rain Taxi Review of Books*, rocks with The New Instructions, and has just completed an anti-memoir entitled *Step-Jew*. His poem, *A Theory*, began with a billboard seen out of the corner of his eye at night, east of St. Paul, Minnesota, coming back from his grandmother's Catholic funeral in Huntley, Illinois. He'd already had a near-death experience outside Madison, Wisconsin. He finds it odd to be writing about this in the third person. In loving memory of Nancy Carollo (1913-2010).

MARY CHRISTINE DELEA is from Long Island and has lived all over the country. She is a former college professor with a PhD in English. Her previous books are *The Skeleton Holding Up the Sky* and two chapbooks, *Ordinary Days in Ordinary Places* and *Moving the Language*. Her chapbook, *Did I Mention There's Gambling and Body Parts?* is forthcoming in early 2012. Besides writing poetry, Delea also writes nonfiction, designs and makes quilts, and creates beaded jewelry and altered art. She lives in Oregon with one husband, five cats, and too many books to count. Delea is also a semi-finalist in the Knightville poetry contest this year, for her poem, *Purr*.

ROB DENNIS is a poet and fiction writer whose work has appeared in *The Paris Review*, *Fence*, *Tin House*, and *Another Chicago Magazine*. His work has also been anthologized in *Satellite Convulsions: Poems from Tin House*. He is active in the arts community, sitting on the executive board of *Fence/Fence Books* as well as on the Advisory board of the Millay Colony for the Arts. He lives in New York City.

JAYDN DEWALD, an MFA candidate at Pacific University, currently lives with his wife in San Francisco, California, where he writes and plays bass for the DeWald/Taylor Quintet. His work has appeared or is forthcoming in *Bellevue Literary Review*, *Columbia Poetry Review*, *New York Quarterly*, *West Branch*, *Witness*, and others.

NICOLE DICELLO'S work has appeared in publications such as *Poetry East*, the *Mid-America Poetry Review*, *Nimrod International Journal of Prose and Poetry*, *Concho River Review*, and *Ballard Street Poetry Journal*. In addition, her manuscript, *Redshift*, was a finalist for the Bordighera Poetry Prize. She won second place in the 2011 Blue Mesa Review

Poetry Contest judged by Lisa Gill, Richard Vargas, and Danny Solis; and was one of twelve poets selected by Marge Piercy to attend a poetry writing intensive workshop in 2012. She is an MFA candidate in the Creative Writing Poetry program at Emerson College, and a reader for *Ploughshares*.

WILLIAM DORESKI teaches at Keene State College in New Hampshire. His most recent collection of poetry is *Waiting for the Angel* (2009). He has published three critical studies, including a piece on Robert Lowell's *Shifting Colors*. His essays, poetry, fiction, and reviews have appeared in many journals, including *Massachusetts Review*, *Atlanta Review*, *Notre Dame Review*, *The Alembic*, *New England Quarterly*, *Harvard Review*, *Modern Philology*, *Antioch Review*, and *Natural Bridge*.

IRIS JAMAHL DUNKLE teaches writing at University of California, Santa Cruz. Her manuscript, *Alphabet of Bones*, was a finalist for the Four Way Books Levis Prize in Poetry in 2011. Her chapbook, *Inheritance*, was published by Finishing Line in 2010. Her poetry, creative nonfiction and scholarly articles have appeared in numerous publications including *Fence*, *LiNQ*, *Boxcar Poetry Review*, *Weave*, *Verse Wisconsin*, Talking Writing.com, *Yalobusha Review*, and *The Mom Egg*.

SOMA MEI SHENG FRAZIER'S poetry has been nominated for the Pushcart Prize, and earned an honorable mention from poet Nikki Giovanni. Her fiction chapbook, *Face*, received a special mention from Robert Olen Butler. Soma's work has appeared in the *Mississippi Review* and other literary journals, and has placed as winner/finalist/ semi-finalist in 2011 contests offered by *RopeWalk Press*, *Black Lawrence Press*, *Slope Editions* and *Glimmer Train*; 2010 contests offered by *Hyphen Magazine*/Asian American Writers' Workshop and *The Pinch*; and 2009 contests offered by *Mississippi Review*, *The Journal*, *Carve Magazine* and *Mudfish Magazine*. She is working on a novel. Soma is also a Machigonne Fiction Contest semi-finalist this year for her story, *She Must Remember*.

ROBIN MICHEL is a San Francisco Bay Area poet earning her living working for nonprofits and in education, with a focus on communications and development. Her first exposure to poetry was the songs and nursery rhymes her mother taught her when she was a young child. One nursery rhyme in particular haunts Robin to this day: "There was a little girl, with a little curl right in the middle of her forehead. When she was good, she was very, very good. When she was bad, she was horrid." She is currently working on a poetry collection exploring this and other dualities.

MARCIA POPP is a retired university professor and the author of several textbooks and biographies. She received the 2008 Robert Greer Cohn Prose Poetry Award for the title poem of *Comfort in Small Rooms*, a collection that chronicles the experience of being a grandchild in the 1940s. A poem from this collection was anthologized in *Best New Poets 2008*, edited by Mark Strand; another poem from the book was read on

The Writer's Almanac by Garrison Keillor, and included in the online anthology *In the Heyday of His Eyes*, a resource for high school English teachers. Poems have appeared in *The Naugatuck River Review*, *The New Guard*, *Memoir (and)*, *The Mom Egg*, and several issues of *Avocet*.

MELISSA ROBERTS-FISHMAN is a student in the MFA Program for Writers at Warren Wilson College. She lives in Maine.

DON SCHOFIELD'S poems, essays and translations have appeared in numerous American journals, including *Partisan Review*, *New England Review*, and *Poets & Writers*, as well as in journals in Europe and Asia. He was the recipient of the 2010 John D. Criticos Prize (UK) and the 2005 Allen Ginsberg Award. He has received honors, among others, from Anhinga Press and *The Southern California Anthology*. He also served as a Princeton University Stanley J. Seeger Writer-in-Residence. His poetry volumes include the chapbook *Of Dust* (1991), *Approximately Paradise* (2002), *Kindled Terraces: American Poets in Greece* (2004), and *The Known: Selected Poems of Nikos Fokas, 1981–2000* (2010). A resident of Greece for many years, he currently lives in Thessaloniki, where he is the Dean of Special Programs at Perrotis College.

TERESE SVOBODA'S fifth book of poetry contains poems which have appeared in *The Times Literary Supplement*, *The Paris Review*, *The New Yorker*, and *Tin House*. Her first book, *All Aberration* (1985), was an American Library Association Notable Book nominee. Her second, *Laughing Africa* (1990), won the Iowa Prize. Her third, *Mere Mortals* (1995), was featured in *The New York Times Book Review*. Her fourth, *Treason* (2002), was a Booksense Pick-of-the-Week and reviewed in *The Los Angeles Times*. Her sixth novel, *Bohemian Girl*, has just been published.

KEN TAYLOR lives and writes in North Carolina. His poetry has appeared or is forthcoming in *The Chattahoochee Review*, *The Stony Thursday Book*, *elimae*, *MiPOesias*, *Whale Sound*, *Eclectica Magazine*, *OCHO*, *Poets and Artists*, *HAM Literature*, and *Gigantic Sequins*. He is the 2011 winner of the Fish Publishing Poetry Prize.

ELAINE ZIMMERMAN is a state and national policy leader for children, an essayist and a poet. Recent publications include poetry in *Coal Hill Review*, *Lilith*, *Caduceus*, *Winning Writers*, *New Millennium Writings*, *Long River Run*, *Friends of Acadia Journal*, and anthologies including *Everybody Says Hello*, *Sleeping with One Eye Open: Women Writers and the Art of Survival*, and *Worlds in Our Words: Contemporary American Women Writers*. She is a Pushcart nominee and a Philbrick Poetry Project and Israeli Poetry Peace Prize finalist. She lives in Connecticut with her family and various wild animals.

KNIGHTVILLE SEMI-FINALISTS*

AUSTIN ALLEN is an MFA poetry candidate and teaching fellow in the Johns Hopkins Writing Seminars. He lives in Baltimore.

HEATHER ALTFELD is a lecturer in composition at California State University, Chico. She helped to found, and now serves on, the board of a local public Waldorf school where she volunteers time as a poet-teacher. She has been grateful to spend several recent summers with the Squaw Valley Community of Writers. She has published poetry in *Tule Review, The Squaw Valley Review, Antique Children: A Mischievous Literary Arts Journal, Clackamas Literary Review, ZYZZYVA*, and has poems forthcoming in *Pleiades* and *The Arroyo Literary Review*. She has just completed her first manuscript of poems, entitled *Letters from the Lake of Stars*.

After being raised on a yacht built by his father and mooring at various points around the Cornish coast, LUKE BRAMLEY moved to the Midlands where he studied English Literature at Birmingham University. He has since lived in the States and New Zealand and is currently teaching English at Ecole Active Bilingue Jeannine Manuel in Lille, France. He has written several short stories and poems and a novel entitled *The Kingdom Within*, which was shortlisted for the Yeovil Literary Prize. He is currently working on several writing projects including a second novel entitled *The Soldrums*.

LYNN TUDOR DEMING'S work has appeared in numerous journals, including *Atlanta Review, new south*, and *The Ledge*. Her chapbook, *Heady Rubbish*, was selected by Robert Pinsky for the 2005 Philbrick Poetry Prize. Other awards include second place in Atlanta Review's International Poetry Competition; and National Runner-up in the 2011 National Cape Cod Poetry Competition, selected by Gerald Stern. Her full-length collection, *Their Imperishable Burn*, was a semi-finalist in the 2009 Crab Orchard First Book Contest. Lynn is a clinical psychologist who lives and practices in Connecticut.

CHAD FRISBIE graduated from Bates College in 2010 with a BA in English and creative writing. His poems have appeared in *Jellyfish Magazine* and *Chroma: A Queer Literary Journal*, and he was a poetry contributor at the 2011 Bread Loaf Writers' Conference.

LYALL F. HARRIS is an award-winning painter and writer. She is currently the inaugural candidate at Mills College in the nation's first MFA Program in Book Art and Creative Writing. This year her poetry appeared in *The Prose-Poem Project*, received Honorable Mention for the Mary Merritt Henry Poetry Prize in Poetry, and placed as finalist in the Bunchgrass Poetry Prize. Her creative nonfiction was also recently featured in *The Montréal Review* and her artwork in *La Petite Zine*.

KENYA T. JENNINGS is a native of Detroit, Michigan, residing in a metro suburb and pursuing a degree in English/Creative Writing. A working professional in the construction and building trades field, she frequents spoken word and open mic venues and is currently working on a collection of poetry, prose, and short stories.

MATTHEW KEUTER'S writing has appeared in journals across the US and has twice been nominated to the Pushcart Prize. *The Short Imposition of Living*, a book-length collection of poetry, is available from *Rain Mountain Press*. His plays have been produced in Arkansas, Arizona, California, Colorado, New York City, and London.

DESMOND KON ZHICHENG-MINGDÉ has new work anthologized in *Coast, Read Write [Hand]: A Multi-disciplinary Nick Cave Reader*, and *[C.]: An MLP Stamp Stories Anthology*. Trained in book publishing at Stanford, with a theology masters in World Religions from Harvard and an MFA in Creative Writing from Notre Dame, Desmond has edited more than ten books and co-produced three audio books. He is a recipient of the PEN Shorts Prize, the Singapore Internationale Grant, Swale Life Poetry Prize, and the Dr. Hiew Siew Nam Academic Award. He also works in clay; commemorative pieces are housed in museums and private collections in India, the Netherlands, the UK and the US.

WULF LOSEE was born and raised in rural Connecticut. After receiving a BA in Anthropology from the University of Connecticut, he fled to the West Coast and then on to Hong Kong. He lost track of his muse for about two decades during his journeys. He now has renewed his rocky relationship with the muse, and he and his muse reside in northern California with two cats who like to knock over his piles of books.

SHAHÉ MANKERIAN is the winner of the Erika Mumford Prize from the New England Poetry Club. His recent poems have won Honorable Mentions in the 2011 Allen Ginsberg Poetry Awards and in *Arts & Letters Journal of Contemporary Culture*. His poems have been published in *Nebo: A Literary Journal, Spillway, Riverwind*, and *Ellipsis: Literature and Art*. He is the principal of St. Gregory Hovsepian School in Pasadena, California. Every summer Shahé co-directs the Los Angeles Writing Project.

NIKOLAS JAMES PEREZ lives in Minneapolis, MN, where he balances his time between distractedly working at a book store and distractedly pursuing his efforts in writing, photography, and supporting the local (and brilliant) artistic community. He is twenty-eight years of age, brown-eyed, likes to wear fake flowers and dance, and struggles incessantly with the 100-word bio.

JEANIE TOMASKO is the author of *Sharp as Want*, a poetry/artwork collaboration with Sharon Auberle, and a chapbook, *Tricks of Light*. Her poems have appeared or are forthcoming in many journals, including *Lilliput Review*, *Verse Wisconsin*, *Wisconsin People and Ideas*, and *The Midwest Quarterly*. Online publications include *Right Hand Pointing*, *Qarrtsiluni*, and *Talking Writing.com*. Born and raised in Madison, Wisconsin, she earned her BSN from University of Wisconsin-Madison and works as a home health nurse in the Madison area.

JULIE MARIE WADE is the author of two collections of poetry, *Without* (2010) and *Postage Due* (forthcoming, 2013) and two collections of lyric nonfiction, *Wishbone: A Memoir in Fractures* (2010) and *Small Fires* (2011). She lives with her partner Angie Griffin in the Bluegrass State, where she is a doctoral candidate and graduate teaching fellow in the Humanities program at the University of Louisville.

*Please see Knightville Finalists for Mary Christine Delea's biography.

The New Guard has had an extremely charmed second year. We've had the support of many incredible writers and artists. Those who've rallied with us this year—there truly is no way to thank you enough. In return, we've gone at it full force, putting our heads down and working hard to make the finest issue we could. Our wish is simple. We are here to support fellow writers in print publication, and to do as our fellows do: write, read, publish, and add our best contribution to the greater letters of the world. Because of the help we've received, we were able to do just that. This issue is a testament to the dedication, faith and innovation of the incredible *TNG* team and the *TNG* community. What an issue. Thank you doesn't cut it.

First, we would like to thank our contest entrants, who submitted poetry and fiction manuscripts from all over the world. Entries came over the desk from Greece, France, England, Ireland, Australia, Singapore, China, Romania, New Zealand, Italy, Canada, Kenya…the list goes on. What a thrill, to read the inspired work of writers hailing from such faraway places, and to experience a connection through a shared passion for the written word. Thank you for caring to submit to our contests. It was an honor to read your writing. Thank you as well to our two winners, and our gracious finalists and our semi-finalists. It is such a pleasure to publish your work.

This year's far reach in culling manuscripts must be due, in large part, to our incredible, awe-inspiring judges: former U.S. Poet Laureate Charles Simic, and award-winning novelist and memoirist David Plante. We couldn't have been prouder to have you both on board. Thank you so much for being a part of this issue and for choosing this year's winners.

Thank you to John Callahan, for having faith in us and giving us the chance to feature this important, never-before published Ralph Ellison manuscript, both in print and with reproductions of the original pages from 1944. It has been a wonder and a joy—and you are a lot of fun to work with!

Thank you to our generous contributors, Theodore Deppe, Cortright McMeel, Tess Gerritsen, Liz Hand, Baron Wormser, Carolina De Robertis, Sarah Braunstein, Tim Seibles, Mike Heppner, Tod Goldberg, Fred Marchant, Michael Kimball, Alexandra Oliver, Ed Skoog, Joe Wenderoth, Jim Zimmerman and Aaron Hamburger. Thank you to this issue's web artists, James Provenzano and Sergei Chaparin; and thank you to our print artists, dave naybor, who created *Type Smash!* just for this issue, and Jeff McCreight, who was on board even from where he lives in Spain. Such a treat to find Jeff's painting over the bar at Local 188 one evening, and to connect with him via the good people of Local 188—thank you every one.

Thank you to our fine 2011 editors: Sarah Kowalski for your boldness and discernment, Bill Roorbach for your humor, agreeable spirit and—humility— you're the best; Suzanne Strempek Shea, for your genuine care; and Scott Wolven for your genius, tireless help, absolute knowing, and for being the one true HBK. You rock. Copyeditors—you hung in there for a second year and helped put out another terrific issue: thank you to Sherry Whittemore for your endless energy, and

David Scribner, for your patience and exactitude. Thank you to our champion layout manager and typesetter Melanie Kratovil, for giving it (more than!) all you had in a very small amount of time. Thank you to our superintern, Siobhan Smith—you were an incredible help. Thank you Peter Maskaluk, for all you did.

Thank you to the incredible and kind Cindy Edwards; thank you to Brandi Neal for your help at the Association of Writers and Writing Programs (AWP) Conference and beyond, thank you to Melissa Falcon Field for helping out with contacts; thank you to Diana Choksey, most cheerful and sweet. Thank you to Scott Vaughan—you are the best at what you do.

Thank you to the wonderful: Peter Scarpaci, Elizabeth Erin, Jotham Burello, Chad Frisbie, Erin Belieu, Joe McDermott, Nathan Eldridge, Susan Culver, Bonnie Coles, Valerie Moore, Rebecca Falzano, David Lydon, Portland Arts & Cultural Alliance, Stephen Kelly, Ramona Koval, Jendi Reiter, Robert Lively, Vanessa Willoughby, Patricia McNair, Tom Morgan of Blue Design, Maine Magazine, The Portland Phoenix and Poets & Writers; and thank you to Adam Eaglin of the Wylie Agency, Peter Guffin of Pierce Atwood and the good people of the Library of Congress. And a thank you goes out to our Facebook and Twitter friends.

Thank you to all the bookstores who've carried us this year: Longfellow Books, Devaney, Doak and Garrett Booksellers, McNally Jackson Books, Skylight Books, Nonesuch Books, Jabberwocky Bookshop, Colby Bookstore and the University of Southern Maine (USM) Bookstore.

Thank you to our Kickstarter backers, a wonderful team of people who helped bolster this year's publication through kind donation: Alysssa Barrett, Adam Birt, Tim Broadrick, Richard Cambridge, Sergei Chaparin, Edie Clark, Malcolm Cochran, Kimberly Connor, Lucinda Coombs, Alan Crichton, Jill Day, Theodore Deppe, Boman Desai, George Drew, Sean Dwyer, Rebecca Falzano, Melissa Falcon Field, Annie Finch, John Fitzpatrick, Nikki Flionis, Megan Grumbling, Lesley Heiser, Gail Hovey, Jen Karetnick, Michael Kimball, Mary Kowalski, Sarah Kowalski, Judy Jones, Theo Kalikow, Jim Kelly, Clark Knowles, Gail Knowles, Mike Langworthy, Donna LaNigra, Rachel Lee, Mike Mack, Jodie Marion, Sibyl Masquelier, Louise McDowell, Lynn McGee, Allison McMahon, David & Kathleen McNair, Diane & Wesley McNair, Indigo Moor, Brandi Neal, Cynthia Neale, Sharon Olds, Helen Peppe, Judith Podell, Marcia Popp, James Provenzano, Bill Roorbach, Penelope Scambly Schott, Elizabeth Searle, David Scribner, Lee Sharkey, Suzanne Strempek Shea, Larry Specht, Bianca Stone, Barbara Sullivan, Gioia Timpanelli, Afaa Michael Weaver, Gail White, Sherry Whittemore, Bradford Winters & Kendall Wyman.

Finally, thank you to last year's team—who helped create the foundation of this growing enterprise, so that *The New Guard* is able to support writers the world over.